Results-Oriented
J O B
Descriptions

Roger J. Plachy • Sandra J. Plachy

RESULTS-ORIENTED JOB DESCRIPTIONS

More than 225 Models to Use or Adapt—
with Guidelines for Creating Your Own

amacom

American Management Association

New York • Atlanta • Boston • Chicago • Kansas City • San Francisco • Washington, D.C.
Brussels • Toronto • Mexico City

Library of Congress Cataloging-in-Publication Data

Plachy, Roger.
    Results-oriented job descriptions / Roger J. Plachy, Sandra J. Plachy.
        p.   cm.
    ISBN 0-8144-7806-9
    1. Job descriptions.   I. Plachy, Sandra J.   II. Title.
    HF5549.5.J613P58   1993
    658.3'06—dc20   93-6946
                                                                 CIP

Printing number

10

For
Jenson
May his life be filled with results

Contents

Alphabetical
List of Job Descriptions

Job Descriptions by Occupation

Introduction
The Why and How
of This Book

Writing job descriptions is not a lot of fun for most people, for whom writing can be tedious and can take up a lot of time. This compendium solves these problems by offering models that you can simply edit and begin using.

The Results-Oriented Format

There are several compendiums of job descriptions on the market, but only this one presents job descriptions in a results-oriented format.

The results-oriented format makes clear *why* work is important. In addition to stating job duties, as most job descriptions do, a results-oriented job description also explains the purpose of the work, what is accomplished by performing the duty.

Focusing work on results changes the emphasis and enhances the usefulness of job descriptions. In recent years, so-called management gurus have denounced job descriptions because they restrict employee attention. These gurus suggest eliminating job descriptions altogether. Given the fact that most job descriptions are written as a laundry list of little things people are required to do, they are not worthwhile. However, we recommend that you improve your job descriptions instead of eliminating them.

We believe in job descriptions. How else can you communicate your organization's purpose and what must be accomplished by each person for the organization to succeed? At the same time, do job descriptions have to be restrictive? Of course not. Flexibility and resourcefulness are issues of style, not elements of a job description. People who advocate the elimination of job descriptions have forgotten what it means to manage, misunderstand solid communication techniques, or have never seen a results-oriented job description.

Who Should Use This Book?

This book is for anyone who needs to communicate job expectations. This includes:

- *Human resources professionals* who analyze, describe, and evaluate jobs, hire and test job candidates, guide reorganizations, negotiate with unions, monitor disciplinary actions and resolve grievances, develop succession plans and career paths, or design pay structures.
- *Supervisors and managers* who define and organize work, orient and train employees, plan, monitor, and appraise employee job results, or encourage employee growth and development.
- *Executives* who chart the course of their organization and want people to focus their efforts on common purposes.

How to Use This Book

The job descriptions included in this compendium represent a cross-section of industries and occupations. They were selected to include those titles most frequently used. Many of these descriptions will probably meet your needs with few alterations. Still, you will undoubtedly need to edit most of the job descriptions to state your organization's specific job requirements.

Chapter 1 explains the concept of the results-oriented job description and illustrates the new focus and structure.

Chapter 2 demonstrates how to edit the models offered in this compendium so you can start using them quickly.

Chapter 3 gives you standard results-oriented statements to help you assemble new job descriptions or adapt our models.

Chapter 4 teaches you how to write results-oriented job description statements, including writing tips and sample forms.

Chapter 5 provides legal guidelines pertinent to the use of job descriptions, including discussions of the Americans with Disabilities Act, the Fair Labor Standards Act, the Equal Pay Act, Title VII of the Civil Rights Act of 1964, and the Occupational Safety and Health Act.

The Many Uses of Job Descriptions

A job description is the basic understanding or "contract" between an employer and an employee. It discusses what needs to be accomplished to fulfill the organization's purpose and describes the employee's commitment.

Job descriptions are an essential element in managing the work of the organization. They are used to:

- Define or revise the organization structure.
- Plan human resources requirements.
- Advertise jobs and recruit candidates.
- Evaluate relative job value.
- Determine exempt/nonexempt status.
- Establish career progressions.
- Analyze work flow and methods.

- Post jobs.
- Interview and select job candidates.
- Orient new employees.
- Identify training requirements.
- Conduct pay surveys.
- Prepare affirmative action plans.
- Comply with employment laws.
- Establish a base for incentive plans.
- Bargain with unions.

The Need for a New Philosophy of Job Descriptions

Job descriptions have been around for a long time. For most of that time, most of what we understood about how people worked concerned desirable traits and behaviors. What people did was put under a microscope.

Not until the middle of the century did managers look up and realize that they were missing the point. What people did made sense only in relation to what they were or were not accomplishing. The philosophy of management-by-objectives taught managers to focus first on the target and then on how they might reach the target.

A results-oriented job description starts the manager-employee relationship off on the right foot. It directs managers and employees to look together at what outcomes are necessary. The first step in this process is to make sure both people understand where they are going.

A results-oriented job description is what good management and good communication are all about.

Part I
A New Philosophy of Job Descriptions

1

Why Use Results-Oriented Job Descriptions?

Results and duties are both stated.

A results-oriented job description states two components of work: the result that must be accomplished and the duties that must be performed in order to accomplish the result.

> For example: **HELPS CUSTOMERS**
> by
> answering the telephone.

Effective managers tell their employees not only what they want them to do—in this case, answer the telephone—but what they want them to accomplish—in this case, help customers.

Employees are taught why work is important.

In clarifying results, managers explain *why* work is important, that is, where a particular task, activity, or behavior fits in the overall scheme of a department function and, thus, where the job fits in as the organization moves toward accomplishing its mission and objectives. A results-oriented job description makes the purpose of work clear and keeps the employee focused on what is truly important about job performance.

Not just duties are stated.

Traditional job descriptions state duties, such as "answers the telephone." Yes, it's logical to assume that an employee would know that the reason for answering the telephone is to help customers. However, it is better management to make this expectation very clear. Surely you have been on the receiving end of telephone answerers who have not helped you—who did not understand *why* their jobs existed.

"Here's what I want you to *do*" may typify the way managers have traditionally talked to employees. Telling employees only what to do on a job is not enough anymore. Actually, it never was.

Accomplishing is emphasized over doing.

If they adhere to a job description written in the traditional duties-oriented style, employees can be "doing" the job without understanding the *why* of the job and without accomplishing important results. An employee who answers the telephone is "doing" the job if that is all the job description requires. Psychologically, a supervisor can be caught in a defensive word game by an employee who has not been told explicitly that the job requirement is to help customers. When the supervisor hands a job description to an employee, the employee can rightly expect that what is printed is what is required.

The focus is on results.

With a results-oriented job description, the focus of managing work switches from doing the work to the results accomplished. Results are easier to manage than duties because results are either accomplished or not accomplished, whereas duties, because they are the process of work, go on interminably.

Focusing on duties easily misses the *why* of work. The supervisor who also wants the employee to answer the fax machine may hear the customary "It's not in my job description," while the customer waits on the line trying to place an order. Focused on helping customers, employees can easily learn to understand the different aspects of the job that add up to the desired outcome.

Focusing on results is a different way of thinking about work. Results describe the strategy of work, whereas duties emphasize the tactics of work. The strategy of the job takes into account where the job fits into the overall scheme of the organization and how the job contributes to the organization's mission. Most of the time, managers and employees merely focus on the work right in front of them, because the language of the job description points them in that narrow direction. Emphasizing results elevates their thinking so they understand why the organization exists and why the organization needs their contribution.

Results and duties are contrasted.

To illustrate the difference between results and duties, consider this sample job description for a Patient Receptionist in a dental clinic, written in two ways. The traditional duties-oriented style is in the left column. In the right column are the same duties, augmented by the result that must be accomplished when the duties are performed.

Duties-Oriented	*Results-Oriented*
1. Greets and refers patients and visitors.	1. PROVIDES INFORMATION by greeting and referring patients and visitors.
2. Notifies dentist of patient's arrival, reviews adherence to schedule, and reminds provider of delays.	2. KEEPS PATIENT APPOINTMENTS ON SCHEDULE by notifying provider of patient's arrival, reviewing adherence to schedule, and reminding provider of delays.

Duties-Oriented	Results-Oriented
3. Anticipates patient anxieties, answers questions, and maintains orderly reception area.	3. COMFORTS PATIENTS by anticipating anxieties, answering questions, and maintaining an orderly reception room.
4. Schedules appointments in person or by telephone.	4. OPTIMIZES PATIENTS' SATISFACTION, PROVIDER TIME, AND TREATMENT ROOM UTILIZATION by scheduling appointments in person or by telephone.
5. Enters and retrieves patient scheduling data on a computer terminal while maintaining confidentiality.	5. COMPLETES AND UPDATES PATIENT SCHEDULING FILE by entering and retrieving data on a computer terminal while maintaining confidentiality.

Most people find that the addition of results clarifies the purpose of the duties, that the duties become more meaningful, that the employee has a much better understanding of why the work is important, and that knowing the result intended actually allows an employee to discover new ways to accomplish results, as long as the results are accomplished.

Results are not buried.

When you pick up an average job description, you generally find only a list of duties. Your job, you are told, is to "interview candidates." On an occasional job description, you may find a few results buried in the verbiage: "Interviews candidates in order to determine their qualifications." This result—to determine qualifications—is easy to miss.

Describing jobs with a focus on results is not just a method of expression. Spelling out the result of work is important in helping an employee understand the work itself. Unlike writing mystery novels, in which building up to the climax is the whole point, the goal of educating and instructing employees is to start with the answer: "This is where you need to arrive. Now, this is how you get there."

DETERMINES CANDIDATES' QUALIFICATIONS
by
conducting interviews.

Without a focal point for concentration, the employee's mind searches for meaning among the duties and instructions.

The writing style is clear.

The job descriptions in this compendium follow a formula so that each expectation is clearly stated both in terms of the result that must be accomplished and the duty(ies) that must be performed. Both are necessary to understand the expectation.

The formula is: **THE RESULT TO BE ACCOMPLISHED**
by
the duty(ies) to be performed.

Descriptions are easier to read and simpler to understand.

Graphically, the result to be accomplished is printed in capital boldface letters in order to bring obvious emphasis to the statement. Right away the employee knows that something is different here.

Written in this style, job descriptions are easier to read and simpler to understand. The writing style is clear and concise. Most job descriptions are just too wordy, and their meaning is obscured.

Employees quickly see the connection between the work that they will do and the results they will have to accomplish; together, the result to be accomplished and the duty(ies) to be performed make sense. Such a job description offers supervisors two ways to discuss job expectations—what is being accomplished and what is being done.

The presentation formula is strictly followed.

The result to be accomplished and the duty(ies) to be performed are separated by the word "by" and are printed on three separate lines.

HELPS CUSTOMERS
by
answering the telephone.

The expectation could be printed "**HELPS CUSTOMERS** by answering the telephone" to save space, but using three lines brings dramatic attention to each portion of the requirement.

There are nearly as many styles of writing job descriptions as there are job description writers. Some writers merely write one long paragraph. Some writers offer an exhaustive list of items in an attempt to be thorough. Some writers say nearly the same thing over and over trying to make their point clear. Some writers use different categories that seem to say the same thing—expectations, accountabilities, and responsibilities. The formula used in this compendium is simple and straightforward. In this way, supervisors and employees get used to the regular, predictable presentation.

The result and duty are read together.

The result to be accomplished and the duty to be performed must be read as one statement to distinguish between jobs. Some jobs may have the same result but different duties. For example:

SERVES CLIENTS
by
analyzing programming needs.

and

SERVES CLIENTS
by
writing programs.

The highlighted focus gives supervisors help in demonstrating common objectives.

Results make the uses of job descriptions more relevant.

Results-oriented job descriptions serve the traditional uses of job descriptions better than ancestral models. Job descriptions are often used to:

- Recruit candidates.
- Interview candidates.
- Test candidates.
- Orient employees.
- Train employees.
- Plan job results.
- Monitor job results.
- Appraise job results.
- Coach employees.
- Discipline employees.

Because results-oriented job descriptions answer the question, "why is this job important?," management and employee actions become more relevant. Recruiting candidates focuses on job outcomes needed and legitimate requirements, instead of personal characteristics. Interviewing candidates focuses on ability to reason, instead of skill to perform specific tasks. Testing candidates focuses on applicability of skills, instead of skills aptitude. Orienting employees focuses on the reasons that the job exists, instead of things to do and places to go. Training employees focuses on use of learning, instead of classroom performance. Coaching and disciplining employees focuses on improved outcomes, instead of personal weaknesses or punishment. Planning, monitoring, and appraising job results focuses on work outcomes, instead of personal attitudes and behaviors.

Results make job descriptions useful.

Anyone who has seen the often inferior and generally uneven quality that is typical of job descriptions will not be surprised at their poor reputation. Writing and using job descriptions often occurs only when the personnel department requires them.

The job description gives life to the employment relationship between the employer and the employee, just as the charter gives life to the corporation. The job description deserves a quality of writing equal to its role, which is to guide supervisors and employees as they accomplish the work of the organization.

Furthermore, job descriptions must be changed when job requirements change. One reason the lowly job description never achieved much status in the past was that keeping it current meant having it completely retyped whenever requirements changed. Word processing and the attendant ease of editing may be the technological development that allows the job description to be elevated to its proper role.

2
Editing Job Descriptions in This Compendium

Although you may find many of the job descriptions in this book ready to use, chances are you will need to adapt others to fit your organization's particular needs. Here's how to edit a job description to conform to your specifications.

Study the Job You Need to Describe

Start with an understanding of the responsibilities of the job you are describing. You will need to conduct some form of job analysis to understand these responsibilities, perhaps interviewing the job incumbent and the supervisor or asking them to complete a questionnaire. You may also observe the job yourself.

Find the Job Description You Need

Find the job in the compendium that matches, or most closely matches, the responsibilities of the job you want to describe. Look through related job titles to see whether statements in other jobs might be helpful even though the job titles may appear to describe somewhat different requirements.

Revise the Job Statements

To revise the job statement to fit your needs, follow these steps:

1. Eliminate results and duties that do not apply.
2. Add, delete, or substitute words in the results and duties statements to meet your exact requirements.
   a. The precise wording of the result may vary from one organization to another as each organization spells out its special values. Defining the result is a useful tactic for managers and employees to help them develop a common understanding of expectations.

     b. Specific duties will vary according to the size and structure—and thus, the work assignments—of each organization.

  3. Add results and duties that need to be included.

     a. Edit standard result-by-duty statements in Chapter 3.

     b. Write new statements according to the guidelines in Chapter 4.

Revision Example 1

For example, suppose that you are writing the job description of a Cook. The closest job description is Chef.

For purposes of illustrating the changes made in the Chef job description, words to be deleted are shown as shaded, and words that are to be added are shown in *italics*.

JOB TITLE: Cook

JOB PURPOSE: **DESIGNS AND PREPARES MEALS**

by

planning and implementing menus; controlling food preparation

following recipes.

ESSENTIAL JOB RESULTS:

% of Time

● IDENTIFIES CURRENT AND FUTURE CUSTOMER FOOD PREFERENCES
by
establishing personal contact and rapport with potential and actual customers and other persons in a position to understand food requirements.

● PLANS MENUS
by
studying marketing conditions, popularity of various dishes, and recency of menu; utilizing food surpluses and leftovers.

● PRICES MEALS
by
analyzing recipes; determining food, labor, and overhead costs.

% of Time

● PURCHASES *ORDERS* FOODSTUFFS AND KITCHEN SUPPLIES
by
identifying and qualifying suppliers; negotiating prices; estimating food consumption; placing and expediting orders. *counting inventory.*

● PREPARES FOOD
by
establishing nutrition and presentation standards; *completing* preparation procedures; measuring results against standards; making necessary production adjustments.

% of
Time

____ ● **APPROVES** *CONFIRMS* **FOOD PRESENTATION**
by
observing methods of preparation; tasting and
smelling prepared dishes; viewing color,
texture, and garnishments; verifying portion
sizes.

____ ● **CONTROLS COSTS**
by
using readily available and seasonal
ingredients; identifying and qualifying
suppliers; setting *adhering to* standards for
quality and quantity.

____ ● **COMPLETES KITCHEN OPERATIONAL**
REQUIREMENTS
by
scheduling and assigning employees; following
up on work results.

____ ● **MAINTAINS KITCHEN STAFF**
by
recruiting, selecting, orienting, and training
employees.

____ ● **MAINTAINS KITCHEN STAFF JOB RESULTS**
by
coaching, counseling, and disciplining
employees; planning, monitoring, and
appraising job results.

% of
Time

____ ● **MAINTAINS PROFESSIONAL AND TECHNICAL KNOWLEDGE**
by
attending educational workshops; reviewing
professional and *technical* publications;
establishing personal networks. participating
in professional societies.

____ ● **MAINTAINS A CLEAN AND SAFE ENVIRONMENT**
by
implementing and *complying* with federal,
state, and local sanitation requirements;
maintaining first aid, CPR, and Heimlich
maneuver certification; instructing others
following procedures in the use of kitchen
utensils and operation of equipment.

____ ● **CONTRIBUTES TO TEAM EFFORT**
by
accomplishing related results as needed.

Revision Example 2

Here is an example of a Receptionist job description that has duties different from the model in the compendium.

JOB TITLE: Receptionist

JOB PURPOSE: **SERVES VISITORS**
by
greeting, welcoming, and directing them; *collecting revenues.* notifying
company personnel of visitor's arrival; maintaining security and
telecommunications system.

ESSENTIAL JOB RESULTS:

% of
Time

____ ● WELCOMES VISITORS
by
greeting them in person; or on the telephone;
answering or referring inquiries.

____ ● *COLLECTS REVENUE*
by
obtaining entrance fees and selling souvenirs.

____ ● DIRECTS VISITORS
by
maintaining employee and department
directories; giving instructions; *providing*
directions and maps.

____ ● MAINTAINS SECURITY
by
following procedures; monitoring logbook;
issuing visitor badges.

____ ● MAINTAINS TELECOMMUNICATION SYSTEM
by
following manufacturer's instructions for house
phone and console operation.

% of
Time

____ ● MAINTAINS SAFE AND CLEAN RECEPTION AREA
by
complying with procedures, rules, and
regulations.

____ ● MAINTAINS CONTINUITY AMONG WORK TEAMS
by
documenting and communicating actions,
irregularities, and continuing needs.

____ ● *MAINTAINS SUPPLIES INVENTORY*
by
checking stock to determine inventory level,
anticipating needed supplies, placing and
expediting orders for supplies, and verifying
receipt of supplies.

____ ● CONTRIBUTES TO TEAM EFFORT
by
accomplishing related results as needed.

3

Standard Job Results and Duties

Many jobs are more similar than they at first appear. Thus, many job results and duties statements can be standardized and then easily used or adapted in cases where you need to write your own job descriptions. Standard job results and duties are included here to help you in this task. For guidance on writing unique job descriptions, refer to Chapter 4.

When you begin to write a job description, search through the following standard statements to find those that describe or nearly decribe your situation. Edit them to fit your organizational requirements.

Standard Statements

The standard results and duties are organized into the following categories:

- Confidentiality and legal requirements
- Education
- Equipment and supplies
- Information
- Management
- Operations
- Problem solving
- Safety
- Service
- Standards and procedures
- Universal

Confidentiality and Legal Requirements

These statements cover safeguarding customer, product, and operational information; as well as complying with legal requirements.

MAINTAINS CUSTOMER CONFIDENCE AND PROTECTS OPERATIONS
by
keeping information confidential.

MAINTAINS ORGANIZATION'S STABILITY AND REPUTATION
by
complying with legal requirements.

MAINTAINS PRODUCT AND COMPANY REPUTATION
by
complying with federal and state regulations.

COMPLIES WITH FEDERAL, STATE, AND LOCAL LEGAL REQUIREMENTS
by
studying existing and new legislation, anticipating legislation, enforcing adherence to requirements, and advising management on needed actions.

Education

These statements concern updating professional and technical knowledge and providing information and learning opportunities to others.

DEVELOPS STAFF
by
providing information, educational opportunities, and experiential growth opportunities.

MAINTAINS PROFESSIONAL AND TECHNICAL KNOWLEDGE
by
attending educational workshops, reviewing professional publications, establishing personal networks, and participating in professional societies.

MAINTAINS TECHNICAL KNOWLEDGE
by
attending educational workshops and reading technical publications.

Equipment and Supplies

Here are statements for completing maintenance and operational requirements, maintaining supplies inventories, and conserving resources.

ENSURES OPERATION OF EQUIPMENT
by
completing preventive maintenance requirements, following manufacturer's instructions, troubleshooting malfunctions, calling for repairs, maintaining equipment inventories, and evaluating new equipment and techniques.

KEEPS EQUIPMENT OPERATIONAL
by
following manufacturer's instructions and established procedures.

MAINTAINS SUPPLIES INVENTORY
by
checking stock to determine inventory level, anticipating needed supplies, placing and expediting orders for supplies, and verifying receipt of supplies.

CONSERVES RESOURCES

by

using equipment and supplies as needed to accomplish job results.

Information

These statements are for obtaining, providing, maintaining, and securing information and for preparing reports.

MAINTAINS DATA BASE

by

writing computer programs and entering and backing up data.

MAINTAINS DATA BASE

by

developing information requirements and designing an information system.

SECURES INFORMATION

by

completing data base backups.

MAINTAINS HISTORICAL RECORDS

by

filing documents.

PROVIDES INFORMATION

by

answering questions and requests.

PREPARES REPORTS

by

collecting, analyzing, and summarizing information and trends.

REPRESENTS THE ORGANIZATION

by

preparing a strategy, collecting data, and presenting information at hearings.

Management

These statements deal with hiring, scheduling, training, and counseling employees and achieving financial objectives.

COMPLETES OPERATIONAL REQUIREMENTS

by

scheduling and assigning employees; following up on work results.

MAINTAINS (DEPARTMENT) STAFF

by

recruiting, selecting, orienting, and training employees.

MAINTAINS (DEPARTMENT) STAFF JOB RESULTS

by

coaching, counseling, and disciplining employees; planning, monitoring, and appraising job results.

ACHIEVES FINANCIAL OBJECTIVES
by
preparing an annual budget; scheduling expenditures; analyzing variances; initiating corrective actions.

Operations

The following statements are for identifying, scheduling, maintaining, and coordinating work flow.

PREPARES WORK TO BE ACCOMPLISHED
by
gathering and sorting documents.

MAINTAINS WORK FLOW
by
sorting and delivering information.

MAINTAINS CONTINUITY AMONG WORK TEAMS
by
documenting and communicating actions, irregularities, and continuing needs.

CONTRIBUTES TO PROGRAM EFFECTIVENESS
by
identifying short-term and long-range issues that must be addressed, providing information and commentary pertinent to deliberations, recommending options and courses of action, and implementing directives.

MAINTAINS INTER- AND INTRADEPARTMENTAL WORK FLOW
by
fostering a spirit of cooperation.

COMPLETES PROJECTS
by
training and guiding technicians.

Problem Solving

These statements concern collecting and analyzing information, evaluating optional courses of action, and resolving problems.

RESOLVES DISCREPANCIES
by
collecting and analyzing information.

ACHIEVES WORK OBJECTIVES
by
gathering pertinent data, identifying and evaluating options, and choosing a course of action.

RESOLVES ASSEMBLY PROBLEMS
by
altering dimensions to meet specifications, and notifying supervisor to obtain additional resources.

Safety

These statements concern complying with and promoting safety requirements and protecting others.

MAINTAINS SAFE AND CLEAN WORKING ENVIRONMENT
by
complying with procedures, rules, and regulations.

PROTECTS PATIENTS AND EMPLOYEES
by
adhering to infection-control policies and protocols.

PROMOTES HEALTHY WORK ENVIRONMENT
by
coordinating and cooperating with federal, state, and local agencies.

Service

These statements cover identifying service requirements and documenting actions.

IDENTIFIES PATIENT SERVICE REQUIREMENTS
by
establishing personal rapport with potential and actual patients and with other persons in a position to understand service requirements.

IDENTIFIES CONCERNS
by
surveying conditions and recommending actions.

DOCUMENTS PATIENT CARE SERVICES
by
completing charting in patient and department records.

IDENTIFIES CURRENT AND FUTURE CUSTOMER SERVICE REQUIREMENTS
by
establishing personal rapport with potential and actual customers and with other persons in a position to understand service requirements.

DOCUMENTS ACTIONS
by
completing production and quality logs.

Standards and Procedures

These statements cover writing, updating, and following procedures, as well as verifying output.

MAINTAINS OPERATIONS
by
following policies and procedures and reporting needed changes.

MAINTAINS GUIDELINES
by
writing and updating policies and procedures.

PRODUCES PRODUCT/SERVICE
by
establishing standards and procedures, measuring results against standards, and making necessary adjustments.

MAINTAINS OPERATIONS
by
initiating, coordinating, and enforcing program, operational, and personnel policies and procedures.

VERIFIES SETTINGS
by
measuring positions, first-run part, and sample workpieces.

MAINTAINS PRODUCTION AND QUALITY
by
observing machine operation, detecting malfunctions, and adjusting settings.

Universal

This statement is for a position that requires flexibility in accepting job assignments.

CONTRIBUTES TO TEAM EFFORT
by
accomplishing related results as needed.

This standard result and duty replaces the traditional "Performs related duties as may be needed," in order to explain why extra demands may be made from time to time. Another possible *why* is "Completes department projects."

The purpose of the universal statement is to communicate to employees that job descriptions are not designed to identify each and every expectation that may be required of an incumbent. This statement makes it clear that there may be times when some result or duty may be required that cannot be anticipated. When those times occur, results or duties will be temporarily added to the job description so that the organization's purposes can be accomplished. Said another way, this is the organization's flexibility statement.

Edited Examples

Here are some examples of how the standard results and duties statements can be edited. Deletions are shown as shaded, and additions are shown in *italics*.

PREPARES *ACCOUNTING* REPORTS
by
collecting, analyzing, and summarizing information and trends.

MAINTAINS CUSTOMER *PATIENT* CONFIDENCE AND PROTECTS *HOSPITAL* OPERATIONS
by
keeping information confidential.

MAINTAINS ORGANIZATION'S STABILITY AND *SERVICE* REPUTATION
by
complying with legal *government* requirements.

DOCUMENTS ACTIONS *FINANCIAL TRANSACTIONS*
by
completing production and quality logs *entering account information.*

RESOLVES *RECONCILES FINANCIAL* DISCREPANCIES
by
collecting and analyzing *account* information.

PROVIDES *ENGINEERING* INFORMATION
by
answering questions and requests.

MAINTAINS *CONSUMER LOAN OPERATIONS* STAFF
by
recruiting, selecting, orienting, and training employees.

4

Writing Results-Oriented Job Descriptions

In many cases you will be able to either use the job descriptions in this compendium just as they are or edit them here and there to match your unique requirements. In some cases, you will need to write new results and duties. Here is the architecture of the statement for you to follow.

The result to be accomplished is stated first, for example:

MAINTAINS COMPANY TELEPHONE DIRECTORY
[*Start with an action verb, then write the object of the action.*]

Then write the connector word:

by

Then write the duty performed in order to accomplish the result (it's possible to have several duties for one result):

updating files with additions, deletions, and changes.
[*What the employee is do"ing"—the verb in the second part of the sentence always ends in "ing."*]

Distinguishing Between Results and Duties

To distinguish between a result and a duty, try placing the job element both before and after the "by." Then complete the sentence to see which order makes more sense. Remember, a result answers the question, *Why* are we doing this? A duty, on the other hand, answers the question, *What* must be done to produce the result?

Here's an example.

(as a result)   =   **UPDATES FILES WITH ADDITIONS, DELETIONS, AND CHANGES**
by . . .

(as a duty)   =   by
                        updating files with additions, deletions, and changes.

When you complete the statement as:

UPDATES FILES WITH ADDITIONS, DELETIONS, AND CHANGES
by
entering data noted on personnel status change forms, retrieving the employee's data
file, deleting information as noted in file, and entering new data.

the duties turn out to be job procedures that belong in an operations manual. Procedures are more
specific than necessary for a job description.

When you complete the statement as:

MAINTAINS COMPANY TELEPHONE DIRECTORY
by
updating files with additions, deletions, and changes.

the result describes what's really important about the job. The telephone directory is the outcome
produced by updating files, the product of the work. Updating files is *how* the directory is maintained.

Are Results Always Results and Duties Always Duties?

One job's duty can be another job's result. Therefore, whether a statement is a result or a duty depends
on the job.

For a Materials Manager

SUPPORTS OPERATIONS
by
maintaining an inventory.

For a Purchasing Assistant

MAINTAINS INVENTORY
by
purchasing supplies.

For a Purchasing Clerk

PURCHASES SUPPLIES
by
preparing requisitions.

Studying the job above and the job below the job you are writing will help you understand the
results and duties.

Recognizing Results and Duties

Here are two statements. Which is the result, and which is the duty?

1. *Inspects work.*
2. *Meets quality standards.*

Remember, a result answers the question, *Why* are we doing this? A duty answers the question, *What* must be done to produce the result?

The result is: MEETS QUALITY STANDARDS
                 by

The duty is: inspecting work.

Here are some more statements for you to compare. Which is the result? Which is the duty? Remember, the duty verb becomes an "ing" word, so try the verbs with "ing" endings to understand which is the result and which is the duty.

1. Directs operations
   by
2. Provides services.

1. Maintains staff job results
   by
2. Conducts planning and appraisal conferences.

1. Serves customers
   by
2. Delivers packages.

1. Maintains staff of employees
   by
2. Recruits, screens, and tests candidates.

Here are the answers:

PROVIDES SERVICES = result
by
directing operations = duty

MAINTAINS STAFF JOB RESULTS = result
by
conducting planning and appraisal conferences = duty

SERVES CUSTOMERS = result
by
delivering packages = duty

MAINTAINS STAFF OF EMPLOYEES = result
by
recruiting, screening, and testing candidates = duties

Some Examples of Duties and Related Results

This is the duty	This is the result
Orienting new employees	Prepares employees for assignments
Typing	Prepares reports
Analyzing data	Recommends action
Counseling employees	Improves job results
Inspecting equipment	Completes preventive maintenance
Participating in meetings	Contributes information and opinion
Assessing a situation	Identifies problem
Supervising employees	Accomplishes job results
Verifying work	Completes assignments
Expediting work	Ensures delivery
Processing orders	Fills customer requests
Making appointments	Organizes time
Recording time	Documents actions
Evaluating action	Determines effect
Delivering supplies	Maintains schedule
Interviewing candidates	Determines eligibility

Identifying Results

One way to identify results is by listing the duties of a job. For example, Column A lists typical duties of a Secretary. Then, ask yourself what result (see Column B) each duty accomplishes.

Column A	Column B
Answering letters	Serves customers
Electronic calendaring	Maintains appointment schedule
Filing	Provides historical reference
Formatting text	Provides info-management support
Inputting text	Provides info-management support
Editing text	Provides info-management support
Drafting letters and documents	Conserves manager's time
Formatting graphics	Provides info-management support
Planning and scheduling meetings	Maintains appointment schedule
Answering inquiries	Serves customers
Ordering and receiving supplies	Maintains office inventory
Developing/maintaining filing system	Provides historical reference
Establishing teleconferences	Maintains appointment schedule

Next, group the duties that produce the same result, and arrange the statements according to the "result-by-duty" formula.

PROVIDES INFO-MANAGEMENT SUPPORT
by
formatting text, inputting text, editing text, and formatting graphics.

SERVES CUSTOMERS
by
answering letters and inquiries.

MAINTAINS APPOINTMENT SCHEDULE
by
electronic calendaring, planning and scheduling meetings, and establishing teleconferences.

CONSERVES MANAGER'S TIME
by
drafting letters and documents.

PROVIDES HISTORICAL REFERENCE
by
developing/maintaining filing system.

MAINTAINS OFFICE INVENTORY
by
ordering and receiving supplies.

Ensuring That the Result Is Correctly Identified

Identifying the result is the toughest part of writing a job description. Duties are more easily recognized than results because that is the way managers and workers have been taught to think about work. Understanding why a duty must be performed is not always so clear. Here's a tip: Generally speaking, what you can see people doing is the duty.

Remember the story about the three bricklayers?

The first said the job was: laying brick
The second said the job was: raising a wall
The third said the job was: building a cathedral

The first saw: a job duty
The second saw: a job result
The third saw: a job purpose

To identify the result, ask yourself:

1. *What* is the outcome of this duty?
2. *Why* is this duty important?
3. *What* does this duty accomplish?

Keep asking these questions until you understand what is really important about the duty, but don't define a result that is beyond the scope of the duty. Building a cathedral is a worthwhile vision of the job, but not the immediate result of laying bricks. The bricklayer will be held accountable for the wall, not for the cathedral.

In the example of the Purchasing Clerk's job, saying that the result is "Supports operations" is too broad; certainly that is beyond the control of the clerk. The immediate outcome of preparing requisitions is "Purchases supplies."

Arranging Results and Duties

The results and duties statements are arranged in the job description to communicate expectations logically, in one of these three sequences:

1. Most important to least important
2. Most time spent to least time spent
3. In the order accomplished

Choosing the Correct Words for Job Results and Duties

Each word in a job description is important to help people understand and clarify job expectations. The correct verb differentiates responsibilities and authorities among jobs. Each of the following verbs defines a different level of job responsibility.

Prepares	purchasing contracts by . . .
Reviews	purchasing contracts by . . .
Audits	purchasing contracts by . . .
Interprets	purchasing contracts by . . .
Enforces	purchasing contracts by . . .

Here is a quick reference to help you select the verb that most accurately describes the job requirement and authority.

Controls	obtains	calculates	manages	assembles
	orders	compiles	oversees	carries
adopts	pays	computes	represents	clears
anticipates	releases	extends	schedules	collates
approves	remits	figures	supervises	disassembles
closes	requires	inventories		enters
collects	routes	invoices	**Distributes**	feeds
consolidates	secures	reconciles	circulates	handles
contracts	selects	totals	disseminates	opens
deletes	signs		furnishes	processes
disburses	traces	**Directs**	issues	stacks
ensures		administers	renders	types
expedites	**Counts**	assigns		
finds		authorizes		
follows up	adds	delegates	**Operates**	
locates	balances	determines		
maintains	bills		aligns	

Originates	***Records***	registers	reviews	checks
arranges	attaches	tabulates	scans	compares
conducts	catalogues	transfers	screens	corrects
creates	charts		searches	edits
defines	classifies	***Studies***	surveys	proofreads
designs	codes		tests	revises
develops	copies	analyzes		
establishes	enters	appraises	***Teaches***	***Writes***
executes	files	ascertains	guides	composes
formulates	indexes	audits	instructs	describes
implements	itemizes	estimates	interprets	drafts
initiates	lays out	evaluates	trains	outlines
institutes	lists	examines		summarizes
organizes	places	inspects	***Verifies***	
plans	posts	investigates	affirms	
prepares	receives	observes	amends	
		rates		

Should Job Standards Be Included in the Results and Duties Statements?

It is not necessary to use evaluative terms in results and duties statements. Do not add words that attempt to define how well the result is to be accomplished or how well the duty is to be performed, as in these examples:

Completes studies *efficiently and competently.*

Designs systems *effectively and appropriately.*

Makes recommendations *that are novel.*

Completes reports *promptly and properly.*

Greets customers *in a courteous manner.*

Qualifying words not only lengthen the statement but blur its meaning. Vague words only make the mind stop and spin as it wonders how to interpret words such as "efficiently" and "appropriately." The goal when writing job standards is to be concrete and clear.

Results and duties, as well as job standards, are more easily understood when they are stated separately but linked in format. When you define job standards for your organization, here is a useful way to present them:

MAINTAINS COMPANY TELEPHONE DIRECTORY
by
updating files with additions, deletions, and changes.

Result required: Additions, deletions, and changes are entered within four hours of receipt. Data entered are verified against personnel status change forms. Discrepancies are questioned.

Stated in this manner, the job description and job standards become the powerful documentation they should be for planning and appraising job outcomes.

Improving Your Writing

Here's a writing tip: *Fewer words are usually better!*

Change this:	*To this:*
Makes sure that shipments are complete.	Completes shipments.
Keeps customers informed.	Informs customers.
Keeps customer accounts up to date.	Maintains customer accounts.
Ensures that automobile fleet is in good condition.	Maintains automobile fleet.
Ensures quality and timeliness of administrative services.	Provides administrative services.
Ensures accuracy of data.	Verifies data.
Makes sure that each manifest is balanced and that product codes agree with customer's order.	Balances manifests and correlating product codes with customer's order.

Writing the Job Purpose

The job purpose is a one-sentence synthesis that tells why a job exists. The job purpose statement follows the result-by-duty formula.

For example, the job purpose of the Telecommunications Specialist is:

HELPS PEOPLE COMMUNICATE
by
referring telephone calls and maintaining telephone directories.

Here's another example. The job purpose of a Quality Assurance Technician is:

ASSURES QUALITY PRODUCT
by
conducting in-process inspections; evaluating finished product.

Some people find it easier to write the job results and duties first and then synthesize them in the job purpose. Others write the job purpose first and then the job results and duties. Write in the sequence that is easier for you.

Where and How Does the Job Fit in the Organization?

The job purpose can be tricky to write. It is more than just a job summary that regurgitates what is written below. The job purpose offers an opportunity to explain where and how the job fits in the scheme of the organization and why the job exists.

Is the purpose realistic?

The job purpose should not be inflated or out of reach for the job described.

If, for example, you are describing a Housekeeper in a hospital and the mission of the hospital is to treat patients, you may be tempted to describe the Housekeeper's job purpose as "Treats patients by maintaining facilities."

While you want the Housekeeper to understand his or her role in the unified effort to treat patients, treating patients is beyond the immediate control of the Housekeeper. If, however, the job description states only "Maintains facilities by providing cleaning services," the necessary participation of the Housekeeper in the delivery system is not recognized.

More accurately, the Housekeeper's job purpose is:

MAINTAINS FACILITIES FOR PATIENTS, VISITORS, AND COWORKERS
by
providing cleaning services.

Is the purpose meaningful?

You can use the job purpose to elevate a job to its true meaning and value. Sometimes just a slight change of words will do. In the case of the Aircraft Mechanic, the purpose of the organization is to transport people and cargo. You could say that the job of the Aircraft Mechanic is: "Transports people and cargo by maintaining aircraft." Yet the Aircraft Mechanic does not transport people.

One option is to identify the job purpose as: "Maintains aircraft by completing preventive maintenance schedules; installing and repairing parts and systems." Still, you want to tie the Aircraft Mechanic's job to the real purpose of the airline because the work is such an integral and obvious part of the business.

Trying different words, you might conclude that the Aircraft Mechanic:

PROVIDES TRANSPORT FOR PEOPLE AND CARGO
by
maintaining, repairing, and overhauling aircraft and aircraft engines.

Gathering Data for a Job Description

There are a number of sources for the information you need to write a job description. These include:

- Job analyses
- Personnel requisitions and job opportunity bulletins
- Goals set in performance planning
- Corporate and department studies and projects
- Job competencies
- Old job descriptions
- Job descriptions for similar jobs
- Sample job descriptions from books or other organizations
- Job procedure lists
- Corporate philosophy and mission statements

- Department mission statements
- Organization charts
- Performance criteria
- Regulatory requirements

Converting Statements to the Result-by-Duty Formula

When you read job descriptions, you may find that they follow a different format than those in this compendium. The expectations may be stated in this manner: The duty is performed *"in order to,"* or, *"to,"* or, *"so that,"* or, *"so,"* or, *"for"* the result accomplished.

Consider this example: "Completes analyses to provide management with cost information." The duty and the result are here, but not in the order we use. You can convert the statement into the result-by-duty formula by rearranging its elements in this way:

PROVIDES MANAGEMENT WITH INFORMATION
by
completing cost analyses.

Some Rules for Writing

Write in any way that is comfortable for you. You can begin by listing all of the duties or by specifying the job results.

Remember that good writing comes from good editing; don't try to write perfectly the first time. Write for a while, and, when you get tired, put the work away. Pick up the work later, and edit your previous work.

Set aside some time to write without interruption so you can concentrate better.

Worksheets

Here are some worksheets you can use to organize and guide your work.

WORKSHEET: Job Description Cover Sheet

JOB TITLE: _____

SECTION: _____

WRITTEN BY: _____

REPORTS TO (JOB TITLE): _____

JOB TITLES SUPERVISED: _____

                                               _____

                                               _____

                                               _____

DATE WRITTEN: _____

REVIEWED BY: _____

APPROVED BY: _____

DATE APPROVED: _____

WORKSHEET: Job Purpose

JOB PURPOSE:

_____

by

_____

WORKSHEET: Job Description Results and Duties

Write either the result or the duty first, whichever is easier for you. Jobs typically have about one dozen specific result and duty statements. Fill in the following:

___ **Result**   =   Why is the duty important? What is accomplished by performing the duty?

   by

   Duty   =   What is the activity being performed?

% of
time

___ **Result**   _____
                                        [Start with an active verb, such as "completes" or "maintains"]

by

Duty   _____
                                        [Start with an "ing" verb, such as "recording" or "evaluating"]

Duty   _____

___ **Result**   _____
                                        [Start with an active verb, such as "completes" or "maintains"]

by

Duty   _____
                                        [Start with an "ing" verb, such as "recording" or "evaluating"]

Duty   _____

___ **Result**   _____
                                        [Start with an active verb, such as "completes" or "maintains"]

by

Duty   _____
                                        [Start with an "ing" verb, such as "recording" or "evaluating"]

Duty   _____

WORKSHEET: Job Qualifications and Job Evaluation Documentation

Job qualifications define the knowledge, skill, and ability an incumbent must have in order to accomplish the job results and to perform the job duties.

Job evaluation documentation defines the job demands made on the job incumbent. These job demands are compared with the demands of other jobs to determine which jobs are worth more to the organization and therefore should carry higher salaries. This process is called job evaluation.

The information that identifies job qualifications and job demands can easily be combined into one document. Although this book is not intended to teach you how to define job qualifications or gauge differing job demands, a worksheet that will help you to assemble that information is included. Be sure to use job-specific examples when completing the worksheet!

KNOWLEDGE
What does the incumbent need to know to perform the job at the entry level, whether the skills are acquired through formal education, experience, or self-learning?

INFORMATION PROCESSING
In what way does the incumbent use information mentally?

SCOPE OF RESPONSIBILITY
What decisions are made by the incumbent?

INTERPERSONAL COMMUNICATION
What is the reason for contacts with others?

IMPACT ON RESULTS
What typically might go wrong as a result of an error by the incumbent?

DESCRIBE CONTROLS
What controls exist to prevent errors?

CONFIDENTIAL AND SENSITIVE INFORMATION
What confidential and sensitive information is available to the incumbent?

_____

_____

_____

SCOPE OF FINANCIAL RESPONSIBILITY
What is the incumbent's responsibility for expenditures and funding/revenue?

_____

_____

_____

ENVIRONMENT
What are the physical and mental strains, stresses, or exposures of the job?

PHYSICAL DEMANDS

☐ Balancing	☐ Crouching	☐ Hearing	Seeing	☐ Sitting
☐ Carrying	☐ Feeling	☐ Kneeling	☐ Close	☐ Standing
☐ Climbing	☐ Fingering	☐ Lifting	☐ Far	☐ Stooping
☐ Crawling	☐ Grasping	☐ Pulling	☐ Color	☐ Talking
			☐ Depth	☐ Walking

EXPOSURES

☐ Airborne particles	☐ Explosives	☐ Muscular strain	☐ Temperature
☐ Caustics	☐ Fumes	☐ Noise	☐ Toxicants
☐ Chemicals	☐ High places	☐ Odors	☐ Vibration
☐ Electrical current	☐ Moving parts	☐ Physical abuse	☐ Vision strain
			☐ Weather

SUPERVISORY-MANAGEMENT RESPONSIBILITY
In what ways does the incumbent direct the work of others?

| ☐ Hire/discipline/terminate | ☐ Assign and check work | ☐ Train |
| ☐ Plan/appraise job results | ☐ Recommend pay increases | |

Number of employees supervised: _____

How many employees are supervised (including those supervised indirectly, namely, those employees supervised by subordinate supervisors)? _____

SAMPLE: Job Description, Job Qualifications, and Job Evaluation
Documentation

I. JOB DESCRIPTION

TITLE: Employee Benefits Assistant

DEPARTMENT: Personnel **FLSA:** N

REPORTS TO: Compensation Manager **GRADE:** 8

JOBS SUPERVISED: None

CAREER PROGRESSION: Employee Benefits Specialist; Compensation Analyst

---

JOB PURPOSE: **PROVIDES EMPLOYEE BENEFITS**

by

answering questions, and initiating and continuing membership.

ESSENTIAL JOB RESULTS:

*% of
Time*

___35%___ 1. RESOLVES EMPLOYEE QUESTIONS AND PROBLEMS
   by
   researching policies and procedures and
   providing answers.

___20%___ 2. INITIATES NEW-HIRE BENEFITS
   by
   obtaining and recording benefit information
   and informing insurance carriers.

___10%___ 3. COMPLETES BILLING
   by
   organizing carrier reports, requesting
   disbursements, and reconciling accounts.

*% of
Time*

___15%___ 4. PRESERVES HISTORICAL REFERENCE
   by
   establishing and maintaining recordkeeping
   system and filing and retrieving department
   information.

___10%___ 5. CONTINUES ELECTIVE RETIREE INSURANCE COVERAGE
   by
   tracking payments and depository funds.

___5%___ 6. MAINTAINS DEPARTMENT SUPPLIES INVENTORY
   by
   anticipating needs, placing orders, and
   verifying delivery.

___5%___ 7. COMPLETES DEPARTMENTAL OPERATIONS
   by
   accomplishing related results as needed.

II. JOB QUALIFICATIONS AND JOB EVALUATION DOCUMENTATION

KNOWLEDGE

EDUCATION:	One year business school preferred.
EXPERIENCE:	Accounts receivable/payable process.
SKILLS AND ABILITIES:	Basic calculator operation. Data entry, 40 wpm. Proven accuracy. Demonstrated telephone operation and courtesy.

INFORMATION PROCESSING
Identifies and answers employee questions and concerns, using defined sources of information.

DECISION MAKING
Identifies correct answer. Transfers and verifies information. Orders supplies.

INTERPERSONAL COMMUNICATION
Clarifies benefits policies and procedures for employees at individual levels of understanding.

IMPACT OF RESULTS
Errors increase expense to the organization. Incorrect information is an inconvenience to employee or the employee's family. Incomplete or inaccurate work causes a negative perception of the department.

DESCRIBE CONTROLS
Insurance company verification. Billing errors can be corrected.

CONFIDENTIAL AND SENSITIVE INFORMATION
All personnel files and salary information.

SCOPE OF FINANCIAL RESPONSIBILITY
Orders supplies. Reconciles benefits accounts.

ENVIRONMENT

PHYSICAL DEMANDS

☐ Balancing	☐ Crouching	☒ Hearing	Seeing	☒ Sitting
☒ Carrying	☐ Feeling	☐ Kneeling	☒ Close	☐ Standing
☐ Climbing	☒ Fingering	☐ Lifting	☐ Far	☒ Stooping
☐ Crawling	☒ Grasping	☐ Pulling	☐ Color	☒ Talking
			☐ Depth	☒ Walking

EXPOSURES

☐ Airborne particles	☐ Explosives	☐ Muscular strain	☐ Temperature
☐ Caustics	☐ Fumes	☐ Noise	☐ Toxicants
☐ Chemicals	☐ High places	☐ Odors	☐ Vibration
☐ Electrical current	☐ Moving parts	☐ Physical abuse	☐ Vision strain
			☐ Weather

SUPERVISORY RESPONSIBILITY

Number of employees supervised:___

___ Hire/discipline/terminate

___ Assign and check work   ___ Train

___ Plan/appraise job results   ___ Recommend pay increases

5
Legal Considerations

Federal law is remarkably silent about job descriptions. What federal law is not silent about, however, is the protection of employee rights. A judge's decision about the abuse of employee rights may well rest on the job results and duties that are (or are not) stated in a job description. If a job description exists but the actual conditions on the job are different from those stated in the job description, the actual conditions take precedence in determining liability. What this means, of course, is that job descriptions must be maintained and audited.

The following federal laws contain a variety of provisions that are not discussed in this book. The guidelines that follow are derived from provisions to which a job description might be relevant.

State laws are not addressed here because of their diversity.

Americans With Disabilities Act

The Americans with Disabilities Act (ADA), which went into effect in 1990, protects people from discrimination based on physical or mental disabilities. A key factor in this protection is the determination of whether a person with a disability can "perform the essential functions" of the job, with or without reasonable accommodation.

Essential Functions

Essential functions can be defined by answering the following questions:

1. Why does the job exist?
2. Would removing the function fundamentally change the job?
3. Is the function marginal or incidental to the job purpose?
4. Is the job specialized, so that the person in the job is hired for his or her expertise to accomplish the function?
5. Is the function actually accomplished by all current incumbents?
6. Was the function required of past incumbents?
7. Does the incumbent spend a substantial amount of time accomplishing the function? [Time spent is only a rough indicator of a function's importance, because some functions require only a little time to accomplish but are crucial to the outcome of the job. To help with this

consideration, we have included a "% of time" space alongside each result and duty statement.]

8. Would the consequences be serious if the function were not accomplished?
9. Is there a limited number of employees available among whom the function can be distributed?
10. Does a collective bargaining agreement identify the function as part of the job?

Determining What Is Essential

A results-oriented job description can help you define essential functions and carry out the intent of the ADA, but you may have to adjust your language a little bit. In the language of the ADA, the issue is whether a person can "perform the essential functions of the job."

Since most job descriptions list only job duties, the question becomes, Which of the duties are essential? Interestingly, some of the examples used in the ADA Handbook, published by the Equal Employment Opportunity Commission and the U.S. Department of Justice, recognize that defining what is "essential" may not be as easy as you might think.

For example, the handbook notes that "the ability to access, input, and retrieve information from a computer" may not mean that the person has to "enter information manually, or visually read the information on the computer screen. Adaptive devices or computer software can enable a person without arms or a person with impaired vision to perform the essential functions of the job."

Focusing on Results to Clarify What Is Essential

The results-oriented job description helps clarify the issue.

The result is:	MAINTAINS DATA BASE
	by
The duties are:	accessing, inputting, and retrieving information from a computer.

Here the emphasis is on the data base rather than accessing, inputting, and retrieving. The implication is that as long as the data base is maintained, how it is maintained is not as significant. Focusing on the result, instead of on the duties, helps open the door to new and other ways of accomplishing the same outcome.

The result is not necessarily the same as the essential function, because some duties may be essential. Focusing on the result helps clarify what is essential. A close examination of the job description is required.

The Job Description as Evidence

The ADA does not require you to develop and maintain job descriptions, but a written job description prepared before advertising for, or interviewing, applicants for a job can serve as evidence in documenting functions.

The ADA does not require that you limit your job descriptions to a definition of essential functions or even that essential functions be identified. However, if you wish to use a job description to document what functions are essential, you should identify those functions as important in accomplishing the purpose of the job.

Do you have to rewrite all of your job descriptions? That depends on the state of your current job descriptions. If your descriptions list only job duties, then your explanation of job expectations is incomplete, by the reasoning employed in this book. Applicants and employees who are disabled can teach managers new ways to accomplish traditional job results.

What Constitutes Reasonable Accommodation?

Debates regarding the ADA will probably center not on the definition of essential functions but on whether a qualified individual with a known physical or mental disability can be reasonably accommodated without undue hardship to the employer.

"Reasonable accommodation" is a modification or adjustment to a job, the work environment, or the way things are usually done that enables a qualified individual with a disability to enjoy an equal employment opportunity. An equal employment opportunity is defined as the opportunity to attain the same level of performance or to enjoy the same benefits and privileges of employment that are available to an average similarly situated employee without a disability.

Reasonable accommodations may include:

- Making facilities readily accessible and usable
- Restructuring the job by reallocating or redistributing nonessential job functions
- Offering part-time or modified work schedules
- Obtaining or modifiying equipment or devices
- Providing qualified readers and interpreters
- Providing reserved parking for a person with a mobility impairment

Legal challenges to the law will probably address the questions of what constitutes an "undue hardship" and how to define "the way things are usually done."

Given two candidates with different disabilities, both requesting that job requirements be reallocated, employers may find they can accommodate one candidate but not the other. Therefore, what is deemed essential at first may not be essential in the final analysis.

What Is Written Is Essential

We suggest that you start with the position that anything you write in a job description is essential. To label some job expectations as unessential or marginal sends an awkward, if not demotivating message to employees. Whether a particular function is in fact essential can be determined when you decide whether it can be modified to accommodate an employee or applicant with a disability.

Fair Labor Standards Act

Generally speaking, under the Fair Labor Standards Act (FLSA), employees must be paid overtime for hours worked in excess of forty per workweek, although there is a variety of requirements, exclusions, exceptions, and exemptions, all of which you must thoroughly research to determine their applicability to your organization. The reference is the United States Code, Title 29, Chapter 8, as well as related laws such as the Portal-to-Portal Act, the Service Contract Act, the Contract Work Hours and Safety Act, the Davis-Bacon Act, the Walsh-Healey Act, and the Railway Labor Act.

Whether an employee is exempt from the law is determined by the employee's actual work requirements, typically defined in a job description. Exemptions from overtime pay are defined in four categories: executives, administrators, professionals, and outside salespersons. Here are the exemptions for your easy reference.

Executive Exemption

An executive employee must:

- Earn at least $250 per week.
- Have the primary duty of management of the enterprise in which employed or of a customarily recognized department or subdivision of that enterprise.
- Customarily and regularly direct the work of two or more other employees in that enterprise.

If the executive earns at least $155 per week but less than $250 per week, in addition to the above requirements, he or she must:

- Have the authority to hire or fire other employees or make particularly influential suggestions and recommendations regarding hiring, firing, advancement, promotion, or other change of status of other employees.
- Customarily and regularly exercise discretionary powers.
- Devote no more than 20 percent (40 percent in the case of an employee in a retail or service establishment) of hours of work in the workweek to activities that are not directly and closely related to the performance of the work described above, unless the person is an owner or operator of an independent establishment or branch establishment.

Administrative Exemption

An administrative employee must:

- Earn at least $250 per week.
- Have the primary duty to exercise discretion and independent judgment.
- Perform office or nonmanual work directly related to management policies or the general business operations of the employer or employer's customers or perform administrative functions in an educational setting in work directly related to the academic instruction or training carried on there.

If the administrative employee earns at least $155 per week but less than $250 per week or is a school administrator whose compensation is on a salary basis, in addition to the above requirements, he or she must:

- Customarily and regularly exercise discretion and independent judgment.
- Regularly and directly assist a business owner or another bona fide executive or administrator or work only under general supervision on tasks that are specialized or technical and require

special training, experience, or knowledge or work only under general supervision on special assignments and tasks.

- Devote no more than 20 percent (40 percent in the case of an employee in a retail or service establishment) of time to activities that are not directly and closely related to the work described above.

Professional Exemption

A professional employee must:

- Earn at least $250 per week (there are some specific exceptions).
- Have primary duties in the performance of a learned or an educational profession entailing work that requires the exercise of discretion and judgment or have primary duties in the performance of work requiring invention, imagination, or talent in a recognized field of artistic endeavor.

If the professional earns at least $155 per week but less than $250 per week, he or she must:

- Have primary duties in the performance of a learned, artistic, or educational profession.
- Consistently exercise discretion and judgment in the performance of the primary duties.
- Accomplish work that is predominantly intellectual and varied in character and that cannot be standardized in relation to time.
- Devote no more than 20 percent of work hours in the workweek to activities that are not an essential part of, and necessarily incident to, the work described above.

Outside Salesperson

An outside salesperson must:

- Customarily and regularly work away from the employer's place of business while making sales or obtaining orders or contracts for services or for the use of facilities for which a consideration will be paid by the client or customer.
- Not engage in work of any other nature for more than 20 percent of the hours worked in the workweek by the employer's nonexempt employees.

These exemptions are explained in detail, with specific examples, in the interpretive bulletin issued by the Department of Labor. Additionally, court cases have clarified specific applications. Note that job titles are not important when determining whether an employee is exempt or whether the company is in compliance with a law. What counts are the job requirements stated under the job title.

Equal Pay Act

Employees may not be discriminated against in pay on the basis of sex when they perform equal work on jobs in the same establishment requiring equal skill, effort, and responsibility and performed under similar working conditions.

The job description of the job accomplished by men is compared to the job description of the job accomplished by women to determine whether they are equal in requirements. Regardless of what is stated in the job description, however, what actually happens on the job is decisive.

Civil Rights Act, Title VII, and Other Antidiscrimination Measures

The Civil Rights Act provides that employees may not be discriminated against because of race, color, sex, pregnancy, religion, or natural origin in regard to hiring, discharge, compensation, terms conditions, or privileges of employment. Executive orders extend the protection to cover age, handicap, and status as a Vietnam veteran. Other laws protecting employees' rights disallow discrimination based on age (Age Discrimination in Employment Act), handicap (Rehabilitation Act), or veteran status (Vietnam Era Veteran's Readjustment Act).

The qualifications listed in job descriptions are often the basis for hiring decisions, so that qualifications that discriminate, or that appear to discriminate, against certain groups of people must be supported by legitimate job results and duties. Be sure that there are no artificial barriers in your job descriptions.

Job Titles

Job titles should not refer to the sex of the incumbent. Use "waitperson" instead of "waiter" or "waitress."

Job Evaluations

Job evaluation plans are used to determine the pay associated with different jobs on the basis of the demands of the job. Job descriptions describe the different job demands.

Appraisals

Appraisals of an employee's accomplishments, which may lead to promotions and pay adjustments, must be substantiated with reference to the description of the employee's job. An appraisal of accomplishments, regardless of the form used, ultimately rests on the job requirements and whether the employee has been able to accomplish them.

Occupational Safety and Health Act

Employers must furnish employees with working conditions free from recognized hazards. Job descriptions are used to warn employees about any possible hazards and to inform employees of requirements regarding safety regulations and procedures.

Part II
Job Descriptions

JOB TITLE: Account Executive

JOB PURPOSE: **SERVES CLIENTS**

by

planning and directing advertising campaigns.

ESSENTIAL JOB RESULTS:

*% of
Time*

_____ 1. DETERMINES CLIENT ADVERTISING CAMPAIGN REQUIREMENTS

by

utilizing product or service knowledge, marketing research, media capabilities, and audience characteristics.

_____ 2. IDENTIFIES CURRENT AND FUTURE CUSTOMER SERVICE REQUIREMENTS

by

establishing rapport with potential and actual customers and other persons in a position to understand customer requirements.

_____ 3. DEVELOPS ADVERTISING BUDGET

by

conferring with agency artists, copywriters, photographers, and other media-production specialists to select media and estimate costs.

_____ 4. OBTAINS CLIENT ACCEPTANCE

by

developing a campaign strategy; preparing and presenting proposals, concepts, storyboards, and other copy and print mock-ups.

_____ 5. GUIDES ADVERTISING PRODUCTION

by

coordinating marketing research, copywriting, art layout, media time and space purchases, special display, and promotional items.

_____ 6. IMPLEMENTS ADVERTISING CAMPAIGNS

by

negotiating newspaper, radio, television, and billboard rates; authorizing contracts.

*% of
Time*

_____ 7. EVALUATES, ADJUSTS, AND REDIRECTS ADVERTISING CAMPAIGNS

by

studying and analyzing sales results, demographics, customer satisfaction surveys, and other market research information.

_____ 8. MAINTAINS CLIENT CONFIDENCE AND PROTECTS ADVERTISING OPERATIONS

by

keeping information confidential.

_____ 9. PROVIDES ACCOUNT INFORMATION

by

answering questions and requests.

_____ 10. PREPARES REPORTS

by

collecting, analyzing, and summarizing information and trends.

_____ 11. MAINTAINS PROFESSIONAL AND TECHNICAL KNOWLEDGE

by

attending educational workshops; reviewing professional publications; establishing personal networks; participating in professional societies.

_____ 12. CONTRIBUTES TO AGENCY EFFECTIVENESS

by

identifying short-term and long-range issues that must be addressed; providing information and commentary pertinent to deliberations; recommending options and courses of action; implementing directives.

_____ 13. CONTRIBUTES TO AGENCY TEAM EFFORT

by

accomplishing related results as needed.

JOB TITLE: Accountant

JOB PURPOSE: PROVIDES FINANCIAL INFORMATION TO MANAGEMENT
by

researching and analyzing accounting data; preparing reports.

ESSENTIAL JOB RESULTS:

% of
Time

____ 1. PREPARES ASSET, LIABILITY, AND CAPITAL ACCOUNT ENTRIES
by
compiling and analyzing account information.

____ 2. DOCUMENTS FINANCIAL TRANSACTIONS
by
entering account information.

____ 3. RECOMMENDS FINANCIAL ACTIONS
by
analyzing accounting options.

____ 4. SUMMARIZES CURRENT FINANCIAL STATUS
by
collecting information; preparing balance sheet, profit and loss statement, and other reports.

____ 5. SUBSTANTIATES FINANCIAL TRANSACTIONS
by
auditing documents.

____ 6. MAINTAINS ACCOUNTING CONTROLS
by
preparing and recommending policies and procedures.

____ 7. GUIDES ACCOUNTING CLERICAL STAFF
by
coordinating activities and answering questions.

____ 8. RECONCILES FINANCIAL DISCREPANCIES
by
collecting and analyzing account information.

____ 9. SECURES FINANCIAL INFORMATION
by
completing data base backups.

% of
Time

____ 10. MAINTAINS FINANCIAL SECURITY
by
following internal controls.

____ 11. PREPARES PAYMENTS
by
verifying documentation, and requesting disbursements.

____ 12. ANSWERS ACCOUNTING PROCEDURE QUESTIONS
by
researching and interpreting accounting policy and regulations.

____ 13. COMPLIES WITH FEDERAL, STATE, AND LOCAL FINANCIAL LEGAL REQUIREMENTS
by
studying existing and new legislation, enforcing adherence to requirements, and advising management on needed actions.

____ 14. PREPARES SPECIAL FINANCIAL REPORTS
by
collecting, analyzing, and summarizing account information and trends.

____ 15. MAINTAINS CUSTOMER CONFIDENCE AND PROTECTS OPERATIONS
by
keeping financial information confidential.

____ 16. MAINTAINS PROFESSIONAL AND TECHNICAL KNOWLEDGE
by
attending educational workshops; reviewing professional publications; establishing personal networks; participating in professional societies.

____ 17. CONTRIBUTES TO TEAM EFFORT
by
accomplishing related results as needed.

JOB TITLE: Accounts Receivable/Payable Clerk

JOB PURPOSE: **OBTAINS REVENUE AND PAYS INVOICES**
by
verifying and completing payable and receivable transactions.

ESSENTIAL JOB RESULTS:

% of Time

____ 1. PREPARES WORK TO BE ACCOMPLISHED
by
gathering and sorting documents and related information.

____ 2. PAYS INVOICES
by
verifying transaction information; scheduling and preparing disbursements; obtaining authorization of payment.

____ 3. OBTAINS REVENUE
by
verifying transaction information; computing charges and refunds; preparing and mailing invoices; identifying delinquent accounts and insufficient payments.

____ 4. COLLECTS REVENUE
by
reminding delinquent accounts; notifying customers of insufficient payments.

____ 5. PREPARES FINANCIAL REPORTS
by
collecting, analyzing, and summarizing account information and trends.

% of Time

____ 6. MAINTAINS ACCOUNTING LEDGERS
by
posting account transactions.

____ 7. VERIFIES ACCOUNTS
by
reconciling statements and transactions.

____ 8. RESOLVES ACCOUNT DISCREPANCIES
by
investigating documentation; issuing stop payments, payments, or adjustments.

____ 9. MAINTAINS FINANCIAL SECURITY
by
following internal accounting controls.

____ 10. SECURES FINANCIAL INFORMATION
by
completing data base backups.

____ 11. MAINTAINS FINANCIAL HISTORICAL RECORDS
by
filing accounting documents.

____ 12. CONTRIBUTES TO TEAM EFFORT
by
accomplishing related results as needed.

JOB TITLE: Administrative Assistant

JOB PURPOSE: **PROVIDES OFFICE SERVICES**

by

implementing administrative systems, procedures, and policies, and monitoring administrative projects.

ESSENTIAL JOB RESULTS:

% of Time

_____ 1. MAINTAINS WORK FLOW
by
studying methods; implementing cost reductions; and developing reporting procedures.

_____ 2. CREATES AND REVISES SYSTEMS AND PROCEDURES
by
analyzing operating practices, recordkeeping systems, forms control, office layout, and budgetary and personnel requirements; implementing changes.

_____ 3. DEVELOPS ADMINISTRATIVE STAFF
by
providing information, educational opportunities, and experiential growth opportunities.

_____ 4. RESOLVES ADMINISTRATIVE PROBLEMS
by
coordinating preparation of reports, analyzing data, and identifying solutions.

_____ 5. ENSURES OPERATION OF EQUIPMENT
by
completing preventive maintenance requirements; calling for repairs; maintaining equipment inventories; evaluating new equipment and techniques.

% of Time

_____ 6. PROVIDES INFORMATION
by
answering questions and requests.

_____ 7. MAINTAINS SUPPLIES INVENTORY
by
checking stock to determine inventory level; anticipating needed supplies; placing and expediting orders for supplies; verifying receipt of supplies.

_____ 8. COMPLETES OPERATIONAL REQUIREMENTS
by
scheduling and assigning administrative projects; expediting work results.

_____ 9. MAINTAINS PROFESSIONAL AND TECHNICAL KNOWLEDGE
by
attending educational workshops; reviewing professional publications; establishing personal networks; participating in professional societies.

_____ 10. CONTRIBUTES TO TEAM EFFORT
by
accomplishing related results as needed.

48

JOB TITLE: Advertising Manager

JOB PURPOSE: PROMOTES PRODUCT/SERVICE

by

defining, developing, and implementing advertising and sales promotion programs.

ESSENTIAL JOB RESULTS:

% of Time

____ 1. DEFINES ADVERTISING OBJECTIVES, CAMPAIGNS, AND BUDGETS
by
studying marketing plans; consulting with product and market managers.

____ 2. SELECTS INTERNAL/EXTERNAL MEDIA VENDORS
by
determining production requirements.

____ 3. ACHIEVES ADVERTISING FINANCIAL OBJECTIVES
by
preparing an annual budget; scheduling expenditures; using combinations of internal/external resources; analyzing variances; initiating corrective actions.

____ 4. ENSURES SUPPLY OF PROMOTIONAL LITERATURE
by
monitoring inventories; keeping product information current.

____ 5. DEVELOPS ADVERTISING AND SALES PROMOTION PROGRAMS
by
utilizing media advertising, direct mail, trade shows, publicity, point-of-purchase, and audiovisual presentations.

____ 6. COMPLETES OPERATIONAL REQUIREMENTS
by
scheduling and assigning employees; following up on work results.

% of Time

____ 7. ACHIEVES ADVERTISING FINANCIAL OBJECTIVES
by
preparing an annual budget; scheduling expenditures; analyzing variances; initiating corrective actions.

____ 8. MAINTAINS ADVERTISING STAFF
by
recruiting, selecting, orienting, and training employees.

____ 9. MAINTAINS ADVERTISING STAFF JOB RESULTS
by
counseling and disciplining employees; planning, monitoring, and appraising job results.

____ 10. MAINTAINS PROFESSIONAL AND TECHNICAL KNOWLEDGE
by
attending educational workshops; reviewing professional publications; establishing personal networks; participating in professional societies.

____ 11. CONTRIBUTES TO TEAM EFFORT
by
accomplishing related results as needed.

JOB TITLE: Aircraft Mechanic

JOB PURPOSE: **PROVIDES TRANSPORT FOR PEOPLE AND CARGO**

by

maintaining, repairing, and overhauling aircraft and aircraft engines.

ESSENTIAL JOB RESULTS:

% of Time

____ 1. ENSURES OPERATION OF AIRCRAFT
by
completing preventive maintenance requirements; following manufacturer's instructions; troubleshooting malfunctions; making repairs; maintaining equipment inventories; evaluating new equipment and techniques.

____ 2. MAINTAINS THE STABILITY AND REPUTATION OF THE AIRLINE
by
complying with Federal Aviation Administration and other legal requirements.

____ 3. DETECTS AND DIAGNOSES MALFUNCTIONS
by
examining engines for cracked cylinders and oil leaks; listening to operating engine for abnormal sounds to detect sticking or burned valves; inspecting turbine blades to detect cracks or breaks; using testing equipment such as ignition analyzer, compression checker, distributor timer, and ammeter.

____ 4. DETERMINES FEASIBILITY OF AND METHOD OF REPAIR OR REPLACEMENT
by
studying and interpreting manufacturer's and airline's maintenance manuals, service bulletins, and other specifications.

____ 5. REPAIRS, REPLACES, AND REBUILDS AIRCRAFT STRUCTURES
by
using hand tools, power tools, machines, and equipment on wings and fuselage and on functional components, including rigging, surface controls, and plumbing and hydraulic units.

% of Time

____ 6. REPAIRS AND REPLACES WORN OR DAMAGED ENGINES AND SYSTEM COMPONENTS
by
disassembling and inspecting parts for wear, warping, or other defects; reassembling, reinstalling, or installing parts; using hand tools, gauges, and testing equipment.

____ 7. MAINTAINS AIRCRAFT ELECTRICAL AND MECHANICAL SYSTEMS
by
adjusting, repairing, or replacing electrical wiring systems; flushing crankcase; cleaning screens; greasing moving parts; checking brakes.

____ 8. MAINTAINS INTER- AND INTRADEPARTMENTAL WORK FLOW
by
fostering a spirit of cooperativeness.

____ 9. MAINTAINS SAFE AND CLEAN WORKING ENVIRONMENT
by
complying with procedures, rules, and regulations.

____ 10. DOCUMENTS ACTIONS
by
completing production and quality logs.

____ 11. MAINTAINS CONTINUITY AMONG WORK TEAMS
by
documenting and communicating actions, irregularities, and continuing needs.

____ 12. KEEPS MAINTENANCE EQUIPMENT OPERATIONAL
by
following manufacturer's instructions and established procedures.

JOB TITLE: Aircraft Mechanic

ESSENTIAL JOB RESULTS:

% of
Time

_____ 13. MAINTAINS MAINTENANCE SUPPLIES INVENTORY
by
checking stock to determine inventory level;
anticipating needed supplies; placing and
expediting orders for supplies; verifying
receipt of supplies.

_____ 14. CONSERVES MAINTENANCE RESOURCES
by
using equipment and supplies as needed to
accomplish job results.

% of
Time

_____ 15. CONTRIBUTES TO TEAM EFFORT
by
accomplishing related results as needed.

JOB TITLE: Air Traffic Controller

JOB PURPOSE: **CONTROLS AIR TRAFFIC**

by

issuing landing, flight and takeoff instructions.

ESSENTIAL JOB RESULTS:

% of Time

___ 1. CONTROLS DEPARTING AIRCRAFT

by

answering radio calls from pilots; scheduling takeoff.

___ 2. ISSUES TAKEOFF INSTRUCTIONS

by

identifying runway to use, taxiing directions, meteorological and navigational data, and information on other aircraft operating in the vicinity.

___ 3. TRANSFERS CONTROL OF FLIGHT

by

notifying air traffic control center.

___ 4. CONTROLS FLIGHTS IN AIR

by

transmitting flight plans to air traffic control center.

___ 5. CONTROLS ARRIVING AIRCRAFT

by

answering radio calls from pilots; operating radarscope; scheduling landing.

___ 6. ISSUES LANDING INSTRUCTIONS

by

identifying runway to use, meteorological and navigational data, information on other aircraft operating in vicinity, and taxiing directions.

% of Time

___ 7. PREPARES FOR EMERGENCIES

by

alerting emergency crews and related services.

___ 8. CONTROLS CROSS-RUNWAY TRAFFIC

by

issuing instructions to vehicle drivers.

___ 9. MAINTAINS OPERATIONS

by

following policies and procedures; reporting needed changes.

___ 10. DOCUMENTS OBSERVATIONS AND ACTIONS

by

entering data; completing reports.

___ 11. ENSURES OPERATION OF EQUIPMENT

by

completing preventive maintenance requirements; following manufacturer's instructions; troubleshooting malfunctions; calling for repairs; evaluating new equipment and techniques.

___ 12. CONTRIBUTES TO TEAM EFFORT

by

accomplishing related results as needed.

JOB TITLE: Analyst/Programmer

JOB PURPOSE: **SOLVES CLIENT'S SOFTWARE REQUIREMENTS**

by

developing and maintaining applications and data bases, and helping clients use computer resources.

ESSENTIAL JOB RESULTS:

% of Time

____ 1. IDENTIFIES CLIENT REQUIREMENTS

by

establishing personal rapport with potential and actual clients and with other persons in a position to understand service requirements.

____ 2. DEVELOPS AND MAINTAINS APPLICATIONS AND DATA BASES

by

evaluating client needs; analyzing requirements; developing software systems.

____ 3. ARRANGES PROJECT REQUIREMENTS IN PROGRAMMING SEQUENCE

by

analyzing requirements; preparing a work flow chart and diagram using knowledge of computer capabilities, subject matter, programming language, and logic.

____ 4. PROGRAMS THE COMPUTER

by

encoding project requirements in computer language; entering coded information into the computer.

____ 5. CONFIRMS PROGRAM OPERATION

by

conducting tests; modifying program sequence and/or codes.

____ 6. PROVIDES REFERENCE FOR USE OF PRIME AND PERSONAL COMPUTERS

by

writing and maintaining user documentation; maintaining a help desk.

% of Time

____ 7. PREPARES CLIENTS TO USE SYSTEM AND SOFTWARE

by

conducting training sessions.

____ 8. MAINTAINS COMPUTER SYSTEMS AND PROGRAMMING GUIDELINES

by

writing and updating policies and procedures.

____ 9. MAINTAINS PROFESSIONAL AND TECHNICAL KNOWLEDGE

by

attending educational workshops; reviewing professional publications; establishing personal networks; participating in professional societies.

____ 10. KEEPS EQUIPMENT OPERATIONAL

by

calling for repairs; following manufacturer's instructions and established procedures; evaluating new equipment.

____ 11. MAINTAINS CLIENT CONFIDENCE AND PROTECTS OPERATIONS

by

keeping information confidential.

____ 12. CONTRIBUTES TO TEAM EFFORT

by

accomplishing related results as needed.

JOB TITLE: Assembler

JOB PURPOSE: **PRODUCES COMPONENTS**

by

assembling parts and subassemblies.

ESSENTIAL JOB RESULTS:

% of Time

____ 1. PREPARES WORK TO BE ACCOMPLISHED
by
studying assembly instructions, blueprint specifications, and parts lists; gathering parts, subassemblies, tools, and materials.

____ 2. POSITIONS PARTS AND SUBASSEMBLIES
by
using templates or reading measurements.

____ 3. ASSEMBLES COMPONENTS
by
examining connections for correct fit; fastening parts and subassemblies.

____ 4. VERIFIES SPECIFICATIONS
by
measuring completed component.

____ 5. RESOLVES ASSEMBLY PROBLEMS
by
altering dimensions to meet specifications; notifying supervisor to obtain additional resources.

____ 6. KEEPS EQUIPMENT OPERATIONAL
by
completing preventive maintenance requirements; following manufacturer's

% of Time

____ 7. MAINTAINS SAFE AND CLEAN WORKING ENVIRONMENT
by
complying with procedures, rules, and regulations.

____ 8. MAINTAINS SUPPLIES INVENTORY
by
checking stock to determine inventory level; anticipating needed supplies; placing and expediting orders for supplies; verifying receipt of supplies.

____ 9. CONSERVES RESOURCES
by
using equipment and supplies as needed to accomplish job results.

____ 10. DOCUMENTS ACTIONS
by
completing production and quality forms.

____ 11. CONTRIBUTES TO TEAM EFFORT
by
accomplishing related results as needed.

54

JOB TITLE: Assembler, Wire Harness

JOB PURPOSE: **COMPLETES WIRE HARNESS**
by
placing and tieing wires, and protecting cable.

ESSENTIAL JOB RESULTS:

*% of
Time*

____ 1. PREPARES WORK TO BE ACCOMPLISHED
by
studying work orders, specifications,
instructions, diagrams, and wire lists;
gathering tools and materials.

____ 2. ASSEMBLES HARNESS
by
selecting and cutting wires; looping wires
between guide pegs following color-coded
lines or sequential numbers; wrapping and
tieing wires.

____ 3. SECURES KNOTS AND PROTECTS CABLE
by
applying sealing liquid.

____ 4. ATTACHES CABLE TO COMPONENTS OR PLUGS
by
soldering or crimping wires and connectors.

____ 5. VERIFIES CONTINUITY
by
testing cable.

____ 6. RESOLVES ASSEMBLY PROBLEMS
by
altering dimensions to meet specifications;
notifying supervisor to obtain additional
resources.

____ 7. KEEPS EQUIPMENT OPERATIONAL
by
completing preventive maintenance
requirements; following manufacturer's
instructions; troubleshooting malfunctions;
calling for repairs.

*% of
Time*

____ 8. MAINTAINS SAFE AND CLEAN WORKING ENVIRONMENT
by
complying with procedures, rules, and
regulations.

____ 9. MAINTAINS WIRE INVENTORY
by
checking stock to determine inventory level;
anticipating needed supplies; placing and
expediting orders for supplies; verifying
receipt of supplies.

____ 10. CONSERVES RESOURCES
by
using equipment and supplies as needed to
accomplish job results.

____ 11. DOCUMENTS HARNESS
by
marking identifying data; completing forms.

____ 12. CONTRIBUTES TO TEAM EFFORT
by
accomplishing related results as needed.

JOB PURPOSE: **PROMOTES AND SERVES MEMBERS' INTERESTS**

by

surveying needs; determining objectives; organizing services.

ESSENTIAL JOB RESULTS:

*% of
Time*

____ 1. PROMOTES MEMBERSHIP
by
explaining benefits in writing or through
personal appearances; developing literature
and audiovisual presentations; contacting
potential or delinquent members.

____ 2. IDENTIFIES CURRENT AND FUTURE MEMBER INTERESTS
AND NEEDS
by
establishing personal rapport with potential
and actual members and other persons in a
position to understand member requirements.

____ 3. ESTABLISHES POLICY WITH BOARD OF DIRECTORS
by
identifying short-term and long-range issues
to be addressed; providing information and
commentary pertinent to the Board's
deliberations; presenting options and
recommending courses of action, especially
where technical and legal considerations are
involved; recruiting Board candidates.

____ 4. KEEPS THE BOARD OF DIRECTORS INFORMED
by
collecting, analyzing, and summarizing
information and trends; remaining accessible;
answering questions and requests.

____ 5. RECOMMENDS PROGRAMS AND SERVICES
by
studying the changing needs of the
membership; identifying and anticipating
service trends; evaluating and offering
options to the Board.

*% of
Time*

____ 6. PROVIDES MEMBER SERVICES
by
establishing and improving a functional
structure; delegating authority; enforcing
Board decisions; developing, monitoring, and
enforcing policies and procedures.

____ 7. MAINTAINS ASSOCIATION STAFF
by
recruiting, selecting, orienting, and training
employees.

____ 8. MAINTAINS ASSOCIATION STAFF JOB RESULTS
by
coaching, counseling, and disciplining
employees; planning, monitoring, and
appraising job results.

____ 9. MAINTAINS PROFESSIONAL AND TECHNICAL KNOWLEDGE
by
attending educational workshops; reviewing
professional publications; establishing
personal networks; participating in
professional societies.

____ 10. ACHIEVES FINANCIAL OBJECTIVES
by
developing and recommending the
association's budget; scheduling
expenditures; analyzing variances; initiating
corrective actions; anticipating long-term
issues.

JOB TITLE: **Association Executive**

ESSENTIAL JOB RESULTS:

% of
Time

_____ 11. COMPLIES WITH FEDERAL, STATE, AND LOCAL LAWS AND REGULATIONS
by
studying existing and new legislation; anticipating future legislation; enforcing adherence to requirements; advising management on needed actions.

% of
Time

_____ 12. CONTRIBUTES TO TEAM EFFORT
by
accomplishing related results as needed.

JOB TITLE: Audiovisual Technician

JOB PURPOSE: ACHIEVES COMMUNICATION OBJECTIVES
by
producing media programs.

ESSENTIAL JOB RESULTS:

% of
Time

____ 1. PRODUCES MEDIA PROGRAMS
by
preparing films, videotapes, photographs, slides, graphics, and audiotapes.

____ 2. COMPLETES PROJECT
by
editing and duplicating program.

____ 3. OPERATES MEDIA EQUIPMENT
by
following manufacturer's procedures.

____ 4. PROVIDES RESOURCE OF PROGRAMS AND EQUIPMENT
by
issuing audiovisual programs, materials, and equipment; training users.

____ 5. ENSURES OPERATION OF AUDIOVISUAL EQUIPMENT
by
completing preventive maintenance requirements.

% of
Time

____ 6. MAINTAINS SUPPLIES INVENTORY
by
checking stock to determine inventory level; anticipating needed supplies; placing and expediting orders for supplies; verifying receipt of supplies.

____ 7. MAINTAINS TECHNICAL KNOWLEDGE
by
attending educational workshops; reviewing publications; establishing personal networks; participating in professional societies.

____ 8. CONTRIBUTES TO TEAM EFFORT
by
accomplishing related results as needed.

JOB TITLE: Auditor

JOB PURPOSE: **PROTECTS ASSETS**

by

ensuring compliance with internal control procedures, and regulations.

ESSENTIAL JOB RESULTS:

% of
Time

_____ 1. ENSURES COMPLIANCE WITH ESTABLISHED INTERNAL CONTROL PROCEDURES
by
examining records, reports, operating practices, and documentation.

_____ 2. VERIFIES ASSETS AND LIABILITIES
by
comparing items to documentation.

_____ 3. COMPLETES AUDIT WORKPAPERS
by
documenting audit tests and findings.

_____ 4. APPRAISES ADEQUACY OF INTERNAL CONTROL SYSTEMS
by
completing audit questionnaires.

_____ 5. MAINTAINS INTERNAL CONTROL SYSTEMS
by
updating audit programs and questionnaires; recommending new policies and procedures.

_____ 6. COMMUNICATES AUDIT FINDINGS
by
preparing a final report; discussing findings with auditees.

% of
Time

_____ 7. COMPLIES WITH FEDERAL, STATE, AND LOCAL SECURITY LEGAL REQUIREMENTS
by
studying existing and new security legislation; enforcing adherence to requirements; advising management on needed actions.

_____ 8. PREPARES SPECIAL AUDIT AND CONTROL REPORTS
by
collecting, analyzing, and summarizing operating information and trends.

_____ 9. MAINTAINS PROFESSIONAL AND TECHNICAL KNOWLEDGE
by
attending educational workshops; reviewing professional publications; establishing personal networks; participating in professional societies.

_____ 10. CONTRIBUTES TO TEAM EFFORT
by
accomplishing related results as needed.

JOB TITLE: Automatic Screw Machine Operator

JOB PURPOSE: **PRODUCES MACHINED PARTS**

by

setting up and operating an automatic screw machine.

ESSENTIAL JOB RESULTS:

% of Time

____ 1. PLANS SEQUENCE OF OPERATIONS
by
studying blueprints.

____ 2. SELECTS CUTTING TOOLS
by
studying dimensions and tolerances of parts.

____ 3. SELECTS CUTTING SPEEDS AND FEED RATES
by
studying properties of metals; making calculations.

____ 4. SETS FEED MECHANISM
by
installing collets, bushings, and stock pushers; setting controls.

____ 5. LOADS FEED MECHANISM
by
lifting stock into position.

____ 6. CONTROLS STOCK AND TOOL MOVEMENT
by
installing and adjusting cams, gears, and stops; setting controls.

____ 7. POSITIONS TOOL
by
adjusting tool holder.

____ 8. VERIFIES SETTINGS
by
measuring positions, first-run part, and sample workpieces.

____ 9. MAINTAINS SPECIFICATIONS
by
observing operations; detecting malfunctions; adjusting controls; sharpening and replacing worn tools.

% of Time

____ 10. RESOLVES PRODUCTION PROBLEMS
by
altering process to meet specifications; notifying supervisor to obtain additional resources.

____ 11. ENSURES OPERATION OF EQUIPMENT
by
completing preventive maintenance requirements; following manufacturer's instructions; troubleshooting malfunctions; calling for repairs.

____ 12. MAINTAINS STOCK INVENTORY
by
checking stock to determine amount available; anticipating needed stock; placing and expediting orders for stock; verifying receipt of stock.

____ 13. MAINTAINS CONTINUITY AMONG WORK TEAMS
by
documenting and communicating actions, irregularities, and continuing needs.

____ 14. DOCUMENTS ACTIONS
by
completing production and quality logs.

____ 15. CONTRIBUTES TO TEAM EFFORT
by
accomplishing related results as needed.

60

JOB TITLE: Automatic Teller Machine Clerk

JOB PURPOSE: **SERVES CUSTOMERS**

by

processing automatic teller machine transactions; providing information.

ESSENTIAL JOB RESULTS:

% of Time

____ 1. BALANCES AUTOMATIC TELLER MACHINES TO SYSTEM
by
verifying deposits and withdrawals; making adjustments; verifying totals.

____ 2. BALANCES SYSTEM TO POSTINGS
by
comparing transactions processed; researching and resolving differences; processing general ledger entries for in-process accounts; researching unposted items; processing or recovering items; balancing interfaces; and preparing entries for proof processing.

____ 3. RESOLVES AUTOMATIC TELLER MACHINE BALANCES
by
comparing system and settlement sheet differences; comparing posting reports with audit tapes; preparing entries to in-process accounts.

____ 4. CONTROLS SETTLEMENT DOCUMENTATION
by
verifying documentation; preparing documentation for retention.

____ 5. COMPLETES CARD APPLICATIONS
by
researching customer information; reviewing account activity, balances, and statuses; obtaining required information; issuing or denying card.

% of Time

____ 6. COMPLETES CARD REQUESTS
by
researching the card and account statuses; restricting, replacing, destroying the current card, or preparing and mailing a new card.

____ 7. HELPS CUSTOMERS
by
resolving problems customers have operating the automatic teller machines; identifying automatic teller machine sites; notifying customers of adjusting errors.

____ 8. COMPLETES SERVICE CHARGE ELECTIONS
by
researching customer's account; determining status of election on account; investigating and correcting errors.

____ 9. SECURES ACCOUNT AND TRANSACTION INFORMATION
by
completing data base backups.

____ 10. MAINTAINS CUSTOMER CONFIDENCE AND PROTECTS OPERATIONS
by
keeping account information confidential.

____ 11. CONTRIBUTES TO TEAM EFFORT
by
accomplishing related results as needed.

JOB TITLE: Automobile Fleet Maintenance Manager

JOB PURPOSE: PROVIDES TRANSPORTATION
by

maintaining automobile fleet.

ESSENTIAL JOB RESULTS:

*% of
Time*

____ 1. PROCURES AUTOMOBILES
by
researching and recommending standard
make and model of the fleet; recommending
timing and type of vehicle replacement;
negotiating purchases; preparing new
vehicles.

____ 2. ACHIEVES FINANCIAL OBJECTIVES
by
preparing an annual budget; recommending
additions or deletions to fleet; scheduling
expenditures; analyzing variances; initiating
corrective actions.

____ 3. PROTECTS USERS
by
requiring mechanical checks and inspections;
following state Department of Transportation
procedures; maintaining inventory of
replacement parts, fuel, and supplies.

____ 4. DETERMINES PRESENT AND FUTURE AUTOMOBILE NEEDS
by
collecting and analyzing vehicle records,
operating, repair, and replacement parts
costs, mileage and gasoline consumption,
and rental/lease/purchase options.

____ 5. KEEPS AUTOMOBILES AVAILABLE
by
tracking temporary and permanent
assignments; utilizing rental and lease
arrangements.

*% of
Time*

____ 6. COMPLETES AUTOMOBILE FLEET OPERATIONAL
REQUIREMENTS
by
scheduling and assigning employees;
following up on work results.

____ 7. MAINTAINS AUTOMOBILE FLEET STAFF
by
recruiting, selecting, orienting, and training
employees.

____ 8. MAINTAINS AUTOMOBILE FLEET STAFF JOB RESULTS
by
counseling and disciplining employees;
planning, monitoring, and appraising job
results.

____ 9. MAINTAINS PROFESSIONAL AND TECHNICAL KNOWLEDGE
by
attending educational workshops; reviewing
professional publications; establishing
personal networks; participating in
professional societies.

____ 10. CONTRIBUTES TO TEAM EFFORT
by
accomplishing related results as needed.

JOB TITLE: Benefits Manager

JOB PURPOSE: MAINTAINS COMPENSATION AND INCOME-SECURITY
PROGRAMS

by

evaluating, recommending, and administering benefit programs.

ESSENTIAL JOB RESULTS:

*% of
Time*

_____ 1. RECOMMENDS BENEFITS PROGRAMS TO MANAGEMENT
by
studying employee requirements and trends
and developments in benefits offered by other
organizations.

_____ 2. SUPPORTS MANAGEMENT'S DECISION MAKING
by
analyzing benefit options and predicting
future costs.

_____ 3. IDENTIFIES BENEFIT OPTIONS
by
studying programs; obtaining advice from
consultants.

_____ 4. COMPLIES WITH FEDERAL, STATE, AND LOCAL LEGAL
REQUIREMENTS
by
studying existing and new legislation;
obtaining qualified opinions; enforcing
adherence to requirements; advising
management on needed actions.

_____ 5. INFORMS EMPLOYEES OF BENEFIT USAGE
by
preparing and distributing benefit reports.

_____ 6. MAINTAINS BENEFIT RECORDS
by
developing recordkeeping systems; initiating
new-hire benefits; recording changes.

_____ 7. RESOLVES EMPLOYEE QUESTIONS AND PROBLEMS
by
interpreting benefit policies and procedures.

_____ 8. EXPEDITES DELIVERY OF BENEFITS
by
establishing and maintaining working
relationships with benefit providers.

*% of
Time*

_____ 9. RECONCILES BENEFITS ACCOUNTS
by
approving billing statements.

_____ 10. COMPLETES OPERATIONAL REQUIREMENTS
by
scheduling and assigning employees;
following up on work results.

_____ 11. MAINTAINS BENEFITS STAFF
by
recruiting, selecting, orienting, and training
employees.

_____ 12. MAINTAINS BENEFITS STAFF JOB RESULTS
by
coaching, counseling, and disciplining
employees; planning, monitoring, and
appraising job results.

_____ 13. MAINTAINS PROFESSIONAL AND TECHNICAL KNOWLEDGE
by
attending educational workshops; reviewing
professional publications; establishing
personal networks; participating in
professional societies.

_____ 14. ACHIEVES FINANCIAL OBJECTIVES
by
preparing the benefits and department
operational budgets; scheduling expenditures;
analyzing variances; initiating corrective
actions.

_____ 15. PREPARES SPECIAL REPORTS
by
collecting, analyzing, and summarizing
information and trends.

_____ 16. CONTRIBUTES TO TEAM EFFORT
by
accomplishing related results as needed.

63

JOB TITLE: Benefits Specialist

JOB PURPOSE: **PROVIDES EMPLOYEE BENEFITS**

by

answering benefits questions; initiating and continuing membership in programs.

ESSENTIAL JOB RESULTS:

*% of
Time*

____ 1. INITIATES NEW-HIRE BENEFITS AND CHANGES OF INFORMATION
by
obtaining, verifying, and recording employee information, and informing insurance carriers of new or changed information.

____ 2. INFORMS EMPLOYEES ABOUT BENEFITS
by
explaining benefit programs.

____ 3. RESOLVES EMPLOYEE QUESTIONS AND PROBLEMS REGARDING BENEFITS
by
researching benefit policies and procedures; providing answers to questions and resolutions to problems.

____ 4. EXPEDITES DELIVERY OF BENEFITS
by
maintaining working relationships with benefit providers.

____ 5. COMPLETES BENEFITS BILLING
by
reconciling carrier reports; requesting benefit disbursements; reconciling benefit accounts.

*% of
Time*

____ 6. RETAINS HISTORICAL REFERENCE OF BENEFITS ACCOUNTS
by
maintaining benefits recordkeeping system; filing and retrieving benefit information.

____ 7. CONTINUES ELECTIVE RETIREE INSURANCE COVERAGE
by
tracking employee payments; reconciling depository funds.

____ 8. MAINTAINS DEPARTMENT SUPPLIES INVENTORY
by
checking stock to determine inventory level; anticipating needed supplies; placing and expediting orders for supplies; verifying receipt of supplies.

____ 9. CONTRIBUTES TO TEAM EFFORT
by
accomplishing related results as needed.

JOB TITLE: Billing Clerk

JOB PURPOSE: **BILLS CUSTOMERS**

by

gathering purchase documentation; calculating charges; issuing invoices and statements.

ESSENTIAL JOB RESULTS:

% of Time

_____ 1. PREPARES WORK TO BE ACCOMPLISHED
by
gathering and sorting documents and information.

_____ 2. COMPILES AMOUNT TO BILL
by
collecting and utilizing information from purchase orders, sales tickets, charge slips, shipping costs, and point-of-purchase tax requirements.

_____ 3. PREPARES INVOICES
by
calculating or computing billing amounts.

_____ 4. ISSUES BILLS OF LADING
by
listing weight and serial numbers of sold items.

% of Time

_____ 5. GENERATES SHIPPING LABELS
by
entering customer data listed on shipping specifications.

_____ 6. ISSUES CREDIT MEMORANDUMS
by
identifying returned or incorrectly billed merchandise.

_____ 7. MAINTAINS ACCOUNTS PAYABLE
by
entering transactions into accounting system.

_____ 8. CONTRIBUTES TO TEAM EFFORT
by
accomplishing related results as needed.

JOB TITLE: Blood Bank Manager

JOB PURPOSE:

SERVES PATIENTS

by

providing blood bank diagnostic and therapeutic information, products, and services.

ESSENTIAL JOB RESULTS:

% of Time

_____ 1. PROVIDES BLOOD BANK DIAGNOSTIC AND THERAPEUTIC INFORMATION, PRODUCTS, AND SERVICES
by
completing specimen preparation; developing and implementing analytical procedures; evaluating laboratory information; consulting with pathologists; reporting results according to protocols mandated by the hospital and the Public Health Department.

_____ 2. MAINTAINS EQUIPMENT PERFORMANCE
by
developing operations, quality, and troubleshooting procedures; ensuring staff compliance; arranging equipment replacement, service, and repair.

_____ 3. MAINTAINS BLOOD BANK SUPPLIES INVENTORY
by
checking stock to determine inventory level; anticipating needed supplies; placing and expediting orders for supplies; verifying receipt of supplies.

_____ 4. MAINTAINS PRODUCTIVITY
by
monitoring workload of blood bank functional areas; identifying peak and slack periods; making operational or staffing adjustment.

% of Time

_____ 5. MAINTAINS QUALITY RESULTS
by
certifying instrument performance; participating in the hospital quality assurance program; consulting with pathologists; performing proficiency surveys; reviewing quality control and assurance programs; implementing infection control and hazardous waste policies; making adjustments in policies and procedures; generating reports; retaining records.

_____ 6. MAINTAINS LABORATORY INFORMATION SYSTEM
by
identifying information needs and problems; recommending improvements; establishing priorities; testing; writing user manuals; training employees; maintaining security and confidentiality.

_____ 7. IMPLEMENTS NEW PROGRAMS, TESTS, METHODS, INSTRUMENTATION, AND PROCEDURES
by
investigating alternatives; preparing proposals; developing and performing parallel testing; monitoring progress.

_____ 8. COMPLETES OPERATIONAL REQUIREMENTS
by
scheduling and assigning employees; following up on work results.

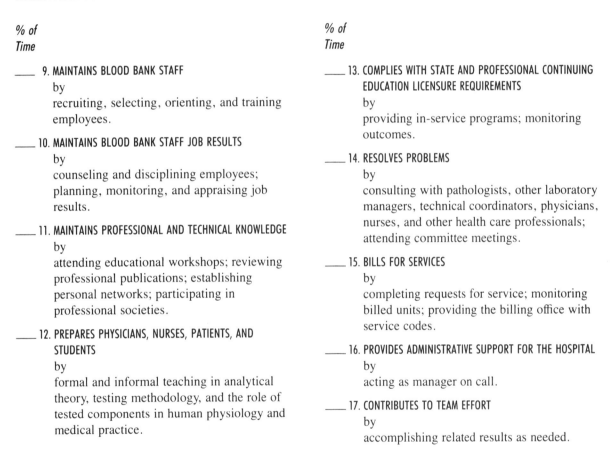

JOB TITLE: **Blood Bank Manager**

ESSENTIAL JOB RESULTS:

% of
Time

____ 9. MAINTAINS BLOOD BANK STAFF
by
recruiting, selecting, orienting, and training
employees.

____ 10. MAINTAINS BLOOD BANK STAFF JOB RESULTS
by
counseling and disciplining employees;
planning, monitoring, and appraising job
results.

____ 11. MAINTAINS PROFESSIONAL AND TECHNICAL KNOWLEDGE
by
attending educational workshops; reviewing
professional publications; establishing
personal networks; participating in
professional societies.

____ 12. PREPARES PHYSICIANS, NURSES, PATIENTS, AND
STUDENTS
by
formal and informal teaching in analytical
theory, testing methodology, and the role of
tested components in human physiology and
medical practice.

% of
Time

____ 13. COMPLIES WITH STATE AND PROFESSIONAL CONTINUING
EDUCATION LICENSURE REQUIREMENTS
by
providing in-service programs; monitoring
outcomes.

____ 14. RESOLVES PROBLEMS
by
consulting with pathologists, other laboratory
managers, technical coordinators, physicians,
nurses, and other health care professionals;
attending committee meetings.

____ 15. BILLS FOR SERVICES
by
completing requests for service; monitoring
billed units; providing the billing office with
service codes.

____ 16. PROVIDES ADMINISTRATIVE SUPPORT FOR THE HOSPITAL
by
acting as manager on call.

____ 17. CONTRIBUTES TO TEAM EFFORT
by
accomplishing related results as needed.

JOB TITLE: Bookkeeper

JOB PURPOSE: **MAINTAINS RECORDS OF FINANCIAL TRANSACTIONS**

by

establishing accounts; posting transactions.

ESSENTIAL JOB RESULTS:

*% of
Time*

____ 1. DEVELOPS SYSTEM TO ACCOUNT FOR FINANCIAL TRANSACTIONS

by

establishing a chart of accounts; defining bookkeeping policies and procedures.

____ 2. MAINTAINS SUBSIDIARY ACCOUNTS

by

verifying, allocating, and posting transactions.

____ 3. BALANCES SUBSIDIARY ACCOUNTS

by

reconciling entries.

____ 4. MAINTAINS GENERAL LEDGER

by

transferring subsidiary account summaries.

____ 5. BALANCES GENERAL LEDGER

by

preparing a trial balance; reconciling entries.

____ 6. MAINTAINS HISTORICAL RECORDS

by

filing documents.

____ 7. PREPARES FINANCIAL REPORTS

by

collecting, analyzing, and summarizing account information and trends.

*% of
Time*

____ 8. COMPLIES WITH FEDERAL, STATE, AND LOCAL LEGAL REQUIREMENTS

by

studying requirements; enforcing adherence to requirements; filing reports; advising management on needed actions.

____ 9. PROTECTS OPERATIONS

by

keeping financial information confidential.

____ 10. ENSURES OPERATION OF EQUIPMENT

by

completing preventive maintenance requirements; following manufacturer's instructions; troubleshooting malfunctions; calling for repairs; evaluating new equipment and techniques.

____ 11. CONTRIBUTES TO TEAM EFFORT

by

accomplishing related results as needed.

JOB PURPOSE: ACHIEVES BRANCH BANK OBJECTIVES

by

developing business opportunities; meeting sales quotas; managing staff.

ESSENTIAL JOB RESULTS:

% of Time

___ 1. ATTRACTS NEW BUSINESS AND EXPANDS CURRENT BUSINESS

by

soliciting consumer deposit accounts and mortgage lending from current and prospective clients; cross-selling services within the branch; pursuing consumer loans.

___ 2. QUALIFIES LOANS

by

interviewing, analyzing, and evaluating applicants.

___ 3. ENSURES COMPLIANCE WITH BANK LOAN POLICIES AND GOVERNMENT REGULATIONS

by

maintaining consumer credit and mortgage files; coordinating efforts with audit, loan review, branch operations, and collection departments.

___ 4. IDENTIFIES AND SOLVES COMMUNITY'S CREDIT NEEDS

by

meeting with community groups and offering available products to entire community, including low- and moderate-income areas.

___ 5. DEVELOPS TRUST AND OTHER NONINTEREST FEE INCOME BUSINESS

by

publicizing the branch's service capabilities.

___ 6. GENERATES COMMERCIAL LOANS

by

meeting potential customers in the business community.

% of Time

___ 7. MEETS SALES OBJECTIVES

by

conducting sales meetings; establishing sales quotas; monitoring demographic sales results; applying marketing research; defining strategies.

___ 8. COMPLETES BRANCH OPERATIONAL REQUIREMENTS

by

scheduling and assigning employees; following up on work results.

___ 9. MAINTAINS STAFF

by

recruiting, selecting, orienting, and training employees.

___ 10. MAINTAINS STAFF JOB RESULTS

by

counseling and disciplining employees; planning, monitoring, and appraising job results.

___ 11. MAINTAINS PROFESSIONAL AND TECHNICAL KNOWLEDGE

by

attending educational workshops; reviewing professional publications; establishing personal networks; participating in professional societies.

___ 12. ACHIEVES FINANCIAL OBJECTIVES

by

preparing an annual budget; scheduling expenditures; analyzing variances; initiating corrective actions.

___ 13. CONTRIBUTES TO TEAM EFFORT

by

accomplishing related results as needed.

JOB TITLE: Budget Officer

JOB PURPOSE: **SUPPORTS FINANCIAL DECISION MAKING**
by
assembling and interpreting budgets; monitoring variances.

ESSENTIAL JOB RESULTS:

% of
Time

____ 1. GUIDES PLANNING AND CONTROL PROCESS
by
establishing and enforcing policies and
procedures.

____ 2. ASSEMBLES PLANNING AND CONTROL DATA
by
establishing and monitoring schedules;
consolidating data.

____ 3. PROVIDES MANAGERS WITH PLANNING AND CONTROL
INFORMATION
by
assembling and analyzing historical financial
data; identifying trends; providing forecasts;
explaining processes and techniques;
recommending actions.

____ 4. RECOMMENDS REVISIONS
by
analyzing and interpreting data; making
comparative analyses.

____ 5. PRESENTS BUDGETS
by
explaining data and assumptions.

____ 6. CONFIRMS FINANCIAL STATUS
by
collecting, interpreting, and reporting
revenue and expenditures.

____ 7. PREPARES SPECIAL REPORTS
by
collecting, analyzing, and summarizing
information and trends.

% of
Time

____ 8. COMPLIES WITH FEDERAL, STATE, AND LOCAL LEGAL
REQUIREMENTS
by
studying existing and new requirements;
enforcing adherence to requirements; filing
financial reports; advising management on
needed actions.

____ 9. ENSURES OPERATION OF EQUIPMENT
by
completing preventive maintenance
requirements; calling for repairs; evaluating
new equipment and techniques.

____ 10. COMPLETES OPERATIONAL REQUIREMENTS
by
scheduling, assigning, and training
employees; following up on work results.

____ 11. MAINTAINS PROFESSIONAL AND TECHNICAL KNOWLEDGE
by
attending educational workshops; reviewing
professional publications; establishing
personal networks; participating in
professional societies.

____ 12. PROTECTS OPERATIONS
by
keeping financial information and plans
confidential.

____ 13. SECURES INFORMATION
by
completing data base backups.

____ 14. CONTRIBUTES TO TEAM EFFORT
by
accomplishing related results as needed.

JOB TITLE: Building Custodian

JOB PURPOSE: **MAINTAINS BUILDING AND GROUNDS**

by

providing housekeeping, groundskeeping, and repair services.

ESSENTIAL JOB RESULTS:

% of
Time

_____ 1. MAINTAINS BUILDING INTERIOR

by

dusting and polishing furniture, equipment, mirrors, and fixtures; washing windows, counters, walls, ceilings, and woodwork; sweeping, scrubbing, and waxing floors; cleaning and vacuuming drapes, furniture, and carpeting; resupplying rest rooms; replacing light bulbs.

_____ 2. MAINTAINS BUILDING ACCESSIBILITY AND APPEARANCE

by

picking up papers and trash; removing ice and snow from walkways and parking lot; painting; maintaining the lawn and surrounding landscape; replacing light bulbs.

_____ 3. REMOVES TRASH

by

emptying trash containers; transporting materials to disposal area; recycling materials.

_____ 4. KEEPS CLEANING EQUIPMENT OPERATIONAL

by

following manufacturer's operating and care guidelines; completing operator repairs and parts replacement.

% of
Time

_____ 5. COMPLETES EQUIPMENT AND BUILDING REPAIRS

by

following manufacturer's instructions and maintenance procedures.

_____ 6. MAINTAINS PARTS AND EQUIPMENT INVENTORY

by

checking stock to determine inventory level; anticipating needed parts; anticipating cleaning equipment replacement; placing orders.

_____ 7. MAINTAINS SAFE WORKING ENVIRONMENT

by

complying with procedures, rules, and regulations.

_____ 8. MAINTAINS CONTINUITY BETWEEN SHIFTS

by

documenting cleaning actions; noting areas requiring additional care or monitoring.

_____ 9. CONTRIBUTES TO TEAM EFFORT

by

accomplishing related results as needed.

JOB TITLE: Building Maintenance Supervisor

JOB PURPOSE: **MAINTAINS BUILDING OPERATIONS**

by

directing and controlling maintenance functions; supervising employees.

ESSENTIAL JOB RESULTS:

% of Time

___ 1. PROVIDES BUILDING MAINTENANCE SERVICES

by

establishing standards and procedures; measuring results against standards; making necessary adjustments.

___ 2. ENSURES OPERATION OF EQUIPMENT

by

developing and enforcing preventive maintenance programs; studying manufacturer's instructions; establishing repair and installation policies and procedures; troubleshooting malfunctions; coordinating tradespeople; maintaining equipment inventories; evaluating new equipment and techniques; recommending equipment purchases and replacements.

___ 3. IDENTIFIES MANAGEMENT AND EMPLOYEE CONCERNS

by

surveying environmental, operational, and occupational conditions; recommending building maintenance programs.

___ 4. DETERMINES SERVICE, EQUIPMENT, AND PERSONNEL REQUIREMENTS

by

conducting inspections.

___ 5. PROTECTS EMPLOYEES AND VISITORS

by

maintaining a safe and clean building.

___ 6. ACHIEVES FINANCIAL OBJECTIVES

by

preparing a building maintenance annual budget; scheduling expenditures; analyzing variances; initiating corrective actions.

% of Time

___ 7. COMPLETES BUILDING MAINTENANCE OPERATIONAL REQUIREMENTS

by

scheduling and assigning employees; following up on work results.

___ 8. MAINTAINS BUILDING MAINTENANCE GUIDELINES

by

writing and updating policies and procedures.

___ 9. MAINTAINS BUILDING MAINTENANCE STAFF

by

recruiting, selecting, orienting, and training employees.

___ 10. MAINTAINS BUILDING MAINTENANCE STAFF JOB RESULTS

by

coaching, counseling, and disciplining employees; planning, monitoring, and appraising job results.

___ 11. MAINTAINS PROFESSIONAL AND TECHNICAL KNOWLEDGE

by

attending educational workshops; reviewing professional publications; establishing personal networks; participating in professional societies.

___ 12. COMPLIES WITH FEDERAL, STATE, AND LOCAL LEGAL REQUIREMENTS

by

studying existing and new legislation; anticipating future legislation; enforcing adherence to requirements; advising management on needed actions.

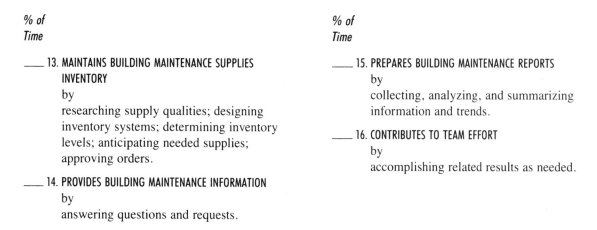

| JOB TITLE: | **Building Maintenance Supervisor** |

ESSENTIAL JOB RESULTS:

% of
Time

_____ 13. MAINTAINS BUILDING MAINTENANCE SUPPLIES INVENTORY
by
researching supply qualities; designing inventory systems; determining inventory levels; anticipating needed supplies; approving orders.

_____ 14. PROVIDES BUILDING MAINTENANCE INFORMATION
by
answering questions and requests.

% of
Time

_____ 15. PREPARES BUILDING MAINTENANCE REPORTS
by
collecting, analyzing, and summarizing information and trends.

_____ 16. CONTRIBUTES TO TEAM EFFORT
by
accomplishing related results as needed.

JOB PURPOSE: **MAINTAINS BUILDING ENVIRONMENT AND ACCESSIBILITY**

by

maintaining building equipment, heating, cooling, electrical, and plumbing systems; maintaining grounds.

ESSENTIAL JOB RESULTS:

% of Time

____ 1. MAINTAINS BUILDING CLIMATE

by

installing, repairing, and servicing heating, ventilating, and air-conditioning equipment.

____ 2. MAINTAINS LIGHTING

by

installing and repairing wiring and fixtures.

____ 3. MAINTAINS EQUIPMENT

by

installing and repairing associated and backup equipment and systems.

____ 4. KEEPS EQUIPMENT, SYSTEMS, AND BUILDING READY FOR USE

by

completing preventive maintenance schedules; following policies and procedures; reporting needed changes.

____ 5. SECURES BUILDING AND OCCUPANTS

by

maintaining alarm and fire protection devices.

____ 6. MAINTAINS SYSTEM FOR CONVEYING LIQUIDS AND LIQUID WASTE

by

installing and repairing plumbing apparatus.

% of Time

____ 7. PROVIDES SYSTEM FOR RECYCLING MATERIALS AND REMOVING TRASH

by

providing containers and monitoring trash disposition.

____ 8. MAINTAINS CONTINUITY BETWEEN SHIFTS

by

documenting maintenance actions; noting system or equipment irregularities requiring continued monitoring.

____ 9. MAINTAINS SAFE AND CLEAN WORKING ENVIRONMENT

by

complying with procedures, rules, and regulations.

____ 10. MAINTAINS PARTS AND EQUIPMENT INVENTORY

by

checking stock to determine inventory level; anticipating needed parts and equipment; placing and expediting orders for parts and equipment; verifying receipt of parts and equipment.

____ 11. CONTRIBUTES TO TEAM EFFORT

by

accomplishing related results as needed.

```
┌─────────────────────────────────────────────────────────────────┐
│  JOB TITLE: Buyer (Manufacturing)                                 │
└─────────────────────────────────────────────────────────────────┘
```

JOB PURPOSE: PROVIDES PARTS, EQUIPMENT, AND MATERIALS

by

identifying manufacturing needs, identifying suppliers, and arranging delivery.

ESSENTIAL JOB RESULTS:

*% of
Time*

_____ 1. DEVELOPS PURCHASING SPECIFICATIONS AND PERFORMANCE TEST REQUIREMENTS
by
analyzing technical data, designs, and manufacturing requirements; consulting with manufacturing personnel.

_____ 2. IDENTIFIES AND RECOMMENDS SUPPLIERS
by
investigating potential suppliers; researching parts, equipment, and materials availability.

_____ 3. PURCHASES PARTS, EQUIPMENT, AND MATERIALS
by
preparing and submitting purchase orders.

_____ 4. DELIVERS PARTS, EQUIPMENT, AND MATERIALS TO LOCATIONS
by
arranging shipping.

_____ 5. FACILITATES INSPECTIONS, SUBSTITUTIONS, AND STANDARDIZATION
by
arranging and participating in conferences between suppliers and company personnel.

*% of
Time*

_____ 6. RESOLVES SHIPMENT QUALITY DISCREPANCIES
by
mediating vendor/manufacturing issues.

_____ 7. PROVIDES PARTS, EQUIPMENT, AND MATERIALS INFORMATION
by
answering questions and requests.

_____ 8. MAINTAINS PROFESSIONAL AND TECHNICAL KNOWLEDGE
by
attending educational workshops; reviewing professional publications; establishing personal networks; participating in professional societies.

_____ 9. PREPARES REPORTS
by
collecting, analyzing, and summarizing information and trends.

_____ 10. CONTRIBUTES TO TEAM EFFORT
by
accomplishing related results as needed.

JOB TITLE: Buyer (Merchandising)

JOB PURPOSE: **PROVIDES MERCHANDISE FOR CUSTOMERS**

by

purchasing, delivering, and pricing goods; training sales staff.

ESSENTIAL JOB RESULTS:

*% of
Time*

_____ 1. PURCHASES MERCHANDISE
by
studying needs, preferences, and buying patterns of customers.

_____ 2. DELIVERS MERCHANDISE TO LOCATIONS
by
scheduling shipments.

_____ 3. APPROVES MERCHANDISE DELIVERY
by
authorizing payment; directing returns.

_____ 4. RESOLVES DISCREPANCIES
by
collecting and analyzing vendor or merchandise information.

_____ 5. SUPERVISES MERCHANDISE PRICING AND IDENTIFICATION
by
determining markups; identifying manufacturer style numbers and seasonal codes.

_____ 6. PROVIDES MERCHANDISE INFORMATION
by
answering questions and requests.

_____ 7. MAINTAINS PROFESSIONAL AND TECHNICAL KNOWLEDGE
by
attending educational workshops; reviewing professional publications; establishing personal networks; participating in professional societies.

*% of
Time*

_____ 8. IDENTIFIES CURRENT AND FUTURE CUSTOMER REQUIREMENTS
by
establishing rapport with potential and actual customers and other persons in a position to understand merchandise requirements.

_____ 9. PREPARES SPECIAL REPORTS
by
collecting, analyzing, and summarizing information and trends.

_____ 10. PREPARES SALES STAFF
by
developing and conducting merchandise-specific, in-service training programs.

_____ 11. CONTRIBUTES TO TEAM EFFORT
by
accomplishing related results as needed.

JOB TITLE: Cafeteria Line Attendant

JOB PURPOSE: **SERVES CUSTOMERS**

by

maintaining food for selection.

ESSENTIAL JOB RESULTS:

% of
Time

____ 1. PREPARES FOODLINE

by

placing and displaying food in serving containers.

____ 2. PROVIDES INFORMATION TO CUSTOMERS

by

answering food preparation questions; resolving special requests.

____ 3. FILLS CUSTOMER REQUESTS

by

arranging chosen food items; adding prescribed garnishes; handing meal to customer.

____ 4. KEEPS EQUIPMENT OPERATIONAL

by

following manufacturer's instructions and established procedures.

% of
Time

____ 5. MAINTAINS FOODLINE

by

notifying kitchen of shortages; replenishing food at work station.

____ 6. PROTECTS CUSTOMERS AND EMPLOYEES

by

adhering to sanitation policies and procedures; maintaining a safe and clean working environment.

____ 7. CONTRIBUTES TO TEAM EFFORT

by

accomplishing related results as needed.

JOB PURPOSE: **FABRICATES, CONSTRUCTS, AND REPAIRS STRUCTURAL WOODWORK AND WOOD PRODUCTS**

by

following blueprints, drawings, and oral instructions; using carpentry tools and equipment.

ESSENTIAL JOB RESULTS:

% of Time

____ 1. PRODUCES CARPENTRY PRODUCTS AND SERVICES

by

following standards and procedures; measuring results against standards; making necessary adjustments.

____ 2. DETERMINES MATERIAL REQUIREMENTS AND DIMENSIONS OF STRUCTURE OR FIXTURE TO BE FABRICATED

by

studying blueprints, sketches, or building plans.

____ 3. MAINTAINS CARPENTRY SUPPLIES INVENTORY

by

checking stock to determine inventory level; anticipating needed supplies; placing and expediting orders for supplies; verifying receipt of supplies.

____ 4. PREPARES LAYOUT

by

following carpentry procedures for fabrication of counters, cabinets, benches, partitions, floors, doors, and building framework and trim, using rule, framing square, and calipers.

____ 5. CONSTRUCTS, REPAIRS, AND INSTALLS STRUCTURE OR FIXTURE

by

marking cutting and assembly lines on materials; shaping materials to measurements; assembling and fastening cut and shaped materials; using carpenter's hand tools, power tools, and woodworking machinery.

% of Time

____ 6. ENSURES CONSTRUCTION QUALITY

by

verifying trueness of structure with plumb bob, carpenter's level, and other measurements.

____ 7. COMPLIES WITH FEDERAL, STATE, AND LOCAL BUILDING CODES

by

adhering to requirements; advising management on needed actions.

____ 8. MAINTAINS SAFE AND CLEAN WORKING ENVIRONMENT

by

complying with procedures, rules, and regulations.

____ 9. CONSERVES CARPENTRY RESOURCES

by

using equipment and supplies as needed to accomplish job results.

____ 10. ENSURES OPERATION OF CARPENTRY EQUIPMENT

by

completing preventive maintenance requirements; following manufacturer's instructions; troubleshooting malfunctions; calling for repairs; maintaining equipment inventories; evaluating new equipment and techniques.

____ 11. PROVIDES CARPENTRY INFORMATION

by

answering questions and requests.

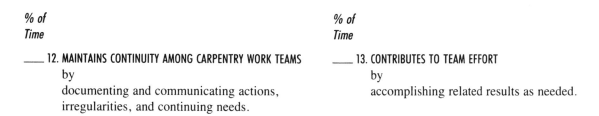

JOB TITLE: Carpenter

ESSENTIAL JOB RESULTS:

% of
Time

____ 12. MAINTAINS CONTINUITY AMONG CARPENTRY WORK TEAMS
by
documenting and communicating actions,
irregularities, and continuing needs.

% of
Time

____ 13. CONTRIBUTES TO TEAM EFFORT
by
accomplishing related results as needed.

JOB TITLE: Caseworker

JOB PURPOSE: **PROVIDES INCOME TO INDIVIDUALS AND FAMILIES**

by

determining applicant's eligibility.

ESSENTIAL JOB RESULTS:

% of Time

____ 1. PREPARES WORK TO BE ACCOMPLISHED
by
gathering documents.

____ 2. OBTAINS REQUIRED INFORMATION
by
interviewing applicants, family members, and others; completing application.

____ 3. CONFIRMS APPLICATION
by
verifying information.

____ 4. DETERMINES ELIGIBILITY
by
applying regulations and memorandums.

____ 5. OBTAINS APPROVAL OF APPLICATION
by
submitting determination for review.

____ 6. EDUCATES APPLICANTS/CLIENTS
by
explaining program requirements, options, interpretations, and determination.

____ 7. OBTAINS ASSISTANCE FOR APPLICANTS/CLIENTS
by
referring them to other programs.

% of Time

____ 8. VERIFIES CLIENT'S CONTINUED ELIGIBILITY
by
reviewing and verifying updated information in client's file.

____ 9. MAINTAINS OPERATIONS
by
following policies and procedures; participating in quality reviews; reporting needed changes.

____ 10. COMPLIES WITH FEDERAL, STATE, AND LOCAL LEGAL REQUIREMENTS
by
studying existing and new legislation and tolerance levels; enforcing adherence to requirements; informing management of needed actions.

____ 11. MAINTAINS CLIENT CONFIDENCE AND PROTECTS OPERATIONS
by
keeping information confidential.

____ 12. CONTRIBUTES TO TEAM EFFORT
by
accomplishing related results as needed.

JOB TITLE: Cash Clerk

JOB PURPOSE:

CONTROLS CASH

by

receiving and disbursing funds; recording transactions.

ESSENTIAL JOB RESULTS:

*% of
Time*

____ 1. ACCEPTS FUNDS
by
recording cash, checks, and credit card transactions.

____ 2. VERIFIES FUNDS
by
counting cash; completing authorization procedures for checks and credit card transactions.

____ 3. RECEIVES FUNDS
by
issuing change; cashing checks; accepting credit cards; issuing receipts.

____ 4. BALANCES CASH DRAWER
by
comparing cash register totals with currency, checks, and credit card transactions.

____ 5. DEPOSITS AND WITHDRAWS FUNDS
by
preparing bank deposit and withdrawal slips.

____ 6. DISBURSES FUNDS
by
writing vouchers and checks.

*% of
Time*

____ 7. BALANCES ACCOUNTS
by
posting and reconciling data.

____ 8. PREPARES REPORTS
by
compiling collection, disbursement, and bank reconciliation information.

____ 9. PROVIDES INFORMATION
by
answering questions and requests.

____ 10. MAINTAINS OPERATIONS
by
following policies and procedures; reporting needed changes.

____ 11. KEEPS EQUIPMENT OPERATIONAL
by
following manufacturer's instructions and established procedures.

____ 12. CONTRIBUTES TO TEAM EFFORT
by
accomplishing related results as needed.

JOB TITLE: Cashier/Checker

JOB PURPOSE: **OBTAINS PAYMENT FOR GOODS**

by

itemizing and totaling customer's purchases.

ESSENTIAL JOB RESULTS:

% of Time

____ 1. ITEMIZES AND TOTALS PURCHASES

by

recording prices, departments, taxable and nontaxable items; operating a cash register.

____ 2. ENTERS PRICE CHANGES

by

referring to price sheets and special sale bulletins.

____ 3. DISCOUNTS PURCHASES

by

redeeming coupons.

____ 4. COLLECTS PAYMENTS

by

accepting cash, check, or charge payments from customers; making change for cash customers.

____ 5. VERIFIES CREDIT ACCEPTANCE

by

reviewing and recording driver's license number; operating credit card authorization system.

% of Time

____ 6. BALANCES CASH DRAWER

by

counting cash at beginning and end of work shift.

____ 7. PROVIDES PRICING INFORMATION

by

answering questions.

____ 8. MAINTAINS CHECKOUT OPERATIONS

by

following policies and procedures; reporting needed changes.

____ 9. MAINTAINS SAFE AND CLEAN WORKING ENVIRONMENT

by

complying with procedures, rules, and regulations.

____ 10. CONTRIBUTES TO TEAM EFFORT

by

accomplishing related results as needed.

JOB TITLE: Ceramic Engineer

JOB PURPOSE: DEVELOPS CERAMIC MATERIALS AND PROCESSES

by

conducting research; testing materials; designing manufacturing methods.

ESSENTIAL JOB RESULTS:

% of
Time

____ 1. DEVELOPS CERAMIC MATERIALS
by
designing and conducting research programs; applying knowledge of materials' properties and applications.

____ 2. CONFIRMS MATERIALS' CHARACTERISTICS AND QUALITIES
by
designing testing methods; testing physical, chemical, and heat-resistant properties.

____ 3. DEVELOPS CERAMIC PRODUCTS
by
studying customer requirements; researching and testing methods of processing, forming, and firing clays.

____ 4. DEVELOPS MANUFACTURING PROCESSES
by
designing and modifying equipment and apparatus for forming, firing, and handling materials.

____ 5. ASSURES PRODUCT QUALITY
by
designing testing methods; testing finished-product characteristics, such as texture, color, durability, glazing, and refractivity.

____ 6. PREPARES PRODUCT AND MATERIALS REPORTS
by
collecting, analyzing, and summarizing information and trends.

% of
Time

____ 7. PROVIDES ENGINEERING INFORMATION
by
answering questions and requests.

____ 8. MAINTAINS PRODUCT AND COMPANY REPUTATION
by
complying with federal and state regulations.

____ 9. KEEPS EQUIPMENT OPERATIONAL
by
following manufacturer's instructions and established procedures; requesting service.

____ 10. MAINTAINS PRODUCT AND MATERIALS DATA BASE
by
writing programs; entering data.

____ 11. COMPLETES PROJECTS
by
training and guiding technicians.

____ 12. MAINTAINS PROFESSIONAL AND TECHNICAL KNOWLEDGE
by
attending educational workshops; reviewing professional publications; establishing personal networks; participating in professional societies.

____ 13. CONTRIBUTES TO TEAM EFFORT
by
accomplishing related results as needed.

JOB PURPOSE: **DESIGNS AND PREPARES MEALS**

by

planning and implementing menus; controlling food preparation.

ESSENTIAL JOB RESULTS:

% of
Time

____ 1. IDENTIFIES CURRENT AND FUTURE CUSTOMER FOOD PREFERENCES

by

establishing personal contact and rapport with potential and actual customers and other persons in a position to understand food requirements.

____ 2. PLANS MENUS

by

studying marketing conditions, popularity of dishes, recency of menu; utilizing food surpluses and leftovers.

____ 3. PRICES MEALS

by

analyzing recipes; determining food, labor, and overhead costs.

____ 4. PURCHASES FOODSTUFFS AND KITCHEN SUPPLIES

by

identifying and qualifying suppliers; negotiating prices; estimating food consumption; placing and expediting orders.

____ 5. PREPARES FOOD

by

establishing nutrition and presentation standards and preparation procedures; measuring results against standards; making production adjustments.

____ 6. APPROVES FOOD PREPARATION

by

observing methods of preparation; tasting and smelling prepared dishes; viewing color, texture, and garnishments; verifying portion sizes.

% of
Time

____ 7. CONTROLS COSTS

by

using readily available and seasonal ingredients; identifying and qualifying suppliers; setting standards for quality and quantity.

____ 8. COMPLETES KITCHEN OPERATIONAL REQUIREMENTS

by

scheduling and assigning employees; following up on work results.

____ 9. MAINTAINS KITCHEN STAFF

by

recruiting, selecting, orienting, and training employees.

____ 10. MAINTAINS KITCHEN STAFF JOB RESULTS

by

coaching, counseling, and disciplining employees; planning, monitoring, and appraising job results.

____ 11. MAINTAINS PROFESSIONAL AND TECHNICAL KNOWLEDGE

by

attending educational workshops; reviewing professional publications; establishing personal networks; participating in professional societies.

____ 12. MAINTAINS A CLEAN AND SAFE ENVIRONMENT

by

implementing federal, state, and local sanitation requirements; maintaining first aid, CPR, and Heimlich maneuver certification; instructing others in the use of kitchen utensils and operation of equipment.

____ 13. CONTRIBUTES TO TEAM EFFORT

by

accomplishing related results as needed.

JOB TITLE: Chemist

JOB PURPOSE: **DEVELOPS CHEMICAL PRODUCTS AND PROCESSES**
by
conducting research, analysis, synthesis, and experimentation.

ESSENTIAL JOB RESULTS:

*% of
Time*

____ 1. DETERMINES PRODUCT SPECIFICATIONS
by
studying consumer requirements; conferring with management and engineering staff.

____ 2. DETERMINES PROCESS STANDARDS
by
developing formulas and methods.

____ 3. IDENTIFIES CHEMICAL AND PHYSICAL PROPERTIES OF SUBSTANCES
by
conducting analyses such as chromatography, spectroscopy, and spectrophotometry.

____ 4. RESEARCHES NEW PRODUCTS AND PROCESSES
by
conducting experiments involving the composition, structure, properties, relationships, and reactions of matter induced by heat, light, energy, and chemical catalysts.

____ 5. PREPARES TECHNICAL REPORTS
by
collecting, analyzing, and summarizing information and trends.

____ 6. MAINTAINS ORGANIZATION'S STABILITY AND REPUTATION
by
complying with government regulations.

*% of
Time*

____ 7. ENSURES OPERATION OF EQUIPMENT
by
completing preventive maintenance requirements; following manufacturer's instructions; troubleshooting malfunctions; calling for repairs; evaluating new equipment and techniques.

____ 8. MAINTAINS DATA BASE
by
writing computer programs; entering and backing up data.

____ 9. MAINTAINS PROFESSIONAL AND TECHNICAL KNOWLEDGE
by
attending educational workshops; reviewing professional publications; establishing personal networks; participating in professional societies.

____ 10. MAINTAINS SAFE AND CLEAN WORKING ENVIRONMENT
by
establishing and complying with procedures, rules, and regulations.

____ 11. CONTRIBUTES TO TEAM EFFORT
by
accomplishing related results as needed.

JOB TITLE: City Manager

JOB PURPOSE: **SERVES CITIZENS**

by

identifying, evaluating, and meeting community living needs.

ESSENTIAL JOB RESULTS:

% of Time

____ 1. RECOMMENDS PROGRAMS AND SERVICES

by

studying the changing needs of the city; identifying and anticipating community service trends; evaluating and offering options to the Board of Managers.

____ 2. PROVIDES CITY SERVICES

by

establishing and improving a functional structure; delegating authority.

____ 3. MAINTAINS CITY STAFF

by

recruiting, selecting, orienting, and training employees.

____ 4. MAINTAINS CITY STAFF JOB RESULTS

by

coaching, counseling, and disciplining employees; planning, monitoring, and appraising job results.

____ 5. MAINTAINS PROFESSIONAL AND TECHNICAL KNOWLEDGE

by

attending educational workshops; reviewing professional publications; establishing personal networks; participating in professional societies.

____ 6. ACHIEVES FINANCIAL OBJECTIVES

by

developing and recommending an annual budget; scheduling expenditures; analyzing variances; initiating corrective actions; anticipating long-term issues.

% of Time

____ 7. ENFORCES BOARD'S DECISIONS

by

developing, monitoring, and enforcing policies and procedures.

____ 8. COMPLIES WITH FEDERAL, STATE, AND LOCAL LAWS AND REGULATIONS

by

studying existing and new legislation; anticipating future legislation; enforcing adherence to requirements; advising management on needed actions.

____ 9. PROMOTES CITY SERVICES

by

coordinating and cooperating with federal, state, and other local units of government.

____ 10. KEEPS THE MAYOR AND THE BOARD INFORMED

by

collecting, analyzing, and summarizing information and trends; remaining accessible; answering questions and requests.

____ 11. MAINTAINS RAPPORT WITH THE COMMUNITY

by

meeting with citizens and advisory groups; reaching out to resolve concerns; settling disputes.

____ 12. CONTRIBUTES TO TEAM EFFORT

by

accomplishing related results as needed.

JOB PURPOSE: **COMPLETES CONSTRUCTION PROJECTS**

by

preparing engineering design and documents; confirming specifications.

ESSENTIAL JOB RESULTS:

*% of
Time*

___ 1. DESIGNS CONSTRUCTION PROJECTS
by
studying project concept, architectural
drawings, and models.

___ 2. PREPARES ENGINEERING DESIGN
by
collecting and studying reports, maps,
drawings, blueprints, aerial photographs and
tests on soil composition, terrain,
hydrological characteristics, and related
topographical and geologic data.

___ 3. DETERMINES PROJECT COSTS
by
calculating labor, material, and related costs.

___ 4. PREPARES FEASIBILITY STUDY
by
analyzing engineering design; conducting
environmental impact studies; assembling
data.

___ 5. PREPARES ENGINEERING DOCUMENTS
by
developing construction specifications, plans,
and schedules.

___ 6. CONFIRMS ADHERENCE TO CONSTRUCTION
SPECIFICATIONS AND SAFETY STANDARDS
by
monitoring project progress; inspecting
construction site; verifying calculations and
placements.

*% of
Time*

___ 7. FULFILLS PROJECT REQUIREMENTS
by
training and guiding operators.

___ 8. MAINTAINS OPERATIONS
by
enforcing project and operational policies and
procedures.

___ 9. PROVIDES ENGINEERING INFORMATION
by
answering questions and requests.

___ 10. COMPLIES WITH FEDERAL, STATE, AND LOCAL LEGAL
REQUIREMENTS
by
studying existing and new legislation;
anticipating future legislation; enforcing
adherence to requirements; advising
management on needed actions.

___ 11. MAINTAINS PROJECT DATA BASE
by
writing computer programs; entering data;
completing backups.

___ 12. CONTRIBUTES TO TEAM EFFORT
by
accomplishing related results as needed.

JOB TITLE: Claims Adjuster

JOB PURPOSE: **RESOLVES CLAIMS**

by

investigating losses; negotiating out-of-court settlements; presenting evidence in legal proceedings.

ESSENTIAL JOB RESULTS:

% of
Time

_____ 1. DETERMINES INSURANCE COVERAGE
by
examining claim forms, policies, and other records; interviewing claimant and witnesses; consulting police and hospital records; inspecting property damage.

_____ 2. PREPARES REPORTS
by
collecting, analyzing, and summarizing information.

_____ 3. RESOLVES QUESTIONABLE CLAIMS
by
investigating claim; comparing claim information with evidence.

_____ 4. SETTLES CLAIMS
by
determining insurance carrier's liability; reaching agreement with claimant according to policy provisions.

_____ 5. RECOMMENDS LITIGATION
by
analyzing negotiated settlement options; evaluating evidence.

% of
Time

_____ 6. PRESENTS EVIDENCE AT LEGAL PROCEEDINGS
by
testifying and producing reports and other documents as evidence.

_____ 7. MAINTAINS INSURANCE PRODUCT AND COMPANY REPUTATION
by
complying with federal and state regulations.

_____ 8. MAINTAINS PROFESSIONAL AND TECHNICAL KNOWLEDGE
by
attending educational workshops; reviewing professional publications; establishing personal networks; participating in professional societies.

_____ 9. CONTRIBUTES TO TEAM EFFORT
by
accomplishing related results as needed.

JOB PURPOSE: **COMPLETES (DEPARTMENT) DOCUMENTS**

by

entering data, completing reports, and filing.

ESSENTIAL JOB RESULTS:

*% of
Time*

____ 1. PREPARES WORK TO BE ACCOMPLISHED
by
gathering and sorting department documents
and information.

____ 2. DETERMINES PRIORITY, FORMAT, AND OTHER
REQUIREMENTS
by
reviewing instructions or references.

____ 3. VERIFIES (DEPARTMENT) INFORMATION
by
comparing information to original source;
recalculating totals.

____ 4. COMPLETES (DEPARTMENT) DOCUMENTS
by
entering/typing data from source materials or
recordings.

____ 5. REVISES (DEPARTMENT) DOCUMENTS
by
entering/retyping edited data.

____ 6. VERIFIES (DEPARTMENT) DOCUMENTS
by
proofreading and rechecking requirements.

____ 7. REPRODUCES (DEPARTMENT) DOCUMENTS
by
operating a copy machine.

*% of
Time*

____ 8. MAINTAINS (DEPARTMENT) HISTORICAL RECORDS
by
filing documents.

____ 9. SECURES (DEPARTMENT) INFORMATION
by
completing data base backups.

____ 10. MAINTAINS (DEPARTMENT) SUPPLIES INVENTORY
by
checking stock to determine inventory level;
anticipating needed supplies; placing and
expediting orders for supplies; verifying
receipt of supplies.

____ 11. MAINTAINS (DEPARTMENT) WORK FLOW
by
sorting and delivering information.

____ 12. PROVIDES INFORMATION
by
answering questions and requests.

____ 13. CONTRIBUTES TO (DEPARTMENT) TEAM EFFORT
by
accomplishing related results as needed.

JOB TITLE: Clinical Engineer

JOB PURPOSE: **PREPARES MEDICAL EQUIPMENT FOR OBSERVING AND TREATING PATIENTS**

by

designing, modifying, and testing mechanical, electrical, and electronic instruments and devices.

ESSENTIAL JOB RESULTS:

% of Time

1. DESIGNS AND DEVELOPS MEDICAL EQUIPMENT
   by
   studying human biobehavioral systems; determining requirements for observing and treating patients; applying knowledge of electrical, mechanical, chemical, and related engineering principles, materials compatible with body tissues, and human anatomy and physiology.

2. DESIGNS AND DEVELOPS DISPLAY AND WARNING SYSTEMS
   by
   applying knowledge of computers, graphics, and related technologies.

3. APPROVES PURCHASED EQUIPMENT
   by
   conducting tests; ensuring adherence to codes; making modifications.

4. ENSURES OPERATION OF EQUIPMENT
   by
   completing preventive maintenance requirements; following manufacturer's instructions; troubleshooting and repairing malfunctions; calling for special service; evaluating service contracts; maintaining equipment inventories.

5. EVALUATES PROPOSED EQUIPMENT
   by
   designing and conducting tests.

% of Time

6. MAINTAINS PROFESSIONAL AND TECHNICAL KNOWLEDGE
   by
   attending educational workshops; reviewing professional publications; establishing personal networks; participating in professional societies.

7. PREPARES BIOMEDICAL REPORTS
   by
   collecting, analyzing, and summarizing information and trends.

8. COMPLIES WITH FEDERAL, STATE, AND LOCAL LEGAL REQUIREMENTS
   by
   studying existing and new legislation; anticipating future legislation; enforcing adherence to requirements; advising management on needed actions.

9. MAINTAINS PATIENT CONFIDENCE AND PROTECTS OPERATIONS
   by
   keeping information confidential.

10. MAINTAINS SAFE WORKING ENVIRONMENT
    by
    recommending and complying with procedures; training and guiding medical and health care personnel.

11. CONTRIBUTES TO TEAM EFFORT
    by
    accomplishing related results as needed.

JOB PURPOSE: **SERVES CLIENTS**

by

evaluating, diagnosing, and treating mental and emotional disorders.

ESSENTIAL JOB RESULTS:

% of
Time

_____ 1. DIAGNOSES DISORDER

by
selecting, administering, and interpreting intelligence, achievement, interest, personality, and other psychological tests; studying medical, emotional, and social histories; interviewing and observing the client.

_____ 2. DEVELOPS TREATMENT PLAN

by
establishing treatment goals and methodologies.

_____ 3. TREATS CLIENT

by
utilizing psychological techniques and therapies; discussing progress toward goals with client; monitoring development; evaluating and adjusting treatment; collaborating with other specialists.

_____ 4. MAINTAINS HISTORICAL RECORDS

by
documenting treatment events.

% of
Time

_____ 5. ASSURES QUALITY SERVICE FOR CLIENTS

by
enforcing rules, regulations, and legal requirements with clients; documenting events of the treatment process.

_____ 6. MAINTAINS PROFESSIONAL KNOWLEDGE

by
attending educational workshops; reviewing professional publications; establishing personal networks.

_____ 7. COMPLETES RESEARCH PROJECTS

by
establishing hypothesis, design, sample, methodology, and evaluation.

_____ 8. CONTRIBUTES TO TEAM EFFORT

by
accomplishing related results as needed.

JOB TITLE: Clinical Social Work Therapist

JOB PURPOSE: **SERVES CLIENTS**

by

providing therapeutic counseling.

ESSENTIAL JOB RESULTS:

% of Time

___ 1. DIAGNOSES CLIENT'S PROBLEMS
by
collecting and evaluating information about the client's situation.

___ 2. DEVELOPS TREATMENT PLAN
by
establishing treatment goals with the client; determining treatment methodologies.

___ 3. ADVISES CLIENT
by
suggesting and exploring resolutions; discussing progress toward goals.

___ 4. OBTAINS SERVICES
by
initiating referrals.

___ 5. MONITORS PROGRESS TOWARD TREATMENT GOALS
by
evaluating and adjusting services provided.

___ 6. ASSURES QUALITY SERVICE FOR CLIENTS
by
enforcing rules, regulations, and legal requirements with clients; documenting events of the therapeutic process.

___ 7. MAINTAINS PROFESSIONAL AND TECHNICAL KNOWLEDGE
by
attending educational workshops; reviewing professional publications; establishing personal networks; conducting research projects.

% of Time

___ 8. MAINTAINS AGENCY CREDIBILITY
by
establishing working relationships with sponsoring, advisory, and related service agencies.

___ 9. PROMOTES THE AGENCY
by
ensuring an understanding of program services available for clients; publicizing activities and accomplishments; adhering to a professional code of ethics.

___ 10. PROVIDES A CLINICAL EXPERIENCE FOR SOCIAL WORK STUDENTS
by
negotiating learning objectives; supervising practice and caseload management; teaching theory and its application; evaluating skills and personal and professional growth; ensuring identification with the social work profession.

___ 11. CONTRIBUTES TO THE SOCIAL WORK PROFESSION
by
participating in meetings and conferences; consulting with other professionals; advocating professional values.

___ 12. CONTRIBUTES TO TEAM EFFORT
by
accomplishing related results as needed.

JOB TITLE: Collection Manager

JOB PURPOSE: RECOVERS ORGANIZATION'S ASSETS

by

collecting delinquent accounts; supervising employees.

ESSENTIAL JOB RESULTS:

% of
Time

____ 1. MAINTAINS COLLECTION GUIDELINES
by
writing and updating collection policies and
procedures.

____ 2. EVALUATES COLLECTION POLICIES AND PROCEDURES
by
assessing accounts recovered in relation to
effort, methods, and costs involved.

____ 3. PREPARES COLLECTION REPORTS
by
collecting, analyzing, and summarizing
account information and trends.

____ 4. COLLECTS DELINQUENT ACCOUNTS
by
locating and notifying customers with
delinquent accounts; establishing repayment
schedules through contacts with customers by
telephone, in person, or by other means.

____ 5. MONITORS COLLECTION EFFORTS
by
auditing accounts and reports; directing new
approaches.

____ 6. MINIMIZES LOSSES
by
referring bad-debt accounts to outside agency
or attorney.

____ 7. DETERMINES LOSSES
by
writing off bad-debt accounts.

____ 8. UNCOVERS FRAUDULENT ACTIVITIES
by
investigating account documentation.

% of
Time

____ 9. DETERMINES LEGAL COURSE OF ACTION
by
conferring with attorneys; estimating
probability of successful recovery.

____ 10. PREVENTS LOSSES
by
notifying credit department of risks.

____ 11. MAINTAINS HISTORICAL RECORDS
by
ensuring that documents are completed and
filed according to policy and procedure.

____ 12. MAINTAINS CUSTOMER CONFIDENCE AND PROTECTS
OPERATIONS
by
keeping collection information confidential.

____ 13. COMPLETES COLLECTION OPERATIONAL REQUIREMENTS
by
scheduling and assigning employees;
following up on work results.

____ 14. MAINTAINS COLLECTION STAFF
by
recruiting, selecting, orienting, and training
employees.

____ 15. MAINTAINS COLLECTION STAFF JOB RESULTS
by
counseling and disciplining employees;
planning, monitoring, and appraising job
results.

ESSENTIAL JOB RESULTS:

% of
Time

_____ 16. MAINTAINS PROFESSIONAL AND TECHNICAL KNOWLEDGE
by
attending educational workshops; reviewing
professional publications; establishing
personal networks; participating in
professional societies.

_____ 17. COMPLIES WITH FEDERAL, STATE, AND LOCAL
COLLECTION AND INFORMATION LEGAL REQUIREMENTS
by
studying existing and new legislation;
enforcing adherence to requirements;
advising management on needed actions.

% of
Time

_____ 18. CONTRIBUTES TO TEAM EFFORT
by
accomplishing related results as needed.

JOB TITLE: Commercial Loan Account Specialist

JOB PURPOSE:

COMPLETES LOANS

by

gathering, verifying, entering, and retrieving loan data.

ESSENTIAL JOB RESULTS:

% of
Time

_____ 1. VERIFIES LOAN INFORMATION
by
comparing data; identifying discrepancies; notifying the loan officer.

_____ 2. ENCODES NEW-LOAN INPUT FORMS
by
extracting information from the loan data worksheet; coding it for the system.

_____ 3. COMPLETES LOAN RENEWALS
by
verifying new data with current data (i.e., rate, renewal balance); making adjustments; preparing input forms.

_____ 4. REVIEWS LOAN ADVANCES
by
verifying credit limits, commitment expirations, and account statuses; notifying the loan officer.

_____ 5. COMPLETES COMMERCIAL LOAN PAYMENTS
by
verifying distribution of principal and interest; inputting verified amounts.

% of
Time

_____ 6. COMPLETES LOAN ADJUSTMENTS
by
preparing input information; calculating rate changes, interest discrepancies, etc.; referring questionable requests to the loan officer.

_____ 7. CONTROLS LOAN TRANSACTIONS
by
verifying information; researching; and rectifying discrepancies.

_____ 8. PROVIDES LOAN INFORMATION
by
answering questions, and stating procedural requirements.

_____ 9. CONTRIBUTES TO TEAM EFFORT
by
accomplishing related results as needed.

JOB TITLE: Commercial Loan Administration Manager

JOB PURPOSE: CONTROLS COMMERCIAL LOAN PORTFOLIO STATUS

by

establishing and enforcing policies, and recommending actions.

ESSENTIAL JOB RESULTS:

% of Time

___ 1. CONTROLS LOANS
by
establishing, monitoring, and enforcing
policies, procedures, and standards.

___ 2. IDENTIFIES STATUS OF COMMERCIAL LOAN PORTFOLIO
by
tracking delinquencies; verifying; preparing
reports.

___ 3. RECOMMENDS ACTION ON DELINQUENT LOANS
by
analyzing accounts and evaluating options.

___ 4. RECOMMENDS ACTION ON DEFAULTED LOANS
by
evaluating charge-offs.

___ 5. CONTRIBUTES DECISION-MAKING INFORMATION TO CREDIT COMMITTEE
by
analyzing loan requests, notes, terms,
security, etc.; presenting administrative issues
for approval.

___ 6. SUPPORTS THE COMPLIANCE COMMITTEE
by
reviewing new or revised regulations and
policy; reviewing loan documentation.

___ 7. COMPLETES OPERATIONAL REQUIREMENTS
by
scheduling and assigning employees;
following up on work results.

% of Time

___ 8. MAINTAINS COMMERCIAL LOAN ADMINISTRATION STAFF
by
recruiting, selecting, orienting, and training
employees.

___ 9. MAINTAINS COMMERCIAL LOAN ADMINISTRATION STAFF JOB RESULTS
by
coaching, counseling, and disciplining
employees; planning, monitoring, and
appraising job results.

___ 10. MAINTAINS PROFESSIONAL AND TECHNICAL KNOWLEDGE
by
attending educational workshops; reviewing
professional publications; establishing
personal networks; participating in
professional societies.

___ 11. ACHIEVES FINANCIAL OBJECTIVES
by
preparing an annual budget; scheduling
expenditures; analyzing variances; initiating
corrective actions.

___ 12. CONTRIBUTES TO TEAM EFFORT
by
accomplishing related results as needed.

JOB TITLE: Communications Specialist

JOB PURPOSE: **MAINTAINS PUBLIC AND EMPLOYEE AWARENESS OF ORGANIZATION ISSUES**

by

completing external and internal information programs.

ESSENTIAL JOB RESULTS:

% of
Time

____ 1. COMPILES INFORMATION
by
researching activities and events; interviewing participants; writing and proofing copy; obtaining photographs or videos.

____ 2. PREPARES INFORMATION
by
establishing deadlines; arranging for technical assistance; determining formats; coordinating actions.

____ 3. INFORMS PUBLIC AND EMPLOYEES
by
providing information, including fact sheets, news releases, newsletters, photographs, videos, recordings, and personal appearances.

% of
Time

____ 4. MAINTAINS RAPPORT WITH MEDIA REPRESENTATIVES
by
arranging continuing contacts; responding to requests; arranging interviews; resolving concerns.

____ 5. MAINTAINS HISTORICAL REFERENCE
by
filing published media.

____ 6. ACCOMPLISHES SPECIFIC INFORMATION OBJECTIVES
by
conducting special projects; coordinating efforts with lobbyists, consultants, and others.

____ 7. CONTRIBUTES TO TEAM EFFORT
by
accomplishing related results as needed.

JOB PURPOSE: **MEETS COMMUNITY NEEDS**

by

determining and pursuing agency goals; guiding agency operations.

ESSENTIAL JOB RESULTS:

*% of
Time*

____ 1. ESTABLISHES AND MAINTAINS THE MISSION OF THE
AGENCY
by
identifying societal and community needs;
advocating the agency's beliefs.

____ 2. DETERMINES LONG-TERM GOALS OF THE AGENCY
by
assessing client needs; examining agency
resources and capabilities; preparing a
strategic plan.

____ 3. MANAGES AGENCY OPERATIONS
by
employing, supporting, and advising the
chief operating officer.

____ 4. GUIDES AGENCY OPERATIONS
by
approving operating structure, policy, and
procedure.

*% of
Time*

____ 5. MAINTAINS THE AGENCY'S FINANCIAL STABILITY
by
identifying requirements; soliciting funds;
preparing a budget; approving expenditures;
auditing procedures and practices.

____ 6. ASSURES ACHIEVEMENT OF AGENCY MISSION AND
POLICIES
by
reviewing agency performance.

____ 7. MAINTAINS AGENCY BOARD OPERATIONS
by
recruiting and electing Board members;
establishing Board operating structure and
policies.

____ 8. CONTRIBUTES TO TEAM EFFORT
by
accomplishing related results as needed.

JOB PURPOSE: MEETS COMMUNITY NEEDS

by

planning, organizing, implementing, and evaluating therapeutic
counseling programs, and developing agency personnel.

ESSENTIAL JOB RESULTS:

% of
Time

_____ 1. IDENTIFIES ACTUAL AND ANTICIPATED COMMUNITY
SERVICE REQUIREMENTS
by
establishing personal rapport with potential
and actual clients and other persons in a
position to understand the needs of the
community.

_____ 2. ADDRESSES CHANGING COMMUNITY AND PROFESSIONAL
TRENDS
by
inaugurating service programs.

_____ 3. MAINTAINS AND DEVELOPS STAFF
by
supervising, directly and through delegating,
all personnel, including hiring, transferring,
promoting, demoting, disciplining,
counseling, coaching, appraising job results,
and terminating, as well as providing
educational and experiential growth
opportunities and morale-maintaining
consideration.

_____ 4. PLANS FOR AND PROTECTS THE PHYSICAL AND
FINANCIAL RESOURCES OF THE AGENCY
by
inspecting and maintaining facilities;
budgeting and controlling expenses; auditing
practices; initiating and participating in
fundraising activities, including submitting
grant proposals.

_____ 5. MAINTAINS AGENCY OPERATIONS
by
formulating and enforcing program,
operational, and personnel policies and
procedures.

% of
Time

_____ 6. MAINTAINS THE STABILITY AND REPUTATION OF THE
AGENCY
by
complying with, and influencing the
development of, legal and accreditation
requirements.

_____ 7. MAINTAINS AGENCY CREDIBILITY
by
working with the executives and staffs of
funding agencies, other sponsoring groups,
and related service agencies.

_____ 8. PROMOTES POSITIVE AGENCY IMAGE
by
ensuring an understanding in the community
of program services available; publicizing
accomplishments of the agency; adhering to a
professional code of ethics.

_____ 9. CONTRIBUTES TO THE BOARD'S EFFECTIVENESS
by
identifying short-term and long-range issues
to be addressed; providing information and
commentary pertinent to the Board's
deliberations, recommending options and
courses of action, especially where
professional considerations are involved;
implementing directives; recruiting Board
candidates.

_____ 10. MAINTAINS PROFESSIONAL AND TECHNICAL KNOWLEDGE
by
attending educational workshops; reviewing
professional publications; establishing
personal networks; participating in
professional societies.

_____ 11. CONTRIBUTES TO TEAM EFFORT
by
accomplishing related results as needed.

JOB TITLE: Compensation Manager

JOB PURPOSE: **ATTRACTS AND RETAINS EMPLOYEES**

by

maintaining a pay program.

ESSENTIAL JOB RESULTS:

*% of
Time*

____ 1. VALIDATES JOB REQUIREMENTS
by
developing and maintaining a job analysis system; analyzing jobs.

____ 2. DEFINES JOBS
by
developing a job description format; writing job descriptions, job qualifications, and job evaluation documentation.

____ 3. ESTABLISHES INTERNAL EQUITY
by
developing and maintaining a job evaluation system; evaluating and ranking jobs.

____ 4. ESTABLISHES EXTERNAL EQUITY
by
defining the labor market; identifying benchmark jobs; selecting competitor organizations; conducting pay surveys; analyzing pay and related data.

____ 5. MAINTAINS PAY STRUCTURE
by
recommending, planning, and implementing structural adjustments; preparing pay budgets.

____ 6. MAINTAINS TOTAL COMPENSATION
by
studying proportion of pay, benefits, incentives, and intangibles; recommending program adjustments.

____ 7. MAINTAINS PAY DECISION-MAKING GUIDELINES
by
writing and updating pay policies and procedures.

*% of
Time*

____ 8. COMPLETES COMPENSATION REPORTS AND RECOMMENDATIONS
by
gathering, analyzing, and summarizing pay data and trend information.

____ 9. COMPLIES WITH FEDERAL, STATE, AND LOCAL LEGAL REQUIREMENTS
by
studying existing and new employment legislation; enforcing adherence to requirements; advising management on needed actions.

____ 10. ENFORCES MERIT RAISE AND INCENTIVE GUIDELINES
by
comparing recommended pay raises and incentives with budget; notifying supervisors of variances.

____ 11. COMPLETES OPERATIONAL REQUIREMENTS
by
scheduling and assigning employees; following up on work results.

____ 12. MAINTAINS COMPENSATION STAFF
by
recruiting, selecting, orienting, and training employees.

____ 13. MAINTAINS COMPENSATION STAFF JOB RESULTS
by
counseling and disciplining employees; planning, monitoring, and appraising job results.

JOB TITLE: Compensation Manager

ESSENTIAL JOB RESULTS:

% of
Time

____ 14. MAINTAINS PROFESSIONAL AND TECHNICAL KNOWLEDGE
by
attending educational workshops; reviewing professional publications; establishing personal networks; participating in professional societies.

% of
Time

____ 15. CONTRIBUTES TO TEAM EFFORT
by
accomplishing related results as needed.

JOB TITLE: Compensation Specialist

JOB PURPOSE: **MAINTAINS A PAY PROGRAM**

by

analyzing, describing, and evaluating jobs; conducting pay surveys.

ESSENTIAL JOB RESULTS:

% of
Time

____ 1. VALIDATES JOB REQUIREMENTS
by
analyzing jobs, including interviewing knowledgeable persons; studying completed questionnaires; observing jobs being performed.

____ 2. DEFINES JOBS
by
writing job descriptions, job qualifications, and job evaluation documentation.

____ 3. ESTABLISHES INTERNAL EQUITY
by
evaluating and ranking jobs.

____ 4. ESTABLISHES EXTERNAL EQUITY
by
conducting pay surveys; analyzing pay data.

____ 5. MAINTAINS PAY STRUCTURE
by
calculating pay grades and ranges.

% of
Time

____ 6. COMPLETES COMPENSATION REPORTS
by
gathering and analyzing pay data.

____ 7. COMPLIES WITH FEDERAL, STATE, AND LOCAL LEGAL REQUIREMENTS
by
enforcing adherence to requirements.

____ 8. ENFORCES MERIT RAISE AND INCENTIVE GUIDELINES
by
comparing recommended pay raises and incentives with budget; notifying supervisors of variances.

____ 9. MAINTAINS PROFESSIONAL AND TECHNICAL KNOWLEDGE
by
attending educational workshops; reviewing professional publications.

____ 10. CONTRIBUTES TO TEAM EFFORT
by
accomplishing related results as needed.

JOB PURPOSE: **PROVIDES DATA**

by

operating a computer.

ESSENTIAL JOB RESULTS:

% of
Time

____ 1. DETERMINES SEQUENCE OF OPERATIONS
by
studying production schedule.

____ 2. PREPARES EQUIPMENT FOR OPERATIONS
by
accessing software in computer; loading
paper into printers and plotters; preparing for
output.

____ 3. STARTS OPERATIONS
by
entering commands.

____ 4. MAINTAINS OPERATIONS
by
monitoring error and stoppage messages;
observing peripheral equipment; entering
commands to correct errors and stoppages;
reloading paper; making adjustments in
process; notifying supervisor for additional
resources.

____ 5. DOCUMENTS PROBLEMS AND ACTIONS
by
completing production logs.

____ 6. RESOLVES USER PROBLEMS
by
answering questions and requests.

% of
Time

____ 7. ENSURES OPERATION OF EQUIPMENT
by
completing preventive maintenance
requirements and tests; following
manufacturer's instructions; troubleshooting
malfunctions; calling for repairs; maintaining
equipment inventories; evaluating new
equipment and techniques.

____ 8. MAINTAINS SUPPLIES INVENTORY
by
checking stock to determine inventory level;
anticipating needed supplies; placing and
expediting orders for supplies; verifying
receipt of supplies.

____ 9. MAINTAINS CLIENT CONFIDENCE AND PROTECTS
OPERATIONS
by
keeping information confidential.

____ 10. CONTRIBUTES TO TEAM EFFORT
by
accomplishing related results as needed.

JOB TITLE: Computer Programmer

JOB PURPOSE: CREATES AND MODIFIES COMPUTER PROGRAMS

by

converting project requirements into computer language.

ESSENTIAL JOB RESULTS:

*% of
Time*

___ 1. CONFIRMS PROJECT REQUIREMENTS

by

reviewing program objective, input data, and output requirements with analyst, supervisor, and client.

___ 2. ARRANGES PROJECT REQUIREMENTS IN PROGRAMMING SEQUENCE

by

analyzing requirements; preparing a work flow chart and diagram using knowledge of computer capabilities, subject matter, programming language, and logic.

___ 3. ENCODES PROJECT REQUIREMENTS

by

converting work flow information into computer language.

___ 4. PROGRAMS THE COMPUTER

by

entering coded information.

___ 5. CONFIRMS PROGRAM OPERATION

by

conducting tests; modifying program sequence and/or codes.

___ 6. PREPARES REFERENCE FOR USERS

by

writing operating instructions.

*% of
Time*

___ 7. MAINTAINS HISTORICAL RECORDS

by

documenting program development and revisions.

___ 8. MAINTAINS CLIENT CONFIDENCE AND PROTECTS OPERATIONS

by

keeping information confidential.

___ 9. ENSURES OPERATION OF EQUIPMENT

by

following manufacturer's instructions; troubleshooting malfunctions; calling for repairs; evaluating new equipment and techniques.

___ 10. MAINTAINS PROFESSIONAL AND TECHNICAL KNOWLEDGE

by

attending educational workshops; reviewing professional publications; establishing personal networks; participating in professional societies.

___ 11. CONTRIBUTES TO TEAM EFFORT

by

accomplishing related results as needed.

JOB TITLE: Computer Systems Hardware Analyst

JOB PURPOSE: **MAINTAINS COMPUTER SYSTEM HARDWARE CAPABILITIES**

by

designing and monitoring requirements and performance.

ESSENTIAL JOB RESULTS:

% of Time

____ 1. IDENTIFIES SYSTEM WORK LOAD REQUIREMENTS
by
conferring with clients and data processing specialists.

____ 2. IDENTIFIES SYSTEM CAPABILITIES AND LIMITATIONS
by
conferring with users; testing system.

____ 3. DETERMINES HARDWARE CONFIGURATION
by
studying, analyzing, and evaluating system factors, such as scope of projects, number of users, reporting requirements, volume of transactions, access restrictions, cost constraints, power supply specifications, and security conditions.

____ 4. SATISFIES WORK LOAD REQUIREMENTS
by
recommending purchase or modifications of computer and peripheral equipment; planning or revising layout.

____ 5. SATISFIES PHYSICAL LAYOUT REQUIREMENTS
by
recommending equipment to control dust, temperature, and humidity.

____ 6. PREPARES USERS TO OPERATE EQUIPMENT
by
writing reference manuals; conducting training sessions.

% of Time

____ 7. MAINTAINS SYSTEM PERFORMANCE
by
monitoring use and output.

____ 8. MAINTAINS HISTORICAL RECORDS
by
documenting configuration and revisions.

____ 9. PREPARES REPORTS
by
collecting, analyzing, and summarizing information and trends.

____ 10. MAINTAINS PROFESSIONAL AND TECHNICAL KNOWLEDGE
by
attending educational workshops; reviewing professional publications; establishing personal networks; participating in professional societies.

____ 11. MAINTAINS CLIENT CONFIDENCE AND PROTECTS OPERATIONS
by
keeping information confidential.

____ 12. CONTRIBUTES TO TEAM EFFORT
by
accomplishing related results as needed.

JOB TITLE: Conference Planner

JOB PURPOSE: **SATISFIES GUESTS**

by

determining and arranging meeting requirements.

ESSENTIAL JOB RESULTS:

*% of
Time*

_____ 1. DETERMINES MEETING REQUIREMENTS

by

interviewing guests; explaining options; verifying selections.

_____ 2. ESTABLISHES A MEETING PLAN

by

conveying requirements to staff; confirming staff ability to comply; coordinating services among staff; confirming plan with guests; publishing a meeting agenda.

_____ 3. ADJUSTS PLANS

by

receiving and verifying changes with guests; informing staff; confirming ability to change; confirming change with guests; publishing changes to the meeting agenda.

_____ 4. OBTAINS MEETING REQUIREMENTS

by

contracting with outside vendors; expediting services.

_____ 5. VERIFIES PREPARATIONS

by

checking readiness before the meeting; expediting services; confirming expectations with guests.

*% of
Time*

_____ 6. FULFILLS MEETING PLAN

by

resolving problems; assigning employees; expediting delivery of services.

_____ 7. MAINTAINS INTER- AND INTRADEPARTMENTAL WORK FLOW

by

fostering a spirit of cooperation and guest service.

_____ 8. PREPARES INVOICE

by

gathering and verifying records of services provided; forwarding to billing department.

_____ 9. MAINTAINS PROFESSIONAL AND TECHNICAL KNOWLEDGE

by

attending educational workshops; reviewing professional publications; establishing personal networks; participating in professional societies.

_____ 10. CONTRIBUTES TO TEAM EFFORT

by

accomplishing related results as needed.

JOB TITLE: Consumer Loan Operations Supervisor

JOB PURPOSE: **MAINTAINS CONSUMER LOAN ACCOUNTING, CREDIT CARD, AND STUDENT LOAN SYSTEMS**
by
enforcing policies; maintaining staff.

ESSENTIAL JOB RESULTS:

*% of
Time*

____ 1. MAINTAINS CONSUMER NOTE AND CREDIT CARD SYSTEMS
by
reviewing the preparation of entries;
reconciling accounts; reviewing certification
of proof.

____ 2. PROTECTS SYSTEMS
by
auditing outcomes; cautioning manager of
potential or observed system misuse.

____ 3. RESPONDS TO EMPLOYEE QUESTIONS
by
researching and investigating problems;
providing feedback.

____ 4. COORDINATES SYSTEM ALTERATIONS WITH
PROGRAMMING DEPARTMENT
by
preparing and revising documents; converting
branches to the system; preparing user testing
of new product changes; identifying systems
problems; recommending corrective actions.

____ 5. PREPARES PERSONNEL TO USE AND INTERPRET SYSTEMS
by
conducting training in new products and
procedures; preparing and distributing
revisions to the user manual.

____ 6. MAINTAINS PROCESSING OF CONSUMER LOAN INSURANCE
PREMIUMS
by
directing the preparation of reports; issuing
and canceling policies; reviewing billings;
reconciling; preparing proof certification.

*% of
Time*

____ 7. RESOLVES CUSTOMER PROBLEMS
by
investigating credit charge-backs with
merchants; mediating disputes.

____ 8. COMPLETES OPERATIONAL REQUIREMENTS
by
scheduling and assigning employees;
following up on work results.

____ 9. MAINTAINS CONSUMER LOAN OPERATIONS STAFF
by
recruiting, selecting, orienting, and training
employees.

____ 10. MAINTAINS CONSUMER LOAN OPERATIONS STAFF JOB
RESULTS
by
counseling and disciplining employees;
planning, monitoring, and appraising job
results.

____ 11. MAINTAINS PROFESSIONAL AND TECHNICAL KNOWLEDGE
by
attending educational workshops; reviewing
professional publications; establishing
personal networks; participating in
professional societies.

____ 12. MAINTAINS CUSTOMER CONFIDENCE AND PROTECTS
OPERATIONS
by
keeping information confidential.

____ 13. CONTRIBUTES TO TEAM EFFORT
by
accomplishing related results as needed.

JOB TITLE: Contract Administrator

JOB PURPOSE: **PROVIDES MATERIALS AND EQUIPMENT**

by

defining requirements, and awarding and monitoring contracts.

ESSENTIAL JOB RESULTS:

% of Time

____ 1. DETERMINES CONTRACT REQUIREMENTS
by
studying performance requirements, delivery schedules, and estimates of costs of material, equipment, and production.

____ 2. ISSUES REQUESTS FOR PROPOSALS
by
preparing bid process procedures; indicating tests and reports required; identifying potential bidders.

____ 3. AWARDS CONTRACTS
by
identifying bid specification conformity; negotiating price; approving amendments or extensions.

____ 4. PROVIDES CONTRACT INFORMATION
by
answering questions and requests.

____ 5. RESOLVES CONTRACT DISCREPANCIES
by
collecting and analyzing information.

____ 6. PROVIDES INFORMATION
by
answering questions and requests.

% of Time

____ 7. MONITORS CONTRACT PERFORMANCE
by
determining compliance and need for amendments or extensions; arbitrating claims or complaints.

____ 8. MAINTAINS PROFESSIONAL AND TECHNICAL KNOWLEDGE
by
attending educational workshops; reviewing professional publications; establishing personal networks; participating in professional societies.

____ 9. COMPLIES WITH FEDERAL, STATE, AND LOCAL LEGAL REQUIREMENTS
by
studying existing and new legislation; enforcing adherence to requirements; advising management on needed actions.

____ 10. CONTRIBUTES TO TEAM EFFORT
by
accomplishing related results as needed.

JOB PURPOSE: **SUPPORTS JOINT VENTURE CONTRACT ADMINISTRATION**
by
maintaining current and historical references; providing information
when requested.

ESSENTIAL JOB RESULTS:

*% of
Time*

____ 1. PROVIDES ADMINISTRATIVE SUPPORT
by
scheduling meetings; organizing and
circulating materials; providing information
to contract committee members.

____ 2. MAINTAINS CONTRACTS
by
researching language and suggesting
wording.

____ 3. COMPLETES REPORTS
by
gathering and analyzing technical data, using
computer spreadsheets and graphics
packages.

____ 4. MONITORS FINANCIAL STATUS
by
tracking and analyzing current revenues and
expenses; projecting the effect of
modifications to agreements using computer
spreadsheets.

____ 5. PREPARES PRESENTATIONS AND REPORTS
by
collecting, analyzing, and summarizing
information and trends.

*% of
Time*

____ 6. INITIATES ANNUAL FINANCIAL REVIEW
by
preparing requests for data; reviewing
responses; reporting results.

____ 7. MAINTAINS INTERGROUP WORK FLOW
by
fostering a spirit of cooperation.

____ 8. MAINTAINS CONTRACTOR CONFIDENCE AND PROTECTS
OPERATIONS
by
keeping information confidential.

____ 9. MAINTAINS CONTRACT DATA BASE
by
entering and backing up data.

____ 10. CONTRIBUTES TO TEAM EFFORT
by
accomplishing related results as needed.

JOB PURPOSE: **MAXIMIZES RETURN ON FINANCIAL ASSETS**

by

establishing financial policies, procedures, controls, and reporting systems.

ESSENTIAL JOB RESULTS:

% of
Time

___ 1. GUIDES FINANCIAL DECISIONS
by
establishing, monitoring, and enforcing policies and procedures.

___ 2. PROTECTS ASSETS
by
establishing, monitoring, and enforcing internal controls.

___ 3. MONITORS AND CONFIRMS FINANCIAL CONDITION
by
conducting audits; providing information to external auditors.

___ 4. MAXIMIZES RETURN, AND LIMITS RISK, ON CASH
by
minimizing bank balances; making investments.

___ 5. PREPARES BUDGETS
by
establishing schedules; collecting, analyzing, and consolidating financial data; recommending plans.

___ 6. ACHIEVES BUDGET OBJECTIVES
by
scheduling expenditures; analyzing variances; initiating corrective actions.

___ 7. PROVIDES STATUS OF FINANCIAL CONDITION
by
collecting, interpreting, and reporting financial data.

___ 8. PREPARES SPECIAL REPORTS
by
collecting, analyzing, and summarizing information and trends.

% of
Time

___ 9. COMPLIES WITH FEDERAL, STATE, AND LOCAL LEGAL REQUIREMENTS
by
studying existing and new legislation; anticipating future legislation; enforcing adherence to requirements; filing financial reports; advising management on needed actions.

___ 10. ENSURES OPERATION OF EQUIPMENT
by
establishing preventive maintenance requirements and service contracts; maintaining equipment inventories; evaluating new equipment and techniques.

___ 11. COMPLETES OPERATIONAL REQUIREMENTS
by
scheduling and assigning employees; following up on work results.

___ 12. MAINTAINS FINANCIAL STAFF
by
recruiting, selecting, orienting, and training employees.

___ 13. MAINTAINS FINANCIAL STAFF JOB RESULTS
by
coaching, counseling, and disciplining employees; planning, monitoring, and appraising job results.

JOB TITLE: Controller

ESSENTIAL JOB RESULTS:

% of
Time

____ 14. MAINTAINS PROFESSIONAL AND TECHNICAL KNOWLEDGE
by
attending educational workshops; reviewing
professional publications; establishing
personal networks; participating in
professional societies.

____ 15. PROTECTS OPERATIONS
by
keeping financial information and plans
confidential.

% of
Time

____ 16. CONTRIBUTES TO TEAM EFFORT
by
accomplishing related results as needed.

JOB PURPOSE: **PROVIDES FINANCIAL DECISION-MAKING INFORMATION**

by

collecting, analyzing, and reporting cost data.

ESSENTIAL JOB RESULTS:

*% of
Time*

____ 1. DETERMINES COST OF OPERATIONS
by
establishing standard costs; collecting
operational data.

____ 2. GUIDES COST ANALYSIS PROCESS
by
establishing and enforcing policies and
procedures; providing trends and forecasts;
explaining processes and techniques;
recommending actions.

____ 3. RECOMMENDS ACTIONS
by
analyzing and interpreting data and making
comparative analyses; studying proposed
changes in methods and materials.

____ 4. CONFIRMS COSTS
by
collecting, interpreting, and reporting data.

____ 5. PREPARES SPECIAL REPORTS
by
collecting, analyzing, and summarizing
information and trends.

*% of
Time*

____ 6. ENSURES OPERATION OF EQUIPMENT
by
completing preventive maintenance
requirements; calling for repairs; evaluating
new equipment and techniques.

____ 7. MAINTAINS PROFESSIONAL AND TECHNICAL KNOWLEDGE
by
attending educational workshops; reviewing
professional publications; establishing
personal networks; participating in
professional societies.

____ 8. PROTECTS OPERATIONS
by
keeping financial information confidential.

____ 9. SECURES INFORMATION
by
completing data base backups.

____ 10. CONTRIBUTES TO TEAM EFFORT
by
accomplishing related results as needed.

JOB TITLE: Court Clerk

JOB PURPOSE: **MAINTAINS COURT OPERATIONS**

by

organizing case schedule; explaining procedures; recording proceedings.

ESSENTIAL JOB RESULTS:

*% of
Time*

_____ 1. ORGANIZES COURT SCHEDULE
by
preparing case docket.

_____ 2. ADMITS DOCUMENTS
by
confirming adherence to law and court
procedures.

_____ 3. ORGANIZES DOCUMENTS
by
preparing case folders.

_____ 4. INFORMS ATTORNEYS AND PARTIES TO THE CASE
by
explaining procedures and forms; notifying
them when to appear.

_____ 5. OBTAINS INFORMATION FOR THE COURT
by
contacting witnesses, attorneys, and litigants.

_____ 6. AFFIRMS WITNESSES' DETERMINATION TO PROVIDE
TRUTHFUL INFORMATION
by
administering oath.

_____ 7. ESTABLISHES CASE RECORDS
by
recording court proceedings; transcribing
testimony; recording disposition, court
orders, and arrangement for, and payment of,
fees and fines.

*% of
Time*

_____ 8. COLLECTS FEES AND FINES
by
accepting payment.

_____ 9. MAINTAINS SYSTEM OPERATIONS
by
following policies and procedures; reporting
needed changes.

_____ 10. MAINTAINS TECHNICAL KNOWLEDGE
by
attending educational workshops; studying
new requirements.

_____ 11. PREPARES REPORTS
by
collecting, analyzing, and summarizing
information and trends.

_____ 12. CONTRIBUTES TO TEAM EFFORT
by
accomplishing related results as needed.

JOB PURPOSE: SUPPORTS CREDIT LENDING DECISIONS

by

analyzing customer's financial condition and ability to pay.

ESSENTIAL JOB RESULTS:

*% of
Time*

____ 1. DEVELOPS CREDIT HISTORIES
by
compiling financial information.

____ 2. INTERPRETS FINANCIAL AND SPECIFIC INDUSTRY TRENDS AND CUSTOMER PAYMENT HISTORIES
by
creating historical financial spreadsheets on customers; categorizing and entering data; analyzing trends.

____ 3. INVESTIGATES VARIANCES ON CUSTOMERS' FINANCIAL STATEMENTS
by
requesting information from sources; researching development within the industry.

____ 4. SUBMITS CREDIT REPORTS
by
including research data; identifying credit strengths and/or weaknesses.

____ 5. MAINTAINS HISTORICAL STUDIES OF CUSTOMERS
by
compiling and analyzing financial developments; comparing industry statistics with the company's exposure to that industry; conferring with institutions providing loans to that industry.

____ 6. PROVIDES CREDIT INFORMATION TO SOURCES
by
compiling information; issuing reports.

*% of
Time*

____ 7. RECOMMENDS ACTION ON DELINQUENT ACCOUNTS
by
analyzing paying practices of customers.

____ 8. RECOMMENDS CREDIT LINE ADJUSTMENTS
by
evaluating customer records, purchase activity, and payment history.

____ 9. VERIFIES ACCURACY OF CHARGES AND CORRECTS ACCOUNT ERRORS
by reviewing purchasing documentation; interviewing customers.

____ 10. PROVIDES INFORMATION
by
answering questions and requests.

____ 11. COMPLIES WITH FEDERAL, STATE, AND LOCAL LEGAL REQUIREMENTS
by
studying existing and new legislation; enforcing adherence to requirements; advising management on needed actions.

____ 12. MAINTAINS CUSTOMER CONFIDENCE AND PROTECTS OPERATIONS
by
keeping information confidential.

____ 13. CONTRIBUTES TO TEAM EFFORT
by
accomplishing related results as needed.

JOB TITLE: Credit Manager

JOB PURPOSE: **PROTECTS ORGANIZATION'S ASSETS**

by

investigating financial status of customers and potential customers; approving credit; supervising employees.

ESSENTIAL JOB RESULTS:

% of Time

____ 1. ESTABLISHES CREDIT GUIDELINES
by
determining ratio of levels of purchases to levels of disposable income.

____ 2. MAINTAINS CREDIT GUIDELINES
by
writing and updating credit policies and procedures.

____ 3. APPROVES OR REJECTS CREDIT
by
studying customer's or potential customer's application; verifying financial status; evaluating reputation of applicant.

____ 4. APPROVES OR REJECTS CREDIT EXCEPTIONS
by
studying credit request; reviewing credit history of applicant; estimating potential for payment.

____ 5. PREPARES SPECIAL CREDIT REPORTS
by
collecting, analyzing, and summarizing account history and trend information.

____ 6. MAINTAINS CUSTOMER CONFIDENCE AND PROTECTS OPERATIONS
by
keeping credit information confidential.

____ 7. COMPLIES WITH FEDERAL, STATE, AND LOCAL CREDIT AND INFORMATION LEGAL REQUIREMENTS
by
studying existing and new credit and information legislation; enforcing adherence to requirements; advising management on needed actions.

% of Time

____ 8. COMPLETES CREDIT OPERATIONS REQUIREMENTS
by
scheduling and assigning employees; following up on work results.

____ 9. MAINTAINS CREDIT STAFF
by
recruiting, selecting, orienting, and training employees.

____ 10. MAINTAINS CREDIT STAFF JOB RESULTS
by
counseling and disciplining employees; planning, monitoring, and appraising job results.

____ 11. MAINTAINS PROFESSIONAL AND TECHNICAL KNOWLEDGE
by
attending educational workshops; reviewing professional publications; establishing personal networks; participating in professional societies.

____ 12. CONTRIBUTES TO TEAM EFFORT
by
accomplishing related results as needed.

JOB TITLE: Customer Service Manager

JOB PURPOSE: MAINTAINS CUSTOMER SATISFACTION

by

defining and developing product, service, and problem-solving information; training and maintaining staff to provide information and resolve problems.

ESSENTIAL JOB RESULTS:

*% of
Time*

____ 1. MEASURES CUSTOMER PERCEPTIONS AND AWARENESS LEVELS OF PRODUCTS AND SERVICES
by
designing and implementing survey methodologies; validating results; tracking effectiveness of advertising or information campaigns.

____ 2. ASSESSES CUSTOMER SATISFACTION WITH GOODS OR SERVICES
by
designing and implementing satisfaction surveys and other research tools; analyzing and interpreting results; designing and implementing organizationwide customer service training programs.

____ 3. RESOLVES CUSTOMER DISSATISFACTIONS
by
planning and directing the receipt, investigation, evaluation, and settling of complaints and claims; following up with customers; personally resolving difficult situations.

____ 4. RESOLVES DISCREPANCIES
by
consulting with other managerial personnel; collecting and analyzing information.

____ 5. AUTHORIZES RETENTION OF DATA
by
analyzing future applicability of complaint resolution information.

*% of
Time*

____ 6. MAINTAINS CUSTOMER SERVICE OPERATIONS
by
initiating, coordinating, and enforcing program, operational, and personnel policies and procedures.

____ 7. COMPLETES CUSTOMER SERVICE OPERATIONAL REQUIREMENTS
by
scheduling and assigning employees; following up on work results.

____ 8. ACHIEVES FINANCIAL OBJECTIVES
by
preparing an annual budget; scheduling expenditures; analyzing variances; initiating corrective actions

____ 9. MAINTAINS CUSTOMER SERVICE STAFF
by
recruiting, selecting, orienting, and training employees.

____ 10. MAINTAINS CUSTOMER SERVICE STAFF JOB RESULTS
by
coaching, counseling, and disciplining employees; planning, monitoring, and appraising job results.

____ 11. MAINTAINS PROFESSIONAL AND TECHNICAL KNOWLEDGE
by
attending educational workshops; reviewing professional publications; establishing personal networks; participating in professional societies.

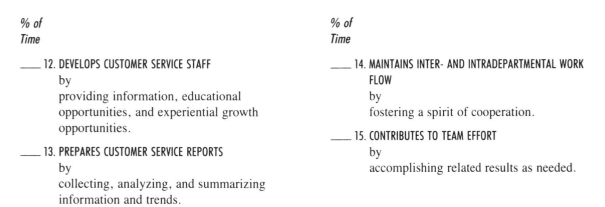

JOB TITLE: Customer Service Manager

ESSENTIAL JOB RESULTS:

% of
Time

____ 12. DEVELOPS CUSTOMER SERVICE STAFF
    by
    providing information, educational
    opportunities, and experiential growth
    opportunities.

____ 13. PREPARES CUSTOMER SERVICE REPORTS
    by
    collecting, analyzing, and summarizing
    information and trends.

% of
Time

____ 14. MAINTAINS INTER- AND INTRADEPARTMENTAL WORK
    FLOW
    by
    fostering a spirit of cooperation.

____ 15. CONTRIBUTES TO TEAM EFFORT
    by
    accomplishing related results as needed.

JOB TITLE: Customer Service Representative

JOB PURPOSE: **SERVES CUSTOMERS**

by

providing product and service information; resolving product and service problems.

ESSENTIAL JOB RESULTS:

% of Time

____ 1. ATTRACTS POTENTIAL CUSTOMERS

by

answering product and service questions; suggesting information about other products and services.

____ 2. OPENS CUSTOMER ACCOUNTS

by

recording account information.

____ 3. MAINTAINS CUSTOMER RECORDS

by

updating account information.

____ 4. RESOLVES PRODUCT OR SERVICE PROBLEMS

by

clarifying the customer's complaint; determining the cause of the problem; selecting and explaining the best solution to solve the problem; expediting correction or adjustment; following up to ensure resolution.

% of Time

____ 5. MAINTAINS FINANCIAL ACCOUNTS

by

processing customer adjustments.

____ 6. RECOMMENDS POTENTIAL PRODUCTS OR SERVICES TO MANAGEMENT

by

collecting customer information and analyzing customer needs.

____ 7. PREPARES PRODUCT OR SERVICE REPORTS

by

collecting and analyzing customer information.

____ 8. CONTRIBUTES TO TEAM EFFORT

by

accomplishing related results as needed.

JOB TITLE: Cutter Operator

JOB PURPOSE: PROVIDES CUT MATERIALS

by

setting up and operating a cutting machine.

ESSENTIAL JOB RESULTS:

% of
Time

____ 1. DETERMINES DIMENSIONS OF SHEETS
by
studying work orders.

____ 2. POSITIONS ROLL ON RACK
by
inserting shaft into core; hoisting roll.

____ 3. POSITIONS MATERIAL
by
threading end of material through feed rollers
and under or across cutting blades; aligning
material against guides.

____ 4. REGULATES LENGTH AND WIDTH OF CUT
by
adjusting tension of material; synchronizing
timing of cutting blades with rate of material
feed.

____ 5. VERIFIES SETTINGS
by
measuring positions, first-run cut, and
sample sheets.

____ 6. COLLECTS CUT MATERIAL
by
adjusting takeoff mechanism.

____ 7. MAINTAINS PRODUCTION AND QUALITY
by
observing machine operation; detecting
malfunctions; adjusting settings; replacing
worn blades.

% of
Time

____ 8. RESOLVES PRODUCTION PROBLEMS
by
altering process to meet specifications;
notifying supervisor to obtain additional
resources.

____ 9. ENSURES OPERATION OF EQUIPMENT
by
completing preventive maintenance
requirements; following manufacturer's
instructions; troubleshooting malfunctions;
calling for repairs.

____ 10. MAINTAINS STOCK INVENTORY
by
checking stock to determine amount
available; anticipating needed stock; placing
and expediting orders for stock; verifying
receipt of stock.

____ 11. MAINTAINS CONTINUITY AMONG WORK TEAMS
by
documenting and communicating actions,
irregularities, and continuing needs.

____ 12. DOCUMENTS ACTIONS
by
completing production and quality logs.

____ 13. CONTRIBUTES TO TEAM EFFORT
by
accomplishing related results as needed.

JOB TITLE: Data Base Analyst

JOB PURPOSE: **MAINTAINS DATA STORAGE AND ACCESS**
by
designing physical data bases.

ESSENTIAL JOB RESULTS:

% of Time

_____ 1. CONFIRMS PROJECT REQUIREMENTS
by
studying user requirements; conferring with others on project team.

_____ 2. DETERMINES CHANGES IN PHYSICAL DATA BASE
by
studying project requirements; identifying data base characteristics, such as location, amount of space, and access method.

_____ 3. CHANGES DATA BASE SYSTEM
by
coding data base descriptions.

_____ 4. PROTECTS DATA BASE
by
developing access system; specifying user level of access.

_____ 5. MAINTAINS DATA DICTIONARY
by
revising and entering definitions.

_____ 6. MAINTAINS USER REFERENCE
by
writing and rewriting data base descriptions.

% of Time

_____ 7. MAINTAINS CLIENT CONFIDENCE AND PROTECTS OPERATIONS
by
keeping information confidential.

_____ 8. MAINTAINS TECHNICAL KNOWLEDGE
by
attending educational workshops; reviewing publications; establishing personal networks; participating in technical societies.

_____ 9. ENSURES OPERATION OF EQUIPMENT
by
completing preventive maintenance requirements; following manufacturer's instructions; troubleshooting malfunctions; calling for repairs; evaluating new equipment and techniques.

_____ 10. CONTRIBUTES TO TEAM EFFORT
by
accomplishing related results as needed.

JOB TITLE: Data Entry Clerk

JOB PURPOSE: **MAINTAINS DATA BASE**

by

entering new and updated customer and account information.

ESSENTIAL JOB RESULTS:

% of
Time

_____ 1. PREPARES SOURCE DATA FOR COMPUTER ENTRY
by
compiling and sorting information;
establishing entry priorities.

_____ 2. PROCESSES CUSTOMER AND ACCOUNT SOURCE
DOCUMENTS
by
reviewing data for deficiencies; resolving
discrepancies by using standard procedures
or returning incomplete documents to the
team leader for resolution.

_____ 3 ENTERS CUSTOMER AND ACCOUNT DATA
by
inputting alphabetic and numeric information
on keyboard or optical scanner according to
screen format.

_____ 4. MAINTAINS ENTRY REQUIREMENTS
by
following data station program techniques
and procedures.

_____ 5. VERIFIES ENTERED CUSTOMER AND ACCOUNT DATA
by
reviewing, correcting, deleting, or reentering
data; combining data from both systems
when account information is incomplete;
purging files to eliminate duplication of data.

% of
Time

_____ 6. TESTS CUSTOMER AND ACCOUNT SYSTEMS CHANGES AND
UPGRADES
by
inputting new data; reviewing output.

_____ 7. SECURES INFORMATION
by
completing data base backups.

_____ 8. MAINTAINS OPERATIONS
by
following policies and procedures; reporting
needed changes.

_____ 9. MAINTAINS CUSTOMER CONFIDENCE AND PROTECTS
OPERATIONS
by
keeping information confidential.

_____ 10. CONTRIBUTES TO TEAM EFFORT
by
accomplishing related results as needed.

JOB TITLE: Data Processing Manager

JOB PURPOSE: **PROVIDES INFORMATION MANAGEMENT SERVICES**

by

defining and solving user requirements; developing computer applications.

ESSENTIAL JOB RESULTS:

*% of
Time*

____ 1. DEFINES USER INFORMATION REQUIREMENTS
by
conferring with users; studying user functions.

____ 2. SOLVES USER INFORMATION REQUIREMENTS
by
developing information procedures; recommending computer system applications.

____ 3. PREPARES PROGRAMS
by
writing, testing, modifying, and documenting programming language.

____ 4. PREPARES USERS TO OPERATE INFORMATION SYSTEM
by
conducting training sessions; providing individual coaching.

____ 5. PROVIDES SYSTEM RESOURCE
by
documenting procedures; maintaining a library of user manuals; answering questions.

____ 6. SECURES INFORMATION AND PROGRAMS
by
completing data base and program backups.

____ 7. IMPROVES PROGRAMS
by
devising new applications; updating procedures.

____ 8. PRODUCES ROUTINE AND SPECIAL REPORTS
by
scheduling operations; assigning employees; following up on work results.

*% of
Time*

____ 9. IMPROVES SERVICES
by
evaluating system results with users.

____ 10. MAINTAINS DATA PROCESSING STAFF
by
recruiting, selecting, orienting, and training employees.

____ 11. MAINTAINS DATA PROCESSING STAFF JOB RESULTS
by
coaching, counseling, and disciplining employees; planning, monitoring, and appraising job results.

____ 12. MAINTAINS PROFESSIONAL AND TECHNICAL KNOWLEDGE
by
attending educational workshops; reviewing professional publications; establishing personal networks; participating in professional societies.

____ 13. ACHIEVES FINANCIAL OBJECTIVES
by
preparing the data processing annual budget; scheduling expenditures; analyzing variances; initiating corrective actions.

____ 14. CONTRIBUTES TO TEAM EFFORT
by
accomplishing related results as needed.

JOB TITLE: Dental Assistant

JOB PURPOSE: **SUPPORTS DENTAL CARE DELIVERY**

by

preparing treatment room, patient, instruments, and materials; passing instruments and materials; performing procedures in compliance with the Dental Practice Act.

ESSENTIAL JOB RESULTS:

% of Time

____ 1. **PREPARES TREATMENT ROOM FOR PATIENT**
by
following prescribed procedures and protocols.

____ 2. **PREPARES PATIENT FOR DENTAL TREATMENT**
by
welcoming, comforting, seating, and draping patient.

____ 3. **PROVIDES INFORMATION TO PATIENTS AND EMPLOYEES**
by
answering questions and requests.

____ 4. **PROVIDES INSTRUMENTATION**
by
sterilizing and delivering instruments to treatment area; positioning instruments for dentist's access; suctioning; passing instruments.

____ 5. **PROVIDES MATERIALS**
by
selecting, mixing, and placing materials on instruments and in the patient's mouth.

____ 6. **PROVIDES DIAGNOSTIC INFORMATION**
by
exposing and developing radiographic studies; pouring, trimming, and polishing study casts.

____ 7. **MAINTAINS PATIENT APPEARANCE AND ABILITY TO MASTICATE**
by
fabricating temporary restorations; cleaning and polishing removable appliances.

% of Time

____ 8. **HELPS DENTIST MANAGE DENTAL AND MEDICAL EMERGENCIES**
by
maintaining CPR certification, emergency drug and oxygen supply, and emergency telephone directory.

____ 9. **EDUCATES PATIENTS**
by
giving oral hygiene, plaque control, and postoperative instructions.

____ 10. **DOCUMENTS DENTAL CARE SERVICES**
by
charting in patient records.

____ 11. **MAINTAINS PATIENT CONFIDENCE AND PROTECTS OPERATIONS**
by
keeping information confidential.

____ 12. **MAINTAINS SAFE AND CLEAN WORKING ENVIRONMENT**
by
complying with procedures, rules, and regulations.

____ 13. **PROTECTS PATIENTS AND EMPLOYEES**
by
adhering to infection-control policies and protocols.

JOB TITLE: Dental Assistant

ESSENTIAL JOB RESULTS:

% of
Time

____ 14. **ENSURES OPERATION OF DENTAL EQUIPMENT**
by
completing preventive maintenance
requirements; following manufacturer's
instructions; troubleshooting malfunctions;
calling for repairs; maintaining equipment
inventories; evaluating new equipment and
techniques.

____ 15. **MAINTAINS DENTAL SUPPLIES INVENTORY**
by
checking stock to determine inventory level;
anticipating needed supplies; placing and
expediting orders for supplies; verifying
receipt of supplies.

% of
Time

____ 16. **CONSERVES DENTAL RESOURCES**
by
using equipment and supplies as needed to
accomplish job results.

____ 17. **MAINTAINS PROFESSIONAL AND TECHNICAL KNOWLEDGE**
by
attending educational workshops; reviewing
professional publications; establishing
personal networks; participating in
professional societies.

____ 18. **CONTRIBUTES TO TEAM EFFORT**
by
accomplishing related results as needed.

JOB PURPOSE: **PROMOTES DENTAL HEALTH**

by

completing dental prophylaxis; providing oral cancer screening, radiographic studies; charting conditions of decay and disease; performing procedures in compliance with the Dental Practice Act.

ESSENTIAL JOB RESULTS:

*% of
Time*

____ 1. PREPARES TREATMENT ROOM FOR PATIENT
by
adhering to prescribed procedures and protocols.

____ 2. PREPARES PATIENT FOR DENTAL HYGIENE TREATMENT
by
welcoming, soothing, seating, and draping patient.

____ 3. PROVIDES INFORMATION TO PATIENTS AND EMPLOYEES
by
answering questions and requests.

____ 4. MAINTAINS INSTRUMENTATION FOR DENTAL HYGIENE TREATMENT
by
sharpening, sterilizing, and selecting instruments.

____ 5. SELECTS MATERIALS AND EQUIPMENT FOR DENTAL HYGIENE VISIT
by
evaluating patient's oral health.

____ 6. COMPLETES DENTAL PROPHYLAXIS
by
cleaning deposits and stains from teeth and from beneath gum margins.

____ 7. DETECTS DISEASE
by
completing oral cancer screening; feeling and visually examining gums; using probes to locate periodontal disease and to assess levels of recession; exposing and developing radiographic studies.

*% of
Time*

____ 8. ARRESTS DENTAL DECAY
by
applying fluorides and other cavity-preventing agents.

____ 9. MAINTAINS PATIENT APPEARANCE AND ABILITY TO MASTICATE
by
fabricating temporary restorations; cleaning and polishing removable appliances; placing, carving, and finishing amalgam restorations; removing cement from crowns and bridges.

____ 10. HELPS DENTIST MANAGE DENTAL AND MEDICAL EMERGENCIES
by
maintaining CPR certification, emergency drugs and oxygen supply, and directory of emergency numbers.

____ 11. EDUCATES PATIENTS
by
giving oral hygiene and plaque control instructions and postoperative instructions; providing reminders of time of next dental hygiene visit.

____ 12. DOCUMENTS DENTAL HYGIENE SERVICES
by
recording vital signs and medical and dental histories; charting in patient records.

____ 13. MAINTAINS PATIENT CONFIDENCE AND PROTECTS OPERATIONS
by
keeping information confidential.

JOB TITLE: Dental Hygienist

ESSENTIAL JOB RESULTS:

*% of
Time*

_____ 14. MAINTAINS SAFE AND CLEAN WORKING ENVIRONMENT
by
complying with procedures, rules, and
regulations.

_____ 15. PROTECTS PATIENTS AND EMPLOYEES
by
adhering to infection-control policies and
protocols.

_____ 16. ENSURES OPERATION OF DENTAL EQUIPMENT
by
completing preventive maintenance
requirements; following manufacturer's
instructions; troubleshooting malfunctions;
calling for repairs; maintaining equipment
inventories; evaluating new equipment and
techniques.

_____ 17. MAINTAINS DENTAL SUPPLIES INVENTORY
by
checking stock to determine inventory level;
anticipating needed supplies; placing and
expediting orders for supplies; verifying
receipt of supplies.

*% of
Time*

_____ 18. CONSERVES DENTAL RESOURCES
by
using equipment and supplies as needed to
accomplish job results.

_____ 19. MAINTAINS PROFESSIONAL AND TECHNICAL KNOWLEDGE
by
attending educational workshops; reviewing
professional publications; establishing
personal networks; participating in
professional societies.

_____ 20. CONTRIBUTES TO TEAM EFFORT
by
accomplishing related results as needed.

JOB PURPOSE: **SUPPORTS PRODUCT MANUFACTURING**

by

constructing and repairing dies; machining parts.

ESSENTIAL JOB RESULTS:

*% of
Time*

____ 1. DEVELOPS DIE FUNCTION AND STRUCTURE

by

studying blueprints of die, product, and prototypes; applying knowledge of material under stress, machining and assembly methods, and mathematics.

____ 2. MACHINES PARTS

by

measuring, marking, and scribing stock; setting up and operating lathe, mill, radial drill, shaper, grinder, etc.

____ 3. CONFIRMS PARTS

by

comparing measurements to specifications.

____ 4. ASSEMBLES DIE

by

shaping, smoothing, and fitting parts with grinders, files, stones, etc.

____ 5. CONFIRMS ASSEMBLY

by

verifying dimensions, clearances, and alignment of parts and components with micrometers, thickness gauges, gauge blocks, dial indicators, etc.

____ 6. COMPLETES ASSEMBLY

by

bolting and doweling parts and components together with hammers, wrenches, etc.; connecting wiring and hydraulic lines.

____ 7. CONFIRMS PERFORMANCE OF DIE

by

installing die; inspecting operation of die; making adjustments; comparing finished product to specifications.

*% of
Time*

____ 8. RESOLVES ASSEMBLY PROBLEMS

by

altering assembly to meet specifications; notifying supervisor to obtain additional resources.

____ 9. ENSURES OPERATION OF EQUIPMENT

by

completing preventive maintenance requirements; following manufacturer's instructions; troubleshooting malfunctions; calling for repairs.

____ 10. MAINTAINS SUPPLIES INVENTORY

by

checking supplies to determine amount available; anticipating needed supplies; placing and expediting orders for supplies; verifying receipt of supplies.

____ 11. MAINTAINS CONTINUITY AMONG WORK TEAMS

by

documenting and communicating actions, irregularities, and continuing needs.

____ 12. DOCUMENTS ACTIONS

by

completing logs.

____ 13. CONTRIBUTES TO TEAM EFFORT

by

accomplishing related results as needed.

JOB TITLE: Dietitian

JOB PURPOSE: **HELPS CLIENTS MAINTAIN HEALTH**

by

developing and implementing nutritious meals; teaching patients food-management techniques.

ESSENTIAL JOB RESULTS:

% of
Time

____ 1. ESTABLISHES PATIENT DATA BASE
by
consulting with physicians and other health care professionals; reviewing patient record; interviewing patient.

____ 2. DEVELOPS AND IMPLEMENTS DIETARY CARE PLAN
by
assessing nutritional needs; determining resources; coordinating dietary program with health care providers.

____ 3. FORMULATES MENUS AND THERAPEUTIC DIETS
by
integrating patient's menus with institutional menus.

____ 4. CONTROLS SPECIAL DIET MEALS
by
verifying food preparation techniques; checking meals for palatability and appearance.

____ 5. DEVELOPS FOOD SERVICE PERSONNEL
by
designing and teaching nutrition in-service programs; coaching and counseling employees; monitoring results.

% of
Time

____ 6. EDUCATES PATIENTS AND THEIR FAMILIES
by
teaching nutrition principles, diet regimens, and food selection, preparation, and economics.

____ 7. ENCOURAGES CLIENTS
by
promoting goals; reinforcing positive results; offering comfort.

____ 8. PROVIDES INFORMATION
by
answering questions.

____ 9. MAINTAINS PROFESSIONAL AND TECHNICAL KNOWLEDGE
by
attending educational workshops; reviewing professional publications; establishing personal networks; participating in professional societies.

____ 10. CONTRIBUTES TO TEAM EFFORT
by
accomplishing related results as needed.

JOB TITLE: Dining Room Manager

JOB PURPOSE: SERVES PATRONS

by

managing reservations; scheduling, training, and supervising personnel.

ESSENTIAL JOB RESULTS:

*% of
Time*

_____ 1. IDENTIFIES CURRENT AND FUTURE PATRON SERVICE REQUIREMENTS

by

establishing personal contact and rapport with potential and actual customers and other persons in a position to understand service requirements.

_____ 2. DEVELOPS OPERATIONAL GUIDELINES

by

initiating, coordinating, and enforcing program, operational, and personnel policies and procedures.

_____ 3. ESTABLISHES RESERVATION SYSTEM

by

planning use of tables; allocating stations; determining staffing requirements.

_____ 4. FULFILLS DINING RESERVATION SCHEDULE

by

assigning and scheduling staff; following up on work results.

_____ 5. MAINTAINS DINING ROOM STAFF

by

recruiting, selecting, orienting, and training employees.

_____ 6. PREPARES DINING ROOM STAFF

by

introducing menus and teaching food presentation techniques; conducting food and wine tastings; giving instruction in etiquette and serving techniques.

_____ 7. MAINTAINS DINING ROOM STAFF JOB RESULTS

by

coaching, counseling, and disciplining employees; planning, monitoring, and appraising job results.

*% of
Time*

_____ 8. SCHEDULES PATRONS

by

recording dining reservations, arrangements for special parties, and private dining room accommodations.

_____ 9. WELCOMES PATRONS

by

exchanging pleasantries with patrons; escorting them to dining area; seating them; presenting and introducing menus; announcing waitperson's name.

_____ 10. MAINTAINS DINING ROOM AMBIANCE

by

inspecting and monitoring serving stations, table linens, floors, seating, lighting, and music.

_____ 11. PROTECTS PATRONS AND EMPLOYEES

by

maintaining first aid, CPR, and Heimlich maneuver certification; enforcing alcohol control practices; maintaining sanitation procedures, rules, and regulations.

_____ 12. PROTECTS DINING ROOM ASSETS

by

adhering to security policies and procedures.

_____ 13. PREPARES REPORTS FOR FACILITY MANAGEMENT

by

identifying patron service requirements; observing and recording patron reactions to meals, beverages, and restaurant environment.

129

JOB TITLE: Dining Room Manager

ESSENTIAL JOB RESULTS:

% of
Time

___ 14. **MAINTAINS PROFESSIONAL AND TECHNICAL KNOWLEDGE**
by
attending educational workshops; reviewing
professional publications; establishing
personal networks; participating in
professional societies.

% of
Time

___ 15. **CONTRIBUTES TO TEAM EFFORT**
by
accomplishing related results as needed.

JOB TITLE: Drafter

JOB PURPOSE: **PREPARES ENGINEERING PLANS**

by

drawing system, components, and parts.

ESSENTIAL JOB RESULTS:

% of Time

____ 1. PREPARES ROUGH SKETCHES

by
studying engineering specifications; creating a picture of the system, components, and parts.

____ 2. PREPARES FINAL DRAWINGS

by
studying engineering sketches, specifications, and supporting documents; developing a layout of the system, components, and parts; drawing multiple views of the system, components, and parts; depicting relationship of components and parts; identifying dimensions, angles, curvatures, tolerances, and materials.

____ 3. IDENTIFIES AND VERIFIES SPECIFICATIONS

by
examining engineering documents; performing calculations.

____ 4. MODIFIES DRAWINGS

by
studying changes; redrawing system, components, and parts; changing identifications.

% of Time

____ 5. RESOLVES DISCREPANCIES

by
collecting and analyzing information; conferring with engineers.

____ 6. KEEPS EQUIPMENT OPERATIONAL

by
following manufacturer's instructions and established procedures.

____ 7. MAINTAINS DATA BASE

by
entering data; completing backups.

____ 8. MAINTAINS TECHNICAL KNOWLEDGE

by
attending educational workshops; reading technical publications.

____ 9. CONTRIBUTES TO TEAM EFFORT

by
accomplishing related results as needed.

JOB TITLE: Electrical/Electronic Specialist

JOB PURPOSE: **MAINTAINS PRODUCTION**

by

redesigning, modifying, repairing, or installing electrical and electronic components in manufacturing equipment.

ESSENTIAL JOB RESULTS:

% of
Time

_____ 1. RESTARTS PRODUCTION
by
troubleshooting breakdowns; making repairs.

_____ 2. ENSURES OPERATION OF EQUIPMENT
by
completing preventive maintenance requirements; following manufacturer's instructions; notifying supervisor of needed repairs; evaluating new equipment and techniques.

_____ 3. ENHANCES EQUIPMENT PERFORMANCE
by
developing and installing modifications; making adjustments.

_____ 4. DOCUMENTS ACTIONS
by
completing engineering and maintenance logs.

% of
Time

_____ 5. RESOLVES INSTALLATION PROBLEMS
by
altering dimensions to meet specifications; notifying supervisor to obtain additional resources.

_____ 6. MAINTAINS CONTINUITY AMONG WORK TEAMS
by
documenting and communicating actions, irregularities, and continuing needs.

_____ 7. CONFIRMS EQUIPMENT PERFORMANCE
by
conducting tests.

_____ 8. CONTRIBUTES TO TEAM EFFORT
by
accomplishing related results as needed.

JOB PURPOSE: **DESIGNS ELECTRICAL SYSTEMS**

by

developing and testing components.

ESSENTIAL JOB RESULTS:

% of
Time

____ 1. EVALUATES ELECTRICAL SYSTEMS, PRODUCTS, COMPONENTS, AND APPLICATIONS
by
designing and conducting research programs; applying knowledge of electricity and materials.

____ 2. CONFIRMS SYSTEM'S AND COMPONENTS' CAPABILITIES
by
designing testing methods; testing properties.

____ 3. DEVELOPS ELECTRICAL PRODUCTS
by
studying customer requirements; researching and testing manufacturing and assembly methods and materials.

____ 4. DEVELOPS MANUFACTURING PROCESSES
by
designing and modifying equipment for building and assembling electrical components; soliciting observations from operators.

____ 5. ASSURES PRODUCT QUALITY
by
designing electrical testing methods; testing finished products and system capabilities.

____ 6. PREPARES PRODUCT REPORTS
by
collecting, analyzing, and summarizing information and trends.

% of
Time

____ 7. PROVIDES ENGINEERING INFORMATION
by
answering questions and requests.

____ 8. MAINTAINS PRODUCT AND COMPANY REPUTATION
by
complying with federal and state regulations.

____ 9. KEEPS EQUIPMENT OPERATIONAL
by
following manufacturer's instructions and established procedures; requesting repair service.

____ 10. MAINTAINS PRODUCT DATA BASE
by
writing computer programs; entering data.

____ 11. COMPLETES PROJECTS
by
training and guiding technicians.

____ 12. MAINTAINS PROFESSIONAL AND TECHNICAL KNOWLEDGE
by
attending educational workshops; reviewing professional publications; establishing personal networks; participating in professional societies.

____ 13. CONTRIBUTES TO TEAM EFFORT
by
accomplishing related results as needed.

JOB TITLE: Electrical Maintenance Supervisor

JOB PURPOSE: **PROVIDES A SAFE, COMFORTABLE OPERATING ENVIRONMENT**

by

providing and maintaining electrical power.

ESSENTIAL JOB RESULTS:

% of Time

___ 1. PROVIDES LIGHTING

by

determining power sources; defining wiring patterns; selecting fixtures.

___ 2. MAINTAINS EMERGENCY AND ROUTINE ELECTRICAL POWER DISTRIBUTION NETWORK

by

discovering, restoring, and repairing faulty or inoperative facility systems.

___ 3. KEEPS ELECTRICAL EQUIPMENT, SYSTEMS, AND BUILDING READY FOR USE AND SAFE

by

developing, implementing, and evaluating preventive maintenance programs and schedules for the electrical power distribution network, fire and smoke alarms, and sprinkler and other electrical systems; restoring and repairing faulty or inoperative equipment; recommending changes and new electrical installations.

___ 4. COMPLIES WITH LOCAL, STATE, NATIONAL, AND OTHER RELATED ELECTRICAL CODES AND STANDARDS

by

directing and monitoring the work of craftsmen, vendors, contractors, and heating, ventilating, and air-conditioning staff; inspecting the facility, systems, and equipment.

___ 5. IMPLEMENTS CHANGES, EXPANSIONS, AND ADDITIONS TO ELECTRICAL SYSTEMS

by

identifying problems; keeping abreast of new developments; using statistics and equipment history reports.

% of Time

___ 6. ACHIEVES ELECTRICAL MAINTENANCE FINANCIAL OBJECTIVES

by

preparing an annual budget; scheduling expenditures; analyzing variances; initiating corrective actions.

___ 7. COMPLETES ELECTRICAL MAINTENANCE OPERATIONAL REQUIREMENTS

by

scheduling and assigning employees; following up on work results.

___ 8. MAINTAINS ELECTRICAL MAINTENANCE STAFF

by

recruiting, selecting, orienting, and training employees.

___ 9. MAINTAINS ELECTRICAL MAINTENANCE STAFF JOB RESULTS

by

counseling and disciplining employees; planning, monitoring, and appraising job results.

___ 10. MAINTAINS PROFESSIONAL AND TECHNICAL KNOWLEDGE

by

attending educational workshops; reviewing professional publications; establishing personal networks; participating in professional societies.

JOB TITLE: Electrical Maintenance Supervisor

ESSENTIAL JOB RESULTS:

% of
Time

____ 11. MAINTAINS CONTINUITY AMONG WORK TEAMS
   by
   documenting maintenance actions; noting
   system or equipment irregularities requiring
   continued monitoring.

____ 12. MAINTAINS SAFE AND CLEAN WORKING ENVIRONMENT
   by
   developing and enforcing procedures, rules,
   and regulations.

____ 13. MAINTAINS ELECTRICAL PARTS AND EQUIPMENT
   INVENTORY
   by
   checking stock to determine inventory level;
   anticipating needed electrical parts and
   equipment; placing and expediting orders for
   parts and equipment; verifying receipt of
   parts and equipment.

% of
Time

____ 14. CONTRIBUTES TO TEAM EFFORT
   by
   accomplishing related results as needed.

JOB TITLE: Electronics Technician

JOB PURPOSE: **BUILDS ELECTRONIC SYSTEMS, COMPONENTS, AND PARTS**
by
completing assembly and testing procedures.

ESSENTIAL JOB RESULTS:

% of Time

_____ 1. DEVELOPS LAYOUT OF WORK
by
collecting engineering documents and drawings; reviewing requirements with engineers.

_____ 2. BUILDS PROTOTYPE MODEL
by
fabricating parts; assembling circuits and components; analyzing results; recommending changes in circuitry, fabrication, and assembly.

_____ 3. TESTS PROTOTYPE MODEL
by
establishing performance and reliability standards; devising and conducting tests; setting up equipment and apparatus; adjusting, calibrating, aligning, and modifying circuitry, components, and parts; analyzing results and recommending changes.

_____ 4. CONSTRUCTS PRODUCT
by
fabricating parts; assembling circuits, components, and parts; operating bench lathes, drills, and related machine tools.

_____ 5. DESCRIBES SYSTEM, COMPONENTS, AND PARTS OPERATING CHARACTERISTICS AND MALFUNCTIONS
by
writing technical reports; preparing charts, graphs, and schematics.

_____ 6. VERIFIES SYSTEM PERFORMANCE
by
testing functioning of installed equipment.

% of Time

_____ 7. ENSURES OPERATION OF EQUIPMENT
by
completing preventive maintenance requirements; following manufacturer's instructions; troubleshooting malfunctions; calling for repairs; maintaining equipment inventories; evaluating new equipment and techniques.

_____ 8. MAINTAINS PRODUCT AND COMPANY REPUTATION
by
complying with federal and state regulations.

_____ 9. MAINTAINS SUPPLIES INVENTORY
by
checking stock to determine inventory level; anticipating needed supplies; placing and expediting orders for supplies; and verifying receipt of supplies.

_____ 10. MAINTAINS TECHNICAL KNOWLEDGE
by
attending educational workshops; reviewing technical publications.

_____ 11. MAINTAINS CONTINUITY AMONG WORK TEAMS
by
documenting and communicating actions, irregularities, and continuing needs.

_____ 12. MAINTAINS ELECTRONICS SYSTEM, COMPONENTS, AND PARTS DATA BASE
by
entering and backing up data.

_____ 13. CONTRIBUTES TO TEAM EFFORT
by
accomplishing related results as needed.

JOB TITLE: Elementary School Principal

JOB PURPOSE: **MAINTAINS THE EDUCATIONAL DEVELOPMENT OF STUDENTS AND THE PROFESSIONAL DEVELOPMENT OF TEACHERS**

by

developing and implementing policies, programs, and curriculum plans; providing a safe and healthy environment conducive to learning.

ESSENTIAL JOB RESULTS:

% of Time

_____ 1. IDENTIFIES CURRENT AND FUTURE EDUCATIONAL REQUIREMENTS
by
establishing personal rapport with educators, parents, students, and other persons in a position to understand educational requirements; surveying operational and educational conditions; recommending and taking actions.

_____ 2. CONTRIBUTES TO THE SCHOOL'S EFFECTIVENESS
by
identifying short-term and long-range issues that must be addressed; providing information and commentary pertinent to deliberations; recommending options and courses of action; implementing directives.

_____ 3. COMPLIES WITH FEDERAL, STATE, AND LOCAL LEGAL REQUIREMENTS
by
studying existing and new legislation; anticipating future legislation; enforcing adherence to requirements; and advising Superintendent on needed actions.

_____ 4. REPRESENTS THE SCHOOL
by
preparing a strategy; collecting data; presenting information to the Superintendent and at public hearings.

% of Time

_____ 5. ACHIEVES SCHOOL'S FINANCIAL OBJECTIVES
by
preparing an annual budget; scheduling expenditures; analyzing variances; initiating corrective actions.

_____ 6. MAINTAINS BUILDINGS, GROUNDS, EQUIPMENT, AND SUPPLIES
by
developing maintenance programs; conserving resources.

_____ 7. DEVELOPS AN EDUCATIONAL PLAN FOR THE SCHOOL
by
involving faculty, curriculum specialists, other resource personnel, parents, and students.

_____ 8. SUPPORTS THE EDUCATIONAL PLAN
by
designing co- and extracurricular activities; using community resources.

_____ 9. MAINTAINS TEACHING STAFF
by
recruiting, selecting, orienting, and training teachers.

_____ 10. COMPLETES OPERATIONAL REQUIREMENTS
by
scheduling and assigning teachers and support staff; following up on work results.

ESSENTIAL JOB RESULTS:

% of
Time

___ 11. DEVELOPS TEACHERS
by
providing information, educational
opportunities, and experiential growth
opportunities.

___ 12. MAINTAINS TEACHING AND SUPPORT STAFF JOB RESULTS
by
coaching, counseling, and disciplining
teachers and support staff; planning,
monitoring, and appraising job results.

___ 13. PROTECTS TEACHERS AND STUDENTS
by
maintaining a safe transportation system and
educational environment; developing and
enforcing rules of conduct.

___ 14. RESOLVES TEACHER/PARENT/STUDENT CONFLICTS
by
collecting and analyzing information;
mediating or arbitrating discussions.

% of
Time

___ 15. PROVIDES EDUCATIONAL INFORMATION
by
developing communication strategies;
answering questions and requests.

___ 16. PREPARES REPORTS
by
collecting, analyzing, and summarizing
information and trends.

___ 17. MAINTAINS PROFESSIONAL AND TECHNICAL KNOWLEDGE
by
attending educational workshops; reviewing
professional publications; establishing
personal networks; participating in
professional societies.

___ 18. CONTRIBUTES TO TEAM EFFORT
by
accomplishing related results as needed.

JOB PURPOSE: PREPARES STUDENTS FOR MEANINGFUL LIVES

by

contributing to their educational and social development.

ESSENTIAL JOB RESULTS:

% of Time

____ 1. **CONTRIBUTES TO SCHOOL SYSTEM'S EFFECTIVENESS**
by
identifying short-term and long-range issues that must be addressed; providing information and commentary pertinent to deliberations; recommending options and courses of action; implementing directives.

____ 2. **ESTABLISHES AND ADJUSTS COURSE OUTLINES AND OBJECTIVES**
by
following curriculum guidelines and state and local school system goals; modifying plans on the basis of student diagnostic and assessment procedures.

____ 3. **CONVEYS INFORMATION TO STUDENTS**
by
using language concepts, examples, demonstrations, and teaching aids, such as audiovisual equipment and computers.

____ 4. **COMPLETES EDUCATIONAL REQUIREMENTS**
by
scheduling and assigning instructional activities; following up on results.

____ 5. **ASSESSES STUDENT LEARNING**
by
preparing, administering, and scoring tests; reviewing and correcting assignments; eliciting student questions and responses; evaluating application of learning to classroom project results.

____ 6. **MAINTAINS STUDENT LEARNING RESULTS**
by
providing instructional feedback; coaching, counseling, and disciplining students; planning, monitoring, and appraising learning results.

% of Time

____ 7. **MAINTAINS RECORDS**
by
documenting learning accomplishments, attendance, and behavior.

____ 8. **GUIDES STUDENTS' PERSONAL AND SOCIAL DEVELOPMENT**
by
establishing rules and procedures for administrative matters, student verbal participation, and student movement within the classroom, between classrooms, and on the playground.

____ 9. **HELPS PARENTS**
by
providing academic information; suggesting available educational and social resources; addressing parents' concerns; answering questions and requests.

____ 10. **COMPLIES WITH FEDERAL, STATE, AND LOCAL LEGAL REQUIREMENTS**
by
studying existing and new legislation; anticipating future legislation; enforcing adherence to requirements; advising school administration on needed actions.

____ 11. **MAINTAINS SAFE AND CLEAN WORKING ENVIRONMENT**
by
complying with procedures, rules, and regulations.

____ 12. **MAINTAINS PROFESSIONAL AND TECHNICAL KNOWLEDGE**
by
attending educational workshops; reviewing professional publications; establishing personal networks; participating in professional societies.

JOB TITLE: Elementary School Teacher

ESSENTIAL JOB RESULTS:

% of
Time

_____ 13. CONSERVES RESOURCES
by
using equipment and supplies as needed to
accomplish educational results.

% of
Time

_____ 14. CONTRIBUTES TO TEAM EFFORT
by
accomplishing related results as needed.

JOB TITLE: Employee Relations Representative

JOB PURPOSE: **MAINTAINS EMPLOYEE MORALE**

by

resolving conflicts; advising managers; maintaining human resources policies and procedures.

ESSENTIAL JOB RESULTS:

% of Time

___ 1. IDENTIFIES EMERGING HUMAN RESOURCE ISSUES
by
surveying and interviewing employees and managers; studying job results documents.

___ 2. MAINTAINS HUMAN RESOURCES PRACTICES
by
developing and recommending policies and procedures.

___ 3. PREPARES MANAGERS TO INTERACT WITH EMPLOYEES
by
recommending, developing, and conducting training programs; reviewing proposed decisions and actions.

___ 4. RESOLVES MANAGER AND EMPLOYEE DISSATISFACTION
by
investigating complaints and concerns; evaluating and offering possible courses of action; providing advice, guidance, and direction.

___ 5. MAINTAINS HUMAN RESOURCE RECORDS
by
documenting incidents and resolutions of problems.

___ 6. MAINTAINS MANAGER AND EMPLOYEE CONFIDENCE AND PROTECTS REPUTATIONS
by
keeping information confidential.

% of Time

___ 7. COMPLIES WITH FEDERAL, STATE, AND LOCAL LEGAL REQUIREMENTS
by
studying existing and new legislation; obtaining opinions from legal counsel; enforcing adherence to requirements; advising management on needed actions.

___ 8. REPRESENTS THE COMPANY AT HEARINGS
by
preparing a strategy; collecting and presenting information.

___ 9. MAINTAINS OPEN COMMUNICATION CHANNELS WITH EMPLOYEES AND MANAGERS
by
answering questions; explaining policies and procedures; encouraging the use of the appeal system.

___ 10. CONTRIBUTES TO TEAM EFFORT
by
accomplishing related results as needed.

JOB TITLE: Employment Interviewer

JOB PURPOSE: **FILLS JOB VACANCIES**

by

interviewing and screening applicants.

ESSENTIAL JOB RESULTS:

% of Time

_____ 1. ESTABLISHES HIRING CRITERIA
by
analyzing job requirements with supervisors.

_____ 2. ATTRACTS APPLICANTS
by
writing advertisements and job postings
based on hiring criteria.

_____ 3. ASCERTAINS APPLICANT'S QUALIFICATIONS
by
conducting interviews, tests, and reference
checks.

_____ 4. MAINTAINS HUMAN RESOURCE RECORDS
by
filing applications; recording statistics;
documenting interviews and job offers.

_____ 5. PRESENTS QUALIFIED CANDIDATES TO SUPERVISORS
by
scheduling appointments; discussing
qualifications and observations from the
interview and reference checks.

% of Time

_____ 6. DETERMINES REASONS FOR TURNOVER
by
conducting exit interviews.

_____ 7. COMPLIES WITH FEDERAL, STATE, AND LOCAL LEGAL
REQUIREMENTS
by
following policies and procedures.

_____ 8. PREPARES SPECIAL REPORTS
by
collecting, analyzing, and summarizing
information and trends.

_____ 9. CONTRIBUTES TO TEAM EFFORT
by
accomplishing related results as needed.

JOB PURPOSE: MAINTAINS ORGANIZATION STAFF

by

directing a recruitment and selection program.

ESSENTIAL JOB RESULTS:

% of
Time

_____ 1. APPROVES HIRING CRITERIA
   by
   analyzing job requirements.

_____ 2. ATTRACTS APPLICANTS
   by
   identifying sources of applicants; developing
   advertising campaigns; establishing rapport
   with referral sources; organizing internal
   communication programs.

_____ 3. APPROVES CANDIDATES FOR REFERRAL TO SUPERVISORS
   by
   analyzing qualifications; matching with
   hiring criteria.

_____ 4. MEETS SHORT-TERM STAFFING NEEDS
   by
   hiring temporary, part-time, and summer
   employees; instituting intern programs.

_____ 5. MAINTAINS HUMAN RESOURCE RECORDS
   by
   developing and enforcing filing and
   documentation systems.

_____ 6. COUNSELS MANAGEMENT TO REDUCE TURNOVER
   by
   determining causes.

_____ 7. COMPLIES WITH FEDERAL, STATE, AND LOCAL
   EMPLOYMENT LAW
   by
   studying existing and new legislation;
   anticipating new requirements; enforcing
   adherence to requirements; advising
   management on needed actions.

_____ 8. PREPARES SPECIAL REPORTS
   by
   collecting, analyzing, and summarizing
   information and trends.

% of
Time

_____ 9. COMPLETES OPERATIONAL REQUIREMENTS
   by
   scheduling and assigning employees;
   following up on work results.

_____ 10. MAINTAINS EMPLOYMENT STAFF
   by
   recruiting, selecting, orienting, and training
   employees.

_____ 11. MAINTAINS EMPLOYMENT STAFF JOB RESULTS
   by
   coaching, counseling, and disciplining
   employees; planning, monitoring, and
   appraising job results.

_____ 12. MAINTAINS PROFESSIONAL AND TECHNICAL KNOWLEDGE
   by
   attending educational workshops; reviewing
   professional publications; establishing
   personal networks; participating in
   professional societies.

_____ 13. ACHIEVES FINANCIAL OBJECTIVES
   by
   preparing the annual employment and
   advertising budget; scheduling expenditures;
   analyzing variances; initiating corrective
   actions.

_____ 14. CONTRIBUTES TO TEAM EFFORT
   by
   accomplishing related results as needed.

JOB TITLE: Engineering Manager

JOB PURPOSE: **PRODUCES PRODUCTS**

by

creating new designs and modifications.

ESSENTIAL JOB RESULTS:

% of Time

_____ 1. PLANS PROJECTS

by

studying customer requirements, market demand, and competitors' products; identifying and analyzing trends in technology; conferring and collaborating with other members of management.

_____ 2. DETERMINES FEASIBILITY OF PROJECT

by

identifying and forecasting costs and requirements.

_____ 3. COMPLETES PROJECTS

by

directing and approving design and modification activities.

_____ 4. MAINTAINS PROFESSIONAL AND TECHNICAL KNOWLEDGE

by

attending educational workshops; reviewing professional publications; establishing personal networks; participating in professional societies.

_____ 5. COMPLETES ENGINEERING PROJECTS

by

scheduling and assigning employees; following up on work results.

_____ 6. MAINTAINS ENGINEERING STAFF

by

recruiting, selecting, orienting, and training employees.

% of Time

_____ 7. MAINTAINS ENGINEERING STAFF JOB RESULTS

by

coaching, counseling, and disciplining employees; planning, monitoring, and appraising job results.

_____ 8. ACHIEVES FINANCIAL OBJECTIVES

by

preparing the engineering budget; scheduling expenditures; analyzing variances; initiating corrective actions.

_____ 9. COMPLIES WITH FEDERAL, STATE, AND LOCAL LEGAL REQUIREMENTS

by

studying existing and new legislation; anticipating future legislation; enforcing adherence to requirements; advising management on needed actions.

_____ 10. MAINTAINS ENGINEERING OPERATIONS

by

initiating, coordinating, and enforcing project, operational, and personnel policies and procedures.

_____ 11. MAINTAINS ENGINEERING DATA BASE

by

developing information requirements; designing an information system.

_____ 12. CONTRIBUTES TO TEAM EFFORT

by

accomplishing related results as needed.

JOB TITLE: Engineering Technician

JOB PURPOSE: **DEVELOPS MECHANICAL EQUIPMENT**

by

fabricating, assembling, and testing components and parts.

ESSENTIAL JOB RESULTS:

% of Time

_____ 1. DETERMINES PROJECT OBJECTIVES

by

studying engineering blueprints and drawings; reviewing specifications and requirements with engineers.

_____ 2. BUILDS EQUIPMENT

by

devising, fabricating, and assembling components and parts.

_____ 3. EVALUATES EQUIPMENT

by

establishing operating conditions; devising performance tests; setting up apparatus; conducting tests; recording and analyzing results; modifying components and parts; recommending changes.

_____ 4. PREPARES OPERATING MANUAL

by

identifying and describing equipment operating characteristics.

_____ 5. ENSURES OPERATION OF EQUIPMENT

by

completing preventive maintenance requirements; following manufacturer's instructions; troubleshooting malfunctions; calling for repairs; maintaining equipment inventories; evaluating new equipment and techniques.

% of Time

_____ 6. MAINTAINS SUPPLIES INVENTORY

by

checking stock to determine inventory level; anticipating needed supplies; placing and expediting orders for supplies; verifying receipt of supplies.

_____ 7. MAINTAINS TECHNICAL KNOWLEDGE

by

attending educational workshops, and reviewing technical publications.

_____ 8. MAINTAINS ENGINEERING DATA BASE

by

entering and backing up data.

_____ 9. CONTRIBUTES TO TEAM EFFORT

by

accomplishing related results as needed.

JOB PURPOSE: **CONTROLS POLLUTION**

by

identifying sources and methods of control.

ESSENTIAL JOB RESULTS:

*% of
Time*

_____ 1. IDENTIFIES SOURCES OF POLLUTION
by
collecting and analyzing data regarding
emission measurements, atmospheric
monitoring, meteorological and
mineralogical assessments, and soil and
water samples.

_____ 2. IDENTIFIES CITIZEN/CONSUMER REQUIREMENTS
by
conducting surveys and interviews.

_____ 3. PREPARES POLLUTION REPORTS
by
summarizing, interpreting, and displaying
information and trends.

_____ 4. RECOMMENDS CORRECTIONS AND ALLEVIATIONS
by
assessing pollution problems; identifying and
evaluating pollution control approaches;
establishing standards.

_____ 5. COMPLETES RESEARCH PROJECTS
by
establishing project objectives; designing and
developing mathematical, statistical, and
physical science models; determining data
collection methods; directing the collection
of data; synthesizing data; interpreting
results.

*% of
Time*

_____ 6. MAINTAINS PROFESSIONAL AND TECHNICAL KNOWLEDGE
by
attending educational workshops; reviewing
professional publications; establishing
personal networks; participating in
professional societies.

_____ 7. MAINTAINS POLLUTION CONTROL DATA BASE
by
developing information requirements;
designing an information system; writing
computer programs; and entering and
backing up data.

_____ 8. REPRESENTS THE ORGANIZATION
by
preparing a strategy; assembling data;
presenting information at hearings.

_____ 9. COMPLETES PROJECTS
by
training and guiding technicians.

_____ 10. CONTRIBUTES TO TEAM EFFORT
by
accomplishing related results as needed.

JOB TITLE: Environmental Technician

JOB PURPOSE: DETERMINES SOURCES AND METHODS OF CONTROLLING POLLUTANTS

by

conducting tests and field investigations.

ESSENTIAL JOB RESULTS:

% of Time

____ 1. ADDRESSES ENVIRONMENTAL ISSUES

by

identifying short-term and long-range issues that must be addressed; providing information and commentary pertinent to deliberations; recommending options and courses of action; implementing directives.

____ 2. GATHERS ENVIRONMENTAL DATA

by

applying agriculture, chemistry, meteorology, and engineering principles.

____ 3. DETERMINES CHARACTERISTICS OR COMPOSITION OF SOLID, LIQUID, OR GASEOUS MATERIALS AND SUBSTANCES

by

conducting chemical, physical, laboratory, and field tests, using pH meter, chemicals, autoclaves, centrifuge spectrophotometer, microscope, analytical instrumentation, and chemical laboratory equipment.

____ 4. EVALUATES ATMOSPHERIC POLLUTANTS

by

collecting and analyzing samples of gases from smokestacks; gathering other air samples and meteorological data.

____ 5. ASSESSES WATER POLLUTANTS

by

collecting and analyzing water samples from streams and lakes, raw, semiprocessed or processed water, and industrial waste water.

% of Time

____ 6. DETERMINES CHEMICAL COMPOSITION AND NATURE OF LAND POLLUTANTS

by

collecting and analyzing soil, silt, and mud.

____ 7. MAINTAINS ENVIRONMENTAL DATA BASE

by

developing information requirements; designing an information system.

____ 8. PREPARES SUMMARIES AND CHARTS

by

gathering and testing samples; analyzing and summarizing findings and trends.

____ 9. MAINTAINS GAS AND FLUID FLOW SYSTEMS, CHEMICAL REACTION SYSTEMS, MECHANICAL EQUIPMENT, AND OTHER TEST INSTRUMENTATION

by

installing; operating; completing preventive maintenance requirements; following manufacturer's instructions; troubleshooting malfunctions; maintaining equipment inventories; evaluating new equipment and techniques.

____ 10. MAINTAINS SAFE AND CLEAN WORKING ENVIRONMENT

by

complying with procedures, rules, and regulations.

____ 11. COMPLETES RESEARCH

by

conducting bacteriological and other tests.

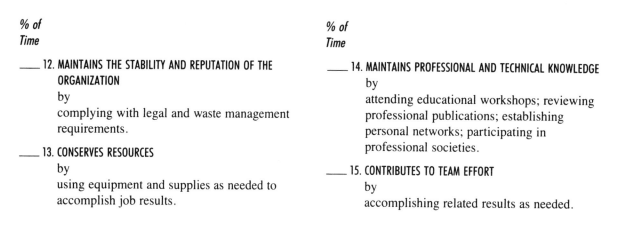

JOB TITLE: **Environmental Technician**

ESSENTIAL JOB RESULTS:

% of
Time

___ 12. MAINTAINS THE STABILITY AND REPUTATION OF THE ORGANIZATION
by
complying with legal and waste management requirements.

___ 13. CONSERVES RESOURCES
by
using equipment and supplies as needed to accomplish job results.

% of
Time

___ 14. MAINTAINS PROFESSIONAL AND TECHNICAL KNOWLEDGE
by
attending educational workshops; reviewing professional publications; establishing personal networks; participating in professional societies.

___ 15. CONTRIBUTES TO TEAM EFFORT
by
accomplishing related results as needed.

JOB PURPOSE: **MAINTAINS MANUFACTURING PROCESS**

by

designing and fabricating production equipment.

ESSENTIAL JOB RESULTS:

% of
Time

_____ 1. IDENTIFIES PRODUCT AND EQUIPMENT REQUIREMENTS
by
conferring with knowledgeable individuals
(including engineering management,
technical operations personnel, research and
development personnel, contractors, vendors,
and consultants); studying sketches,
blueprints, and related engineering material.

_____ 2. DEVELOPS CUSTOM EQUIPMENT SPECIFICATIONS
by
designing pneumatic, electrical, hydraulic,
and associated systems; specifying materials.

_____ 3. COMPLETES EQUIPMENT DESIGN
by
obtaining approval of specifications.

_____ 4. FABRICATES EQUIPMENT PARTS
by
setting up and operating shop equipment;
verifying dimensions.

_____ 5. INSTALLS EQUIPMENT
by
fabricating and assembling parts;
programming electronic components.

% of
Time

_____ 6. VERIFIES EQUIPMENT PERFORMANCE
by
conducting test runs.

_____ 7. MAINTAINS HISTORICAL REFERENCE
by
documenting design and installation actions.

_____ 8. INSTALLS PURCHASED EQUIPMENT
by
modifying pneumatic, electrical, hydraulic,
and associated systems.

_____ 9. MAINTAINS PRODUCTION
by
diagnosing and correcting equipment
failures.

_____ 10. CONTRIBUTES TO TEAM EFFORT
by
accomplishing related results as needed.

JOB TITLE: Estimator

JOB PURPOSE: **PREPARES COST ESTIMATES**

by

analyzing proposals and requirements.

ESSENTIAL JOB RESULTS:

% of
Time

____ 1. PREPARES WORK TO BE ESTIMATED
by
gathering proposals, blueprints,
specifications, and related documents.

____ 2. IDENTIFIES LABOR, MATERIAL, AND TIME REQUIREMENTS
by
studying proposals, blueprints,
specifications, and related documents.

____ 3. COMPUTES COSTS
by
analyzing labor, material, and time
requirements.

____ 4. RESOLVES DISCREPANCIES
by
collecting and analyzing information.

____ 5. PRESENTS PREPARED ESTIMATE
by
assembling and displaying numerical and
descriptive information.

% of
Time

____ 6. PREPARES SPECIAL REPORTS
by
collecting, analyzing, and summarizing
information and trends.

____ 7. MAINTAINS COST DATA BASE
by
entering and backing up data.

____ 8. MAINTAINS TECHNICAL KNOWLEDGE
by
attending educational workshops; reviewing
technical publications.

____ 9. CONTRIBUTES TO TEAM EFFORT
by
accomplishing related results as needed.

JOB TITLE: Facilities Planner

JOB PURPOSE: **SUSTAINS ORGANIZATION'S FUNCTIONS**

by

identifying and planning space requirements.

ESSENTIAL JOB RESULTS:

% of Time

____ 1. IDENTIFIES CURRENT AND FUTURE FACILITIES PLANNING REQUIREMENTS
by
establishing personal rapport with potential and actual users and other persons in a position to understand service requirements; identifying short-term and long-range issues that must be addressed; developing efficiency standards; providing information and commentary pertinent to deliberation; recommending options and courses of action; implementing directives.

____ 2. EVALUATES FACILITY SUITABILITY
by
inspecting buildings and office areas; considering factors of air circulation, lighting, location, and size.

____ 3. DETERMINES SPACE REQUIREMENTS
by
computing space requirements for personnel, equipment, furniture, and storage; measuring and calculating square footage available.

____ 4. DRAWS DESIGN LAYOUTS
by
showing location of furniture, equipment, doorways, partitions, electrical and telephone outlets, and other facilities.

____ 5. PREPARES FACILITIES FOR OCCUPANCY
by
requisitioning and costing modifications.

% of Time

____ 6. COMPLIES WITH FEDERAL, STATE, AND LOCAL LEGAL FACILITY REQUIREMENTS
by
adhering to requirements; advising management on needed actions.

____ 7. PROVIDES FACILITIES PLANNING INFORMATION
by
answering questions and requests.

____ 8. PREPARES FACILITIES PLANNING REPORTS
by
collecting, analyzing, and summarizing information and trends.

____ 9. PLANS SAFE AND CLEAN WORKING ENVIRONMENT
by
complying with procedures, rules, and regulations.

____ 10. MAINTAINS PROFESSIONAL AND TECHNICAL KNOWLEDGE
by
attending educational workshops; reviewing professional publications; establishing personal networks; participating in professional societies.

____ 11. CONTRIBUTES TO TEAM EFFORT
by
accomplishing related results as needed.

JOB TITLE: File Clerk

JOB PURPOSE: **PROVIDES HISTORICAL REFERENCE**
by

preparing, filing, and retrieving documents and micrographs.

ESSENTIAL JOB RESULTS:

% of Time

_____ 1. PREPARES DATA FOR FILING
by
compiling and sorting information; determining filing mechanism according to established procedures; establishing work priorities.

_____ 2. STORES INFORMATION
by
preparing folders and labels for new accounts; rearranging materials for space allotment, filing, or micrographing; filing information in designated areas.

_____ 3. ESTABLISHES PERMANENT RETENTION OF INFORMATION
by
micrographing closed files; maintaining log of micrographed files; storing micrographs.

_____ 4. PROVIDES INFORMATION
by
locating files; reviewing micrograph log records; searching files for misplaced items; retrieving files and micrographs.

_____ 5. MAINTAINS FILE INTEGRITY
by
adhering to filing system procedures.

_____ 6. DUPLICATES FILES
by
following procedures for requests; operating copying and micrographing machines.

% of Time

_____ 7. DISPOSES OF INFORMATION
by
following established obsolescence or retirement schedules, or legal requirements.

_____ 8. MAINTAINS FILING OPERATIONS
by
following policies and procedures; reporting needed changes.

_____ 9. MAINTAINS FILING SUPPLIES INVENTORY AND KEEPS EQUIPMENT OPERATIONAL
by
checking stock to determine inventory level; anticipating needed supplies; placing and expediting orders for supplies; verifying receipt of supplies; following manufacturer's instructions and established procedures when using equipment.

_____ 10. MAINTAINS CUSTOMER CONFIDENCE AND PROTECTS OPERATIONS
by
keeping information confidential.

_____ 11. CONTRIBUTES TO TEAM EFFORT
by
accomplishing related results as needed.

JOB PURPOSE: SUPPORTS FINANCIAL DECISION MAKING

by

analyzing and interpreting economic data and trends.

ESSENTIAL JOB RESULTS:

*% of
Time*

_____ 1. ASSEMBLES ECONOMIC DATA

by

establishing methods, procedures, sources, models, samples, and schedules.

_____ 2. INTERPRETS ECONOMIC INFORMATION

by

consolidating, studying, and analyzing data.

_____ 3. DEVELOPS ECONOMIC RECOMMENDATIONS

by

drawing conclusions from analyzed data.

_____ 4. PRESENTS INFORMATION

by

organizing and explaining data, assumptions, and recommendations; representing the organization at hearings.

_____ 5. PREPARES SPECIAL REPORTS

by

collecting, analyzing, and summarizing economic information and trends.

_____ 6. ENSURES OPERATION OF EQUIPMENT

by

completing preventive maintenance requirements; calling for repairs; evaluating new equipment and techniques.

*% of
Time*

_____ 7. COMPLETES OPERATIONAL REQUIREMENTS

by

scheduling, assigning, and training employees; following up on work results.

_____ 8. MAINTAINS PROFESSIONAL AND TECHNICAL KNOWLEDGE

by

attending educational workshops; reviewing professional publications; establishing personal networks; participating in professional societies.

_____ 9. PROTECTS OPERATIONS

by

keeping information and recommendations confidential.

_____ 10. SECURES ECONOMIC INFORMATION

by

completing data base backups.

_____ 11. CONTRIBUTES TO TEAM EFFORT

by

accomplishing related results as needed.

JOB PURPOSE: **PROTECTS CITIZENS**

by

extinguishing fires; executing rescues.

ESSENTIAL JOB RESULTS:

% of
Time

_____ 1. PREVENTS FIRE DAMAGE

by

conducting surveys and inspections for
hazards; enforcing codes.

_____ 2. PREPARES CITIZENS TO PREVENT FIRE DAMAGE

by

developing and conducting educational and
training programs.

_____ 3. ENSURES AVAILABILITY OF WATER AT FIRE SCENE

by

testing hydrants; requesting and expediting
repairs; verifying repair.

_____ 4. MINIMIZES FIRE DAMAGE

by

responding to alarms; driving and operating
equipment; regulating water pressure;
combating and extinguishing fires; rescuing
and reviving people.

_____ 5. ENSURES OPERATION OF EQUIPMENT

by

completing preventive maintenance
requirements; following manufacturer's
instructions; troubleshooting malfunctions;
notifying supervisor of needed repairs;
evaluating new equipment and techniques.

% of
Time

_____ 6. MAINTAINS OPERATIONS

by

following policies and procedures; reporting
needed changes.

_____ 7. PROVIDES INFORMATION

by

completing reports.

_____ 8. MAINTAINS TECHNICAL KNOWLEDGE

by

attending educational workshops; studying
publications; participating in scheduled
drills.

_____ 9. MAINTAINS FIRE STATION BUILDING, GROUNDS, AND
RELATED EQUIPMENT

by

completing maintenance schedules.

_____ 10. CONTRIBUTES TO TEAM EFFORT

by

accomplishing related results as needed.

JOB TITLE: Fund Development Director

JOB PURPOSE: **OBTAINS FUNDS**

by

promoting the organization's interests and benefits to donors.

ESSENTIAL JOB RESULTS:

*% of
Time*

_____ 1. ESTABLISHES FUND DEVELOPMENT GOALS
by
studying organization objectives and needs;
advising the Board of Directors.

_____ 2. GUIDES FUND DEVELOPMENT EFFORTS
by
formulating fund development policies,
procedures, and programs, including legal
arrangements to transfer funds and goods-in-
kind; obtaining fund development
consultations.

_____ 3. IDENTIFIES POTENTIAL SUPPORTERS
by
examining past records; researching support
given to other organizations; identifying
grant agencies and foundations; establishing
personal networks.

_____ 4. PREPARES PROMOTIONAL LITERATURE AND
PRESENTATIONS
by
composing copy; designing layout; obtaining
graphic arts advice; contracting with printers
and media services.

_____ 5. SOLICITS FUNDS AND PLEDGES
by
completing applications; answering inquiries;
mailing literature; assigning responsibility for
personal solicitation to Board members,
volunteers, and staff members; making
personal visits, speeches, and promotions.

*% of
Time*

_____ 6. ORGANIZES SPECIAL CAMPAIGNS
by
setting objectives; targeting supporters;
developing approaches; making solicitations.

_____ 7. ORGANIZES SPECIAL EVENTS
by
identifying potential guests; developing
announcements and invitations; making and
coordinating arrangements; supervising
activities.

_____ 8. OBTAINS HELP TO ACCOMPLISH OBJECTIVES
by
recruiting, scheduling, training, and
supervising volunteers.

_____ 9. PREPARES FUND DEVELOPMENT REPORTS
by
collecting, analyzing, and summarizing
information and trends.

_____ 10. CONTRIBUTES TO TEAM EFFORT
by
accomplishing related results as needed.

JOB PURPOSE: DEBITS AND CREDITS ACCOUNTS

by

transferring funds.

ESSENTIAL JOB RESULTS:

% of
Time

_____ 1. TRANSFERS FUNDS
by
transmitting and receiving funds; executing
scheduled transfers.

_____ 2. VERIFIES TRANSMITTAL
by
checking source document.

_____ 3. MAINTAINS HISTORICAL RECORDS
by
entering and filing transmittals.

_____ 4. BALANCES ACCOUNTS
by
reconciling transfers with source documents,
correspondent banks, clearing houses, and
Federal Reserve.

_____ 5. MEETS RESERVE REQUIREMENTS
by
monitoring balances and transferring funds
to/from Federal Reserve account.

% of
Time

_____ 6. VERIFIES FUNDS AVAILABLE
by
obtaining credit letters from correspondent
banks.

_____ 7. COMPLIES WITH FEDERAL, STATE, AND LOCAL LEGAL
REQUIREMENTS
by
following procedures; enforcing adherence to
requirements.

_____ 8. MAINTAINS CUSTOMER CONFIDENCE AND PROTECTS
OPERATIONS
by
keeping information confidential.

_____ 9. CONTRIBUTES TO TEAM EFFORT
by
accomplishing related results as needed.

JOB TITLE: Graphic Designer

JOB PURPOSE: PREPARES VISUAL PRESENTATIONS

by

designing art and copy layouts.

ESSENTIAL JOB RESULTS:

*% of
Time*

____ 1. PREPARES WORK TO BE ACCOMPLISHED
by
gathering information and materials.

____ 2. PLANS CONCEPT
by
studying information and materials.

____ 3. ILLUSTRATES CONCEPT
by
designing rough layout of art and copy
regarding arrangement, size, type size and
style, and related aesthetic concepts.

____ 4. OBTAINS APPROVAL OF CONCEPT
by
submitting rough layout for approval.

____ 5. PREPARES FINISHED COPY AND ART
by
operating typesetting, printing, and similar
equipment; purchasing from vendors.

____ 6. PREPARES FINAL LAYOUT
by
marking and pasting up finished copy and
art.

*% of
Time*

____ 7. ENSURES OPERATION OF EQUIPMENT
by
completing preventive maintenance
requirements; following manufacturer's
instructions; troubleshooting malfunctions;
calling for repairs; maintaining equipment
inventories; evaluating new equipment.

____ 8. COMPLETES PROJECTS
by
coordinating with outside agencies, art
services, printers, etc.

____ 9. MAINTAINS TECHNICAL KNOWLEDGE
by
attending design workshops; reviewing
professional publications; participating in
professional societies.

____ 10. CONTRIBUTES TO TEAM EFFORT
by
accomplishing related results as needed.

JOB TITLE: Health Care Administrator

JOB PURPOSE: **PROVIDES HEALTH CARE SERVICES**

by

planning, implementing, controlling, and evaluating health care delivery programs and operations.

ESSENTIAL JOB RESULTS:

% of Time

____ 1. IDENTIFIES PATIENT SERVICE REQUIREMENTS

by

establishing personal rapport with potential and actual patients and other persons in a position to understand service requirements.

____ 2. DELIVERS PATIENT CARE SERVICES

by

identifying markets; establishing standards; developing collaboration among medical, nursing, and administrative staffs.

____ 3. MAINTAINS FISCAL OPERATIONS

by

establishing rates for health care services; defining profit margins; conducting cost studies.

____ 4. MAINTAINS BUILDINGS AND EQUIPMENT

by

planning and controlling space allocations, building additions, and major equipment acquisitions; developing maintenance programs.

____ 5. MAINTAINS THE STABILITY AND REPUTATION OF THE HEALTH CARE FACILITY

by

complying with accreditation requirements.

____ 6. COMPLIES WITH FEDERAL, STATE, AND LOCAL LEGAL REQUIREMENTS

by

studying existing and new legislation; anticipating future legislation; enforcing adherence to requirements; advising the Board of Directors on needed actions.

% of Time

____ 7. MAINTAINS HEALTH CARE STAFF

by

recruiting, selecting, orienting, and training employees.

____ 8. MAINTAINS HEALTH CARE STAFF JOB RESULTS

by

coaching, counseling, and disciplining employees; planning, monitoring, and appraising job results.

____ 9. DEVELOPS HEALTH CARE FACILITY STAFF

by

providing information, educational opportunities, and experiential growth opportunities.

____ 10. MAINTAINS MEDICAL STAFF

by

recruiting physicians, providing support services, and enforcing policies and procedures.

____ 11. MAINTAINS HEALTH CARE FACILITY OPERATIONS

by

initiating, coordinating, and enforcing program, operational, and personnel policies and procedures.

____ 12. REPRESENTS THE HEALTH CARE FACILITY

by

promoting programs, contributing to community programs and groups, and informing and responding to news media.

ESSENTIAL JOB RESULTS:

% of
Time

_____ 13. MAINTAINS PROFESSIONAL AND TECHNICAL KNOWLEDGE
by
attending educational workshops, reviewing
professional publications, establishing
personal networks, and participating in
professional societies.

% of
Time

_____ 14. CONTRIBUTES TO TEAM EFFORT
by
accomplishing related results as needed.

JOB PURPOSE: **PROVIDES FOR WELL-BEING AND COMFORT OF STAFF AND VISITORS**

by

heating, ventilating, and cooling the building environment.

ESSENTIAL JOB RESULTS:

% of Time

____ 1. MAINTAINS WORKING CLIMATE
by
installing, repairing, and servicing heating, ventilating, and air-conditioning (HVAC) systems.

____ 2. KEEPS EQUIPMENT, SYSTEMS, AND BUILDING READY FOR USE
by
completing preventive maintenance schedules; restoring and repairing faulty or inoperative HVAC systems and associated equipment; recommending changes and new HVAC installations.

____ 3. COMPLIES WITH LOCAL, STATE, AND FEDERAL CODES AND STANDARDS
by
directing and monitoring the work of vendors, contractors, and staff; inspecting the HVAC systems and equipment.

____ 4. IMPLEMENTS CHANGES, EXPANSIONS, AND ADDITIONS TO HVAC SYSTEMS
by
identifying problems; keeping abreast of new developments; using statistics and equipment history reports.

____ 5. ACHIEVES HVAC MAINTENANCE FINANCIAL OBJECTIVES
by
preparing an annual budget; scheduling expenditures; analyzing variances; initiating corrective actions.

% of Time

____ 6. COMPLETES HVAC MAINTENANCE OPERATIONAL REQUIREMENTS
by
scheduling and assigning employees; following up on work results.

____ 7. MAINTAINS HVAC MAINTENANCE STAFF
by
recruiting, selecting, orienting, and training employees.

____ 8. MAINTAINS HVAC MAINTENANCE STAFF JOB RESULTS
by
counseling and disciplining employees; planning, monitoring, and appraising job results.

____ 9. MAINTAINS PROFESSIONAL AND TECHNICAL KNOWLEDGE
by
attending educational workshops; reviewing professional publications; establishing personal networks; participating in professional societies.

____ 10. MAINTAINS CONTINUITY AMONG WORK TEAMS
by
documenting maintenance actions; noting system or equipment irregularities requiring continued monitoring.

____ 11. MAINTAINS SAFE AND CLEAN WORKING ENVIRONMENT
by
developing and enforcing procedures, rules, and regulations.

JOB TITLE: Heating/Ventilating/Air-Conditioning
Maintenance Supervisor

ESSENTIAL JOB RESULTS:

% of
Time

___ 12. MAINTAINS HVAC MAINTENANCE PARTS AND EQUIPMENT
INVENTORY
by
checking stock to determine inventory level;
anticipating needed parts and equipment;
placing and expediting orders for parts and
equipment; verifying receipt of parts and
equipment.

% of
Time

___ 13. CONTRIBUTES TO TEAM EFFORT
by
accomplishing related results as needed.

JOB TITLE: Help-Desk Representative

JOB PURPOSE: **RESOLVES COMPUTER USER CONCERNS**

by

answering questions about hardware and software; providing instructions.

ESSENTIAL JOB RESULTS:

*% of
Time*

_____ 1. DETERMINES SOURCE OF CONCERN
by
interviewing user on the telephone.

_____ 2. TEACHES USER
by
answering questions; interpreting operating
instructions; providing references.

_____ 3. DETERMINES SOURCE OF ERROR
by
reviewing procedures and actions taken by
user; instructing user to perform diagnostic
procedures.

_____ 4. RESOLVES PROBLEMS
by
issuing corrective instructions; consulting
with coworkers and vendors.

_____ 5. IMPROVES PROGRAMS
by
notifying programmers of problems; making
recommendations.

*% of
Time*

_____ 6. IMPROVES OPERATING REFERENCES
by
writing revisions.

_____ 7. EVALUATES SOFTWARE
by
testing ease of use and applicability.

_____ 8. MAINTAINS TECHNICAL KNOWLEDGE
by
attending educational workshops; reviewing
technical publications; establishing personal
networks; participating in technical societies.

_____ 9. MAINTAINS CLIENT CONFIDENCE AND PROTECTS
OPERATIONS
by
keeping information confidential.

_____ 10. CONTRIBUTES TO TEAM EFFORT
by
accomplishing related results as needed.

JOB TITLE: Hostperson

JOB PURPOSE: **WELCOMES RESTAURANT PATRONS AND COLLECTS REVENUE**

by

greeting and seating guests; issuing charges; collecting payments.

ESSENTIAL JOB RESULTS:

% of
Time

____ 1. SCHEDULES PATRONS

by
recording dining reservations; giving location of and directions to restaurant; assigning dining areas; referring requests for special parties and accommodations to Dining Room Manager.

____ 2. WELCOMES PATRONS

by
exchanging pleasantries; escorting them to assigned dining area; presenting menus; announcing waitperson's name.

____ 3. PROTECTS ESTABLISHMENT AND PATRONS

by
adhering to sanitation, safety, and alcohol control policies.

____ 4. HELPS DINING ROOM STAFF

by
setting and clearing tables; replenishing water; serving beverages.

____ 5. ISSUES DINING CHARGES

by
verifying orders; calculating taxes; totaling bill.

% of
Time

____ 6. RECEIVES PAYMENTS

by
validating credit charges; approving checks; accepting currency; calculating and issuing change.

____ 7. RECONCILES CASH DRAWER

by
proving cash transactions; listing checks and credit card charges.

____ 8. SAFEGUARDS REVENUES

by
completing cash, check, and credit card deposit slips; arranging for deposit; determining opening cash supply.

____ 9. CONTRIBUTES TO TEAM EFFORT

by
accomplishing related results as needed.

JOB TITLE: Hotel Clerk

JOB PURPOSE: SERVES GUESTS

by

completing registration; controlling room assignments.

ESSENTIAL JOB RESULTS:

% of
Time

____ 1. WELCOMES GUESTS
by
greeting them; answering questions;
responding to requests.

____ 2. REGISTERS GUESTS
by
obtaining or confirming room requirements;
verifying preregistration; assigning room;
obtaining information and signatures; issuing
door cards.

____ 3. ESTABLISHES CREDIT
by
verifying credit cards or obtaining cash.

____ 4. DIRECTS GUESTS TO ROOM
by
showing location on hotel map; calling
bellhop.

____ 5. CONVEYS INFORMATION TO GUESTS
by
receiving and transmitting messages, mail,
facsimiles, packages, etc.

____ 6. PROVIDES INFORMATION TO GUESTS
by
answering inquiries regarding hotel and other
services guests may require, such as
entertainment, shopping, business, and
travel.

% of
Time

____ 7. MAINTAINS RECORDS
by
entering room and guest account data.

____ 8. COLLECTS REVENUE
by
entering services and charges; computing
bill; obtaining payment.

____ 9. MAKES HOTEL AND OTHER RESERVATIONS
by
entering or telephoning requirements;
checking availability; confirming
requirements.

____ 10. SECURES GUESTS' VALUABLES
by
placing valuables in safe deposit box.

____ 11. CONTRIBUTES TO TEAM EFFORT
by
accomplishing related results as needed.

JOB TITLE: Human Resources Clerk

JOB PURPOSE: **SUPPORTS HUMAN RESOURCES OPERATIONS**

by

maintaining records; preparing documents.

ESSENTIAL JOB RESULTS:

% of Time

_____ 1. PREPARES WORK TO BE ACCOMPLISHED
by
gathering and sorting documents.

_____ 2. MAINTAINS HUMAN RESOURCES DATA BASE AND RECORDS
by
entering data from change notices.

_____ 3. PREPARES HUMAN RESOURCES REPORTS
by
assembling and compiling data.

_____ 4. PROVIDES INFORMATION
by
answering questions and requests.

_____ 5. SECURES HUMAN RESOURCES DATA
by
completing data base backups.

% of Time

_____ 6. MAINTAINS EMPLOYEE CONFIDENCE AND PROTECTS OPERATIONS
by
keeping personnel data confidential.

_____ 7. MAINTAINS OPERATION OF EQUIPMENT
by
following operator procedures, and calling for repairs.

_____ 8. COMPLIES WITH FEDERAL, STATE, AND LOCAL LEGAL REQUIREMENTS
by
following policies and procedures.

_____ 9. CONTRIBUTES TO TEAM EFFORT
by
accomplishing related results as needed.

JOB PURPOSE: **MAINTAINS AND ENHANCES THE ORGANIZATION'S HUMAN RESOURCES**

by

planning, implementing, and evaluating employee relations and human resources policies, programs, and practices.

ESSENTIAL JOB RESULTS:

% of Time

____ 1. MAINTAINS THE WORK STRUCTURE
by
updating job requirements and job descriptions for all positions.

____ 2. MAINTAINS ORGANIZATION STAFF
by
establishing a recruiting, testing, and interviewing program; counseling managers on candidate selection; conducting and analyzing exit interviews; recommending changes.

____ 3. PREPARES EMPLOYEES FOR ASSIGNMENTS
by
establishing and conducting orientation and training programs.

____ 4. MAINTAINS A PAY PLAN
by
conducting periodic pay surveys; scheduling and conducting job evaluations; preparing pay budgets; monitoring and scheduling individual pay actions; recommending, planning, and implementing pay structure revisions.

____ 5. ENSURES PLANNING, MONITORING, AND APPRAISAL OF EMPLOYEE WORK RESULTS
by
training managers to coach and discipline employees; scheduling management conferences with employees; hearing and resolving employee grievances; counseling employees and supervisors.

% of Time

____ 6. MAINTAINS EMPLOYEE BENEFITS PROGRAMS AND INFORMS EMPLOYEES OF BENEFITS
by
studying and assessing benefit needs and trends; recommending benefit programs to management; directing the processing of benefit claims; obtaining and evaluating benefit contract bids; awarding benefit contracts; designing and conducting educational programs on benefit programs.

____ 7. ENSURES LEGAL COMPLIANCE
by
monitoring and implementing applicable human resource federal and state requirements; conducting investigations; maintaining records; representing the organization at hearings.

____ 8. MAINTAINS MANAGEMENT GUIDELINES
by
preparing, updating, and recommending human resource policies and procedures.

____ 9. MAINTAINS HISTORICAL HUMAN RESOURCE RECORDS
by
designing a filing and retrieval system; keeping past and current records.

____ 10. MAINTAINS PROFESSIONAL AND TECHNICAL KNOWLEDGE
by
attending educational workshops; reviewing professional publications; establishing personal networks; participating in professional societies.

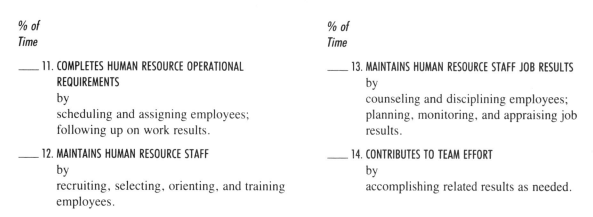

JOB TITLE: Human Resources Manager

ESSENTIAL JOB RESULTS:

% of
Time

_____ 11. COMPLETES HUMAN RESOURCE OPERATIONAL REQUIREMENTS
by
scheduling and assigning employees; following up on work results.

_____ 12. MAINTAINS HUMAN RESOURCE STAFF
by
recruiting, selecting, orienting, and training employees.

% of
Time

_____ 13. MAINTAINS HUMAN RESOURCE STAFF JOB RESULTS
by
counseling and disciplining employees; planning, monitoring, and appraising job results.

_____ 14. CONTRIBUTES TO TEAM EFFORT
by
accomplishing related results as needed.

JOB TITLE: Industrial Engineer

JOB PURPOSE: **ESTABLISHES AND IMPROVES WORK SYSTEMS**

by

studying facility layout, work flow, and work methods.

ESSENTIAL JOB RESULTS:

*% of
Time*

_____ 1. DEVELOPS LABOR STANDARDS
by
analyzing work samples and methods;
measuring work performance.

_____ 2. IMPROVES LABOR UTILIZATION
by
studying work methods; testing
modifications; designing new methods;
recommending job restructuring.

_____ 3. IMPROVES WORK FLOW
by
studying process flowcharts; recommending
modifications in work flow, work stations,
and product; developing new procedures;
recommending equipment modifications and
purchases.

_____ 4. REDUCES WASTE
by
studying methods, equipment, and operator
techniques; recommending changes;
establishing procedures to identify and
analyze waste.

_____ 5. IMPLEMENTS WORK IMPROVEMENT PROGRAMS
by
conferring with management and engineering
staff.

*% of
Time*

_____ 6. PREPARES WORK ANALYSIS REPORTS
by
collecting, analyzing, and summarizing
information and trends.

_____ 7. MAINTAINS INDUSTRIAL ENGINEERING DATA BASE
by
writing computer programs; entering and
backing up data.

_____ 8. COMPLETES WORK IMPROVEMENT PROJECTS
by
training and guiding operators and
supervisors.

_____ 9. MAINTAINS OPERATIONS GUIDELINES
by
writing and updating policies, procedures,
and methods.

_____ 10. MAINTAINS PROFESSIONAL AND TECHNICAL KNOWLEDGE
by
attending educational workshops; reviewing
professional publications; establishing
personal networks; participating in
professional societies.

_____ 11. CONTRIBUTES TO TEAM EFFORT
by
accomplishing related results as needed.

JOB TITLE:	Information Specialist

JOB PURPOSE:

PROVIDES CLIENTS WITH INFORMATION

by

designing methods to collect and retrieve data.

ESSENTIAL JOB RESULTS:

% of
Time

____ 1. IDENTIFIES CLIENT REQUIREMENTS

by

establishing personal rapport with potential and actual clients and other persons in a position to understand service requirements.

____ 2. COLLECTS DATA

by

identifying sources of information; designing survey and collection methods.

____ 3. ORGANIZES INFORMATION

by

studying, analyzing, interpreting, and classifying data.

____ 4. ESTABLISHES AND REVISES DATA BASE

by

conferring with analysts and programmers to code and retrieve data.

____ 5. MAINTAINS DATA BASE

by

entering data.

____ 6. RESOLVES RETRIEVAL PROBLEMS

by

altering design to meet requirements.

% of
Time

____ 7. PREPARES REPORTS

by

collecting, analyzing, and summarizing information.

____ 8. PREPARES REFERENCE FOR USERS

by

writing operating instructions.

____ 9. MAINTAINS HISTORICAL RECORDS

by

documenting system changes and revisions.

____ 10. MAINTAINS CLIENT CONFIDENCE AND PROTECTS OPERATIONS

by

keeping information confidential.

____ 11. MAINTAINS PROFESSIONAL AND TECHNICAL KNOWLEDGE

by

attending educational workshops; reviewing professional publications; establishing personal networks; participating in professional societies.

____ 12. CONTRIBUTES TO TEAM EFFORT

by

accomplishing related results as needed.

JOB TITLE: Inventory Clerk

JOB PURPOSE: **MAINTAINS PRODUCTION**

by

inventorying and disbursing supplies and equipment.

ESSENTIAL JOB RESULTS:

*% of
Time*

____ 1. RECEIVES ITEMS
by
unpacking containers.

____ 2. VERIFIES ITEMS RECEIVED
by
checking identifying information of items;
inspecting condition of items; comparing
count/measure of items to purchase order and
packing list.

____ 3. MAINTAINS INVENTORY
by
marking and placing items in stock;
establishing inventory reorder points;
reporting items to be reordered.

____ 4. DOCUMENTS INVENTORY
by
recording additions, disbursements,
adjustments, losses, and removals of items.

____ 5. FILLS ITEM REQUESTS
by
issuing/delivering items.

*% of
Time*

____ 6. KEEPS INVENTORY AVAILABLE
by
inspecting items for wear and defects;
completing repairs and servicing of items.

____ 7. PREPARES INVENTORY REPORTS
by
collecting and analyzing information on
stock usage.

____ 8. MAINTAINS INVENTORY OPERATIONS
by
following policies and procedures; reporting
needed changes.

____ 9. CONTRIBUTES TO TEAM EFFORT
by
accomplishing related results as needed.

JOB TITLE: Job Analyst

JOB PURPOSE: **DESCRIBES JOBS**

by

collecting, analyzing, and compiling information.

ESSENTIAL JOB RESULTS:

% of
Time

____ 1. IDENTIFIES AND VALIDATES JOB RESULTS, DUTIES, AND QUALIFICATIONS
by
interviewing job incumbents and supervisors; obtaining and studying completed questionnaires; observing jobs being performed.

____ 2. RECORDS JOB REQUIREMENTS
by
writing draft job descriptions.

____ 3. OBTAINS APPROVAL OF JOB DESCRIPTION
by
submitting final copy to management.

____ 4. MAINTAINS JOB DESCRIPTION RECORDS AND DATA BASE
by
filing documents; entering new data and revisions.

% of
Time

____ 5. SUPPORTS THE JOB EVALUATION COMMITTEE
by
collecting job data related to each compensable factor for each job; explaining job information; recording and filing committee decisions; making arrangements for meetings.

____ 6. MAINTAINS AND PRODUCES THE ORGANIZATION CHART
by
entering changes; reformatting; printing copies.

____ 7. PROVIDES JOB INFORMATION
by
answering questions and requests.

____ 8. CONTRIBUTES TO TEAM EFFORT
by
accomplishing related results as needed.

JOB TITLE: Laboratory Manager

JOB PURPOSE: **SERVES PATIENTS**

by

providing medical laboratory diagnostic and therapeutic information,
products, and services.

ESSENTIAL JOB RESULTS:

*% of
Time*

_____ 1. PROVIDES MEDICAL LABORATORY DIAGNOSTIC AND
THERAPEUTIC INFORMATION, PRODUCTS, AND SERVICES
by
establishing specimen preparation
procedures; developing and implementing
analytical procedures; evaluating laboratory
information; consulting with pathologists;
reporting results according to protocols
mandated by the hospital and Public Health
Department.

_____ 2. MAINTAINS MEDICAL LABORATORY EQUIPMENT
PERFORMANCE
by
establishing quality standards; developing
operations, quality, and troubleshooting
procedures; ensuring staff compliance;
certifying instrument performance; arranging
equipment replacement, service, and repair.

_____ 3. MAINTAINS MEDICAL LABORATORY SUPPLIES INVENTORY
by
checking stock to determine inventory level;
anticipating needed supplies; placing and
expediting orders for supplies; verifying
receipt of supplies.

_____ 4. MAINTAINS MEDICAL LABORATORY PRODUCTIVITY
by
monitoring workload of functional areas;
identifying peak and slack periods; making
operational or staffing adjustment.

*% of
Time*

_____ 5. MAINTAINS QUALITY RESULTS
by
participating in the hospital quality assurance
program; consulting with pathologists;
performing proficiency surveys; reviewing
quality control and quality assurance
programs; making adjustments in policy and
procedures; generating reports; maintaining
records.

_____ 6. MAINTAINS MEDICAL LABORATORY INFORMATION SYSTEM
by
identifying information needs and problems;
recommending improvements; establishing
priorities; testing; writing user manuals;
training employees; maintaining security and
confidentiality.

_____ 7. IMPLEMENTS NEW PROGRAMS, TESTS, METHODS,
INSTRUMENTATION, AND PROCEDURES
by
investigating alternatives; preparing
proposals; developing and performing
parallel testing; monitoring progress.

_____ 8. MAINTAINS MEDICAL LABORATORY STAFF
by
recruiting, selecting, orienting, and training
employees.

JOB TITLE: Laboratory Manager

ESSENTIAL JOB RESULTS:

% of Time

_____ 9. COMPLETES OPERATIONAL REQUIREMENTS
by
scheduling and assigning employees; following up on work results.

_____ 10. MAINTAINS MEDICAL LABORATORY STAFF RESULTS
by
counseling and disciplining employees; planning, monitoring, and appraising job results.

_____ 11. MAINTAINS PROFESSIONAL AND TECHNICAL KNOWLEDGE
by
attending educational workshops; reviewing professional publications; establishing personal networks; participating in professional societies.

_____ 12. PREPARES PHYSICIANS, NURSES, PATIENTS, AND STUDENTS
by
teaching analytical theory, testing methodology, and the role of tested components in human physiology and medical practice.

_____ 13. COMPLIES WITH STATE AND PROFESSIONAL CONTINUING EDUCATION LICENSURE REQUIREMENTS
by
providing in-service programs; monitoring outcomes.

% of Time

_____ 14. RESOLVES PROBLEMS
by
consulting with pathologists, other laboratory managers, technical coordinators, laboratory directors, physicians, nurses, and other health care professionals; attending committee meetings.

_____ 15. BILLS FOR SERVICES
by
completing requests for service; monitoring billed units; providing the billing office with service codes.

_____ 16. PROVIDES ADMINISTRATIVE SUPPORT FOR THE HOSPITAL
by
acting as manager on call.

_____ 17. CONTRIBUTES TO TEAM EFFORT
by
accomplishing related results as needed.

JOB TITLE: Laser Technician

JOB PURPOSE: **CONSTRUCTS LASER DEVICES**

by

installing and aligning optical parts.

ESSENTIAL JOB RESULTS:

% of
Time

____ 1. PREPARES WORK TO BE ACCOMPLISHED
by
reviewing work orders, specifications, blueprints, and sketches; conferring with engineers.

____ 2. OBTAINS REQUIRED PARTS
by
clarifying production requirements with production operators regarding mirror blank grinding, mirror surface coating, and parts machining.

____ 3. CONSTRUCTS LASER BODY
by
installing and aligning optical parts with precision instruments.

____ 4. FILLS GAS LASER BODY
by
controlling vacuum pump and transfer equipment.

____ 5. COMPLETES ASSEMBLY
by
installing laser body in chassis; installing and aligning electronic components, tubing, wiring, and controls.

____ 6. CONFIRMS PRODUCT SPECIFICATIONS
by
setting up testing equipment; testing laser devices.

% of
Time

____ 7. PREPARES TEST REPORTS
by
collecting, analyzing, and summarizing data.

____ 8. MAINTAINS PRODUCT AND COMPANY REPUTATION
by
complying with government regulations.

____ 9. MAINTAINS SAFE AND CLEAN WORKING ENVIRONMENT
by
complying with procedures, rules, and regulations.

____ 10. MAINTAINS CONTINUITY AMONG WORK TEAMS
by
documenting and communicating actions, irregularities, and continuing needs.

____ 11. DOCUMENTS ACTIONS
by
completing production and quality logs.

____ 12. CONTRIBUTES TO TEAM EFFORT
by
accomplishing related results as needed.

JOB PURPOSE: ASSESSES LOANS

by

reviewing portfolios; developing policies; supervising staff.

ESSENTIAL JOB RESULTS:

% of Time

____ 1. EVALUATES QUALITY OF LOANS AND ASSIGNS RISK RATINGS

by

assigning portfolios; scheduling, conducting, and overseeing loan reviews; studying verification system information; generating reports.

____ 2. KEEPS BANK BOARD OF DIRECTORS AND CHIEF OFFICERS INFORMED

by

designing, generating, and presenting reports regarding loans that need special attention.

____ 3. MAINTAINS LOAN POLICIES AND PROCEDURES

by

assessing lending practices; recommending changes.

____ 4. REDUCES CHARGE-OFFS, NONPERFORMING ASSETS, AND DELINQUENCIES

by

identifying deteriorating credit situations; assessing action plans; evaluating documentation, collateral, and structure; providing technical advice to lending personnel.

____ 5. CONTROLS SECURED LENDING OPERATIONS

by

conducting field audits on all formula-based loans; reviewing reports on audit results; maintaining secured lending policies and procedures.

____ 6. ACHIEVES FINANCIAL OBJECTIVES

by

preparing an annual budget; scheduling expenditures; analyzing variances; initiating corrective actions.

% of Time

____ 7. MAINTAINS CUSTOMER CONFIDENCE AND PROTECTS OPERATIONS

by

keeping information confidential.

____ 8. COMPLETES OPERATIONAL REQUIREMENTS

by

scheduling and assigning employees; following up on work results.

____ 9. MAINTAINS LOAN REVIEW STAFF

by

recruiting, selecting, orienting, and training employees.

____ 10. MAINTAINS LOAN REVIEW STAFF JOB RESULTS

by

counseling and disciplining employees; planning, monitoring, and appraising job results.

____ 11. MAINTAINS PROFESSIONAL AND TECHNICAL KNOWLEDGE

by

attending educational workshops; reviewing professional publications; establishing personal networks; participating in professional societies.

____ 12. CONTRIBUTES TO TEAM EFFORT

by

accomplishing related results as needed.

JOB TITLE: Machine Cleaner

JOB PURPOSE: **MAINTAINS PRODUCTION**

by

completing preventive maintenance requirements.

ESSENTIAL JOB RESULTS:

% of Time

____ 1. KEEPS EQUIPMENT FUNCTIONING
by
cleaning, lubricating, and greasing parts.

____ 2. PROLONGS ENDURANCE OF EQUIPMENT
by
completing preventive maintenance schedules.

____ 3. DOCUMENTS ACTIONS
by
completing maintenance logs.

____ 4. MAINTAINS SAFE AND CLEAN WORKING ENVIRONMENT
by
complying with procedures, rules, and regulations.

____ 5. MAINTAINS CONTINUITY AMONG WORK TEAMS
by
communicating actions, irregularities, and continuing needs.

% of Time

____ 6. MAINTAINS SUPPLIES
by
checking stock; anticipating and requesting needed supplies.

____ 7. CONSERVES RESOURCES
by
using equipment and supplies as needed to accomplish job results.

____ 8. CONTRIBUTES TO TEAM EFFORT
by
accomplishing related results as needed.

JOB TITLE: Machine Operator

JOB PURPOSE: **FORMS PRODUCT**

by

operating fabricating equipment.

ESSENTIAL JOB RESULTS:

% of Time

____ 1. DETERMINES SEQUENCE OF OPERATIONS
by
studying blueprints, specifications, and work orders.

____ 2. PREPARES MACHINE FOR PRODUCTION
by
positioning and securing dies, stops, guides, and turntables.

____ 3. REGULATES MACHINING
by
setting and adjusting controls.

____ 4. PRODUCES PARTS
by
locating and marking reference points on workpiece with rule, compass, template, etc.; positioning or aligning workpiece against stops and guides or with die; operating equipment.

____ 5. MAINTAINS SPECIFICATIONS
by
observing operations; detecting malfunctions; inspecting parts; adjusting controls; replacing dies.

____ 6. RESOLVES PRODUCTION PROBLEMS
by
altering process to meet specifications; notifying supervisor to obtain additional resources.

% of Time

____ 7. ENSURES OPERATION OF EQUIPMENT
by
completing preventive maintenance requirements; following manufacturer's instructions; troubleshooting malfunctions; calling for repairs.

____ 8. MAINTAINS STOCK INVENTORY
by
checking stock to determine amount available; anticipating needed stock; placing and expediting orders for stock; verifying receipt of stock.

____ 9. MAINTAINS CONTINUITY AMONG WORK TEAMS
by
documenting and communicating actions, irregularities, and continuing needs.

____ 10. DOCUMENTS ACTIONS
by
completing production and quality logs.

____ 11. CONTRIBUTES TO TEAM EFFORT
by
accomplishing related results as needed.

JOB TITLE: Mail Clerk

JOB PURPOSE: **TRANSMITS COMMUNICATIONS**

by

distributing and dispatching mail.

ESSENTIAL JOB RESULTS:

% of
Time

____ 1. DISTRIBUTES MAIL

by

retrieving or receiving items from post office
and delivery services; opening and sorting by
addressee, destination, and type; delivering
items.

____ 2. COMPLIES WITH POSTAL SERVICE AND DELIVERY SERVICE
REQUIREMENTS

by

preparing outgoing mail for delivery.

____ 3. PREPARES VOLUME MAILINGS

by

operating stuffing and posting equipment.

____ 4. SUPPORTS COST-CONTROL MEASURES

by

presorting and batching outgoing items for
incentives and discounts.

____ 5. MAINTAINS POSTAGE EQUIPMENT

by

operating and inspecting equipment
according to established procedures;
performing minor repairs; notifying
supervisor or vendor technicians of
problems.

% of
Time

____ 6. MAINTAINS POSTAGE METER RESERVES

by

monitoring balances; completing control
logs; requisitioning postage.

____ 7. PROVIDES MAIL AND PARCEL DELIVERY INFORMATION

by

answering questions and requests.

____ 8. MAINTAINS MAIL OPERATIONS

by

following policies and procedures; reporting
needed changes.

____ 9. MAINTAINS SAFE AND CLEAN WORKING ENVIRONMENT

by

complying with procedures, rules, and
regulations.

____ 10. CONTRIBUTES TO TEAM EFFORT

by

accomplishing related results as needed.

┌───┐
│ **JOB TITLE:** Maintenance Electrician   │
└───┘

JOB PURPOSE: **MAINTAINS PRODUCTION AND QUALITY**

by

ensuring operation of electrical systems, apparatus, and electrical and electronic components of machinery and equipment.

ESSENTIAL JOB RESULTS:

*% of
Time*

____ 1. ENSURES OPERATION OF ELECTRICAL SYSTEMS AND EQUIPMENT

by

completing preventive maintenance requirements on robots, conveyors, programmable controllers, transformers, voltage regulators, and machinery wiring; following electrical code, manuals, schematic diagrams, blueprints, and other specifications; troubleshooting.

____ 2. INSTALLS NEW MACHINES AND EQUIPMENT

by

installing power supply wiring and conduit to and between machines and equipment; using hand tools and test equipment.

____ 3. REPAIRS ELECTRICAL SYSTEMS AND EQUIPMENT

by

diagnosing malfunctioning apparatus, such as transformers, motors, and lighting fixtures; determining faulty wiring; inspecting and testing malfunctioning machinery.

____ 4. CONTROLS DOWNTIME

by

informing production workers of routine electrical preventive maintenance techniques and monitoring compliance.

____ 5. REPAIRS AND REPLACES FAULTY ELECTRICAL COMPONENTS

by

using testing equipment and hand tools to install relays, switches, motors, printed circuit boards, and position-sensing devices.

*% of
Time*

____ 6. PROGRAMS AUTOMATED MACHINERY

by

operating, testing for malfunctions, and verifying repairs to robots, robot controllers, and programmable controllers.

____ 7. MAINTAINS ELECTRICAL EQUIPMENT, PARTS, AND SUPPLIES INVENTORIES

by

checking stock to determine inventory level; anticipating needed equipment, parts, and supplies; placing and expediting orders; verifying receipt.

____ 8. CONSERVES ELECTRICAL MAINTENANCE RESOURCES

by

using equipment and supplies as needed to accomplish job results.

____ 9. PROVIDES ELECTRICAL MAINTENANCE INFORMATION

by

answering questions and requests.

____ 10. PREPARES ELECTRICAL MAINTENANCE REPORTS

by

collecting, analyzing, and summarizing information and trends.

____ 11. MAINTAINS TECHNICAL KNOWLEDGE

by

attending educational workshops; reviewing technical publications; establishing personal networks.

____ 12. MAINTAINS CONTINUITY AMONG WORK TEAMS

by

documenting and communicating actions, irregularities, and continuing needs.

JOB TITLE: Maintenance Electrician

ESSENTIAL JOB RESULTS:

% of
Time

_____ 13. MAINTAINS SAFE AND CLEAN WORKING ENVIRONMENT
    by
    complying with procedures, rules, and
    regulations.

% of
Time

_____ 14. CONTRIBUTES TO TEAM EFFORT
    by
    accomplishing related results as needed.

JOB TITLE: **Maintenance Manager**

JOB PURPOSE: **PROVIDES A SAFE, COMFORTABLE OPERATING ENVIRONMENT**

by

directing installation, maintenance, and repair of machines, tools, equipment, and utility systems.

ESSENTIAL JOB RESULTS:

% of
Time

____ 1. IDENTIFIES CURRENT AND FUTURE MAINTENANCE REQUIREMENTS
by
establishing rapport with management, engineering, and production personnel, tradesmen, technicians, and other persons in a position to understand maintenance requirements.

____ 2. ACHIEVES FINANCIAL OBJECTIVES
by
preparing an annual maintenance budget; scheduling expenditures; analyzing variances; initiating corrective actions.

____ 3. ENSURES PRODUCTION OPERATIONS
by
determining work priorities and scheduling repair, maintenance, and installation of machines, tools, and equipment.

____ 4. SUPPORTS PRODUCT DEVELOPMENT AND IMPROVEMENT
by
reviewing new product plans; discussing equipment needs and modifications with design engineers; coordinating activities of technicians and workers fabricating or modifying machines, tools, or equipment.

____ 5. PROVIDES HEAT, STEAM, ELECTRIC POWER, GAS, AND AIR
by
directing installation of, modifications to, and maintenance activities on utility systems.

% of
Time

____ 6. DESIGNS, IMPLEMENTS, AND MODIFIES PREVENTIVE MAINTENANCE PROGRAMS
by
reviewing production, quality control, and maintenance reports and statistics; inspecting operating machines, equipment, and systems for conformance with operational standards.

____ 7. DIRECTS MAINTENANCE OPERATIONS
by
initiating, coordinating, and enforcing program, operational, and personnel policies and procedures.

____ 8. RESOLVES MAINTENANCE PROBLEMS
by
conferring with management, engineering, and quality control personnel.

____ 9. PROTECTS EMPLOYEES AND VISITORS
by
maintaining a safe and clean working environment.

____ 10. COMPLETES MAINTENANCE OPERATIONAL REQUIREMENTS
by
scheduling and assigning employees; following up on work results.

____ 11. MAINTAINS MAINTENANCE STAFF
by
recruiting, selecting, orienting, and training employees.

JOB TITLE: Maintenance Manager

ESSENTIAL JOB RESULTS:

% of
Time

_____ 12. MAINTAINS MAINTENANCE STAFF JOB RESULTS
by
coaching, counseling, and disciplining
employees; planning, monitoring, and
appraising job results.

_____ 13. MAINTAINS PROFESSIONAL AND TECHNICAL KNOWLEDGE
by
attending educational workshops; reviewing
professional publications; establishing
personal networks; participating in
professional societies.

% of
Time

_____ 14. CONTRIBUTES TO TEAM EFFORT
by
accomplishing related results as needed.

JOB TITLE: Maintenance Mechanic

JOB PURPOSE: **MAINTAINS PRODUCTION AND QUALITY**

by

ensuring operation of machinery and mechanical equipment.

ESSENTIAL JOB RESULTS:

*% of
Time*

___ 1. ENSURES OPERATION OF MACHINERY AND MECHANICAL EQUIPMENT
by
completing preventive maintenance requirements on engines, motors, pneumatic tools, conveyor systems, and production machines; following diagrams, sketches, operations manuals, manufacturer's instructions, and engineering specifications; troubleshooting malfunctions.

___ 2. LOCATES SOURCES OF PROBLEMS
by
observing mechanical devices in operation; listening for problems; using precision measuring and testing instruments.

___ 3. REMOVES DEFECTIVE PARTS
by
dismantling devices; using hoists, cranes, and hand and power tools; examining form and texture of parts.

___ 4. DETERMINES CHANGES IN DIMENSIONAL REQUIREMENTS OF PARTS
by
inspecting used parts; using rules, calipers, micrometers, and other measuring instruments.

___ 5. ADJUSTS FUNCTIONAL PARTS OF DEVICES AND CONTROL INSTRUMENTS
by
using hand tools, levels, plumb bobs, and straightedges.

___ 6. CONTROLS DOWNTIME
by
informing production workers of routine preventive maintenance techniques; monitoring compliance.

*% of
Time*

___ 7. FABRICATES REPAIR PARTS
by
using machine shop instrumentation and equipment.

___ 8. MAINTAINS EQUIPMENT, PARTS, AND SUPPLIES INVENTORIES
by
checking stock to determine inventory level; anticipating needed equipment, parts, and supplies; placing and expediting orders; verifying receipt.

___ 9. CONSERVES MAINTENANCE RESOURCES
by
using equipment and supplies as needed to accomplish job results.

___ 10. PROVIDES MECHANICAL MAINTENANCE INFORMATION
by
answering questions and requests.

___ 11. PREPARES MECHANICAL MAINTENANCE REPORTS
by
collecting, analyzing, and summarizing information and trends.

___ 12. MAINTAINS TECHNICAL KNOWLEDGE
by
attending educational workshops; reviewing technical publications; establishing personal networks.

___ 13. MAINTAINS CONTINUITY AMONG WORK TEAMS
by
documenting and communicating actions, irregularities, and continuing needs.

JOB TITLE: Maintenance Mechanic

ESSENTIAL JOB RESULTS:

% of
Time

_____ 14. MAINTAINS SAFE AND CLEAN WORKING ENVIRONMENT
by
complying with procedures, rules, and
regulations.

% of
Time

_____ 15. CONTRIBUTES TO TEAM EFFORT
by
accomplishing related results as needed.

JOB PURPOSE: **DEVELOPS AND IMPROVES MANUFACTURING PROCESSES**
by

studying product and manufacturing methods.

ESSENTIAL JOB RESULTS:

% of Time

____ 1. EVALUATES MANUFACTURING PROCESSES
by
designing and conducting research programs; applying knowledge of product design, fabrication, assembly, tooling, and materials; conferring with equipment vendors; soliciting observations from operators.

____ 2. DEVELOPS MANUFACTURING PROCESSES
by
studying product requirements; researching, designing, modifying, and testing manufacturing methods and equipment; conferring with equipment vendors.

____ 3. IMPROVES MANUFACTURING EFFICIENCY
by
analyzing and planning work flow, space requirements, and equipment layout.

____ 4. ASSURES PRODUCT AND PROCESS QUALITY
by
designing testing methods; testing finished-product and process capabilities; establishing standards; confirming manufacturing processes.

____ 5. PROVIDES MANUFACTURING DECISION-MAKING INFORMATION
by
calculating production, labor, and material costs; reviewing production schedules; estimating future requirements.

____ 6. PREPARES PRODUCT AND PROCESS REPORTS
by
collecting, analyzing, and summarizing information and trends.

% of Time

____ 7. PROVIDES MANUFACTURING ENGINEERING INFORMATION
by
answering questions and requests.

____ 8. MAINTAINS PRODUCT AND COMPANY REPUTATION
by
complying with government regulations.

____ 9. KEEPS EQUIPMENT OPERATIONAL
by
coordinating maintenance and repair services; following manufacturer's instructions and established procedures; requesting special service.

____ 10. MAINTAINS PRODUCT AND PROCESS DATA BASE
by
writing computer programs; entering data.

____ 11. COMPLETES DESIGN AND DEVELOPMENT PROJECTS
by
training and guiding technicians.

____ 12. MAINTAINS PROFESSIONAL AND TECHNICAL KNOWLEDGE
by
attending educational workshops; reviewing professional publications; establishing personal networks; participating in professional societies.

____ 13. CONTRIBUTES TO TEAM EFFORT
by
accomplishing related results as needed.

JOB TITLE: Manufacturing Manager

JOB PURPOSE: **MANUFACTURES PRODUCTS**

by

designing and developing methods; establishing priorities; supervising personnel.

ESSENTIAL JOB RESULTS:

% of Time

____ 1. ESTABLISHES MANUFACTURING QUALITY STANDARDS, METHODS, FACILITIES, POLICIES, AND PROCEDURES
by
studying product requirements; obtaining engineering consultations; determining equipment and facility budgets.

____ 2. ESTABLISHES AN ORGANIZATION STRUCTURE
by
assigning responsibilities; delegating authority; recruiting, selecting, orienting, and training employees.

____ 3. DEVELOPS PRODUCTION PLAN
by
coordinating requirements with sales, engineering, procurement, and traffic departments.

____ 4. COMPLETES PRODUCTION PLAN
by
establishing priorities; scheduling activities and employees; monitoring progress; revising schedules; resolving problems.

____ 5. ENSURES OPERATION OF EQUIPMENT
by
establishing preventive maintenance requirements; conferring with manufacturers; contracting for special maintenance services; maintaining equipment inventories; evaluating new equipment and techniques.

% of Time

____ 6. MAINTAINS MANUFACTURING STAFF JOB RESULTS
by
coaching, counseling, and disciplining employees; answering grievances; planning, monitoring, and appraising job results.

____ 7. ACHIEVES FINANCIAL OBJECTIVES
by
preparing the manufacturing and maintenance budgets; scheduling expenditures; analyzing variances; compiling and studying costs; initiating corrective actions.

____ 8. PREPARES REPORTS
by
collecting, analyzing, and summarizing information and trends.

____ 9. MAINTAINS PROFESSIONAL AND TECHNICAL KNOWLEDGE
by
attending educational workshops; reviewing professional publications; establishing personal networks; visiting other manufacturing facilities; participating in professional societies.

____ 10. CONTRIBUTES TO TEAM EFFORT
by
accomplishing related results as needed.

JOB TITLE: Marketing Director

JOB PURPOSE: **DEVELOPS MARKETING STRATEGY**
by
studying economic indicators; tracking changes in supply and demand;
identifying customers and their current and future needs; monitoring the
competition.

ESSENTIAL JOB RESULTS:

*% of
Time*

____ 1. CONTRIBUTES TO MARKETING EFFECTIVENESS
by
identifying short-term and long-range issues
that must be addressed; providing
information and commentary pertinent to
deliberations; recommending options and
courses of action; implementing directives.

____ 2. OBTAINS MARKET SHARE
by
developing marketing plans and programs for
each product; directing promotional support.

____ 3. MAINTAINS RELATIONS WITH CUSTOMERS
by
organizing and developing specific customer-
relations programs; determining company
presence at conventions, annual meetings,
trade associations, and seminars.

____ 4. PROVIDES SHORT- AND LONG-TERM MARKET FORECASTS
AND REPORTS
by
directing market research collection,
analysis, and interpretation of market data.

____ 5. INFLUENCES PRESENT AND FUTURE PRODUCTS
by
determining and evaluating current and future
market trends.

____ 6. DEVELOPS NEW USES FOR EXISTING PRODUCTS
by
analyzing statistics regarding market
development; acquiring and analyzing data;
consulting with internal and external sources.

*% of
Time*

____ 7. MAINTAINS RESEARCH DATA BASE
by
identifying and assembling marketing
information.

____ 8. PROVIDES MARKETING INFORMATION
by
answering questions and requests.

____ 9. ACHIEVES FINANCIAL OBJECTIVES
by
preparing an annual budget; scheduling
expenditures; analyzing variances; initiating
corrective actions.

____ 10. COMPLETES MARKETING DEPARTMENT OPERATIONAL
REQUIREMENTS
by
scheduling and assigning employees;
following up on work results.

____ 11. MAINTAINS MARKETING STAFF
by
recruiting, selecting, orienting, and training
employees.

____ 12. MAINTAINS MARKETING STAFF JOB RESULTS
by
counseling and disciplining employees;
planning, monitoring, and appraising job
results.

____ 13. DEVELOPS MARKETING STAFF
by
providing information, educational
opportunities, and experiential growth
opportunities.

JOB TITLE: Marketing Director

ESSENTIAL JOB RESULTS:

% of
Time

____ 14. MAINTAINS PROFESSIONAL AND TECHNICAL KNOWLEDGE
      by
      attending educational workshops; reviewing
      professional publications; establishing
      personal networks; participating in
      professional societies.

% of
Time

____ 15. CONTRIBUTES TO TEAM EFFORT
      by
      accomplishing related results as needed.

JOB PURPOSE: **IDENTIFIES MARKETING OPPORTUNITIES AND RESOLVES MARKETING PROBLEMS**

by

researching and analyzing market data.

ESSENTIAL JOB RESULTS:

% of Time

____ 1. DEVELOPS MARKET RESEARCH DESIGN
by
identifying objectives; selecting research methodologies.

____ 2. CONDUCTS MARKETING RESEARCH
by
interviewing company personnel; contracting for outside consumer testing.

____ 3. TESTS PRODUCTS
by
composing and printing questionnaires; coding answers; analyzing and interpreting data; preparing reports; making product recommendations.

____ 4. PROVIDES HISTORICAL MARKET RESEARCH INFORMATION
by
establishing and maintaining market research data storage and retrieval systems.

____ 5. DEVELOPS TREND DATA
by
establishing disciplines and standards for each type of research.

____ 6. PROVIDES TEST PANELS
by
developing selection, training, and validation techniques.

% of Time

____ 7. RECOMMENDS RESEARCH TECHNIQUES TO BUSINESS UNITS
by
monitoring new developments in research techniques; attending educational workshops; reviewing professional publications; establishing personal networks; participating in professional societies.

____ 8. CONDUCTS TREND ANALYSES
by
participating in special economic and market segmentation studies.

____ 9. ACHIEVES FINANCIAL OBJECTIVES
by
monitoring annual budget; scheduling expenditures; analyzing variances; initiating corrective actions.

____ 10. CONTRIBUTES TO TEAM EFFORT
by
accomplishing related results as needed.

JOB PURPOSE: **MAINTAINS PRODUCTION AND DISTRIBUTION OF PRODUCT**
by
pulling orders from inventory; delivering production materials and
supplies; staging finished product.

ESSENTIAL JOB RESULTS:

*% of
Time*

____ 1. MAINTAINS INVENTORY
by
identifying, labeling, and placing materials
and supplies in stock; recording location of
inventory.

____ 2. LOCATES MATERIALS AND SUPPLIES
by
pulling and verifying materials and supplies
listed on production orders.

____ 3. MAINTAINS IN-PROCESS INVENTORY AT WORK CENTERS
by
delivering and opening materials and
supplies.

____ 4. DOCUMENTS MATERIALS AND SUPPLIES DISPOSITION
by
recording units delivered and location of
units.

____ 5. RECEIVES CREDIT-RETURN MATERIAL AND SUPPLIES FROM
PRODUCTION
by
verifying materials and supplies code and lot
number and quantity; placing materials in
stock.

*% of
Time*

____ 6. PREPARES FINISHED STOCK FOR SHIPMENT
by
identifying, pulling, packing, crating,
loading, and securing product.

____ 7. DOCUMENTS PRODUCT SHIPMENT
by
recording units shipped.

____ 8. MAINTAINS MATERIAL-HANDLING EQUIPMENT
by
completing pre-use inspections; making
operator repairs.

____ 9. CONTRIBUTES TO TEAM EFFORT
by
accomplishing related results as needed.

JOB TITLE: Mechanical Engineer

JOB PURPOSE: **DESIGNS MECHANICAL AND ELECTROMECHANICAL PRODUCTS AND SYSTEMS**

by

developing and testing specifications and methods.

ESSENTIAL JOB RESULTS:

% of Time

____ 1. EVALUATES MECHANICAL AND ELECTROMECHANICAL SYSTEMS AND PRODUCTS

by

designing and conducting research programs; applying principles of mechanics, thermodynamics, hydraulics, heat transfer, and materials.

____ 2. CONFIRMS SYSTEM AND PRODUCT CAPABILITIES

by

designing feasibility and testing methods; testing properties.

____ 3. DEVELOPS MECHANICAL AND ELECTROMECHANICAL PRODUCTS

by

studying customer requirements; researching and testing manufacturing and assembly methods and materials; soliciting observations from operators.

____ 4. DEVELOPS MANUFACTURING PROCESSES

by

designing and modifying equipment for fabricating, building, assembling, and installing components.

____ 5. ASSURES SYSTEM AND PRODUCT QUALITY

by

designing testing methods; testing finished-product and system capabilities; confirming fabrication, assembly, and installation processes.

____ 6. PREPARES PRODUCT REPORTS

by

collecting, analyzing, and summarizing information and trends.

% of Time

____ 7. PROVIDES ENGINEERING INFORMATION

by

answering questions and requests.

____ 8. MAINTAINS PRODUCT AND COMPANY REPUTATION

by

complying with government regulations.

____ 9. KEEPS EQUIPMENT OPERATIONAL

by

coordinating maintenance and repair services; following manufacturer's instructions and established procedures; requesting special services.

____ 10. MAINTAINS SYSTEM AND PRODUCT DATA BASE

by

writing computer programs and entering data.

____ 11. COMPLETES PROJECTS

by

training and guiding technicians.

____ 12. MAINTAINS PROFESSIONAL AND TECHNICAL KNOWLEDGE

by

attending educational workshops; reviewing professional publications; establishing personal networks; participating in professional societies.

____ 13. CONTRIBUTES TO TEAM EFFORT

by

accomplishing related results as needed.

191

JOB TITLE: Media Center Manager

JOB PURPOSE: **SUPPORTS COMMUNICATION OBJECTIVES**

by

selecting audiovisual media; producing media programs.

ESSENTIAL JOB RESULTS:

*% of
Time*

_____ 1. ADVISES PROGRAM MANAGERS
by
recommending media selection and mix,
format, presentation style, editorial content,
site selection, and budget.

_____ 2. ASSEMBLES PROJECT COMPONENTS
by
arranging for equipment, crew, set, lighting,
props, talent, script, graphics, music, etc.

_____ 3. PRODUCES PROGRAM
by
directing activities of crew and performers.

_____ 4. COMPLETES PROJECT
by
editing, duplicating, and packaging program.

_____ 5. SELECTS MEDIA EQUIPMENT
by
identifying communication requirements;
defining specifications; soliciting and
evaluating vendors and service.

_____ 6. MAINTAINS RESOURCE OF PROGRAMS AND EQUIPMENT
by
storing audiovisual programs, materials,
supplies, and equipment; training users.

_____ 7. ENSURES OPERATION OF AUDIOVISUAL EQUIPMENT
by
completing preventive maintenance
requirements; arranging for repairs.

*% of
Time*

_____ 8. MAINTAINS MEDIA STAFF
by
recruiting, selecting, orienting, and training
employees.

_____ 9. MAINTAINS MEDIA STAFF JOB RESULTS
by
coaching, counseling, and disciplining
employees; planning, monitoring, and
appraising job results.

_____ 10. MAINTAINS PROFESSIONAL AND TECHNICAL KNOWLEDGE
by
attending educational workshops; reviewing
professional publications; establishing
personal networks; participating in
professional societies.

_____ 11. ACHIEVES FINANCIAL OBJECTIVES
by
preparing annual media budget; scheduling
expenditures; analyzing variances; initiating
corrective actions.

_____ 12. CONTRIBUTES TO TEAM EFFORT
by
accomplishing related results as needed.

JOB TITLE: Medical Director

JOB PURPOSE: **PROMOTES AND MAINTAINS EMPLOYEE HEALTH**
by
developing health policies and procedures; rendering medical treatment.

ESSENTIAL JOB RESULTS:

*% of
Time*

_____ 1. IDENTIFIES MANAGEMENT AND EMPLOYEE HEALTH CONCERNS
by
surveying environmental, operational, and occupational conditions; recommending preventive health programs.

_____ 2. GUIDES AND PROMOTES HEALTHY WORK PERFORMANCE
by
recommending medical and health policies and procedures.

_____ 3. COMPLIES WITH FEDERAL, STATE, AND LOCAL HEALTH REQUIREMENTS
by
studying existing and new legislation; enforcing adherence to health requirements; advising management on needed actions.

_____ 4. ENFORCES MEDICAL AND HEALTH POLICIES
by
conducting preemployment, periodic, and special medical examinations.

_____ 5. STABILIZES OR CORRECTS PATIENT'S CONDITION
by
rendering first aid and emergency medical care.

_____ 6. COMPLETES TREATMENT PLAN
by
providing continuing observations and consultations.

_____ 7. COMPLIES WITH STANDARDS OF PRACTICE
by
supervising the professional and technical activities of medical staff.

*% of
Time*

_____ 8. PROMOTES HEALTHY WORK ENVIRONMENT
by
coordinating and cooperating with local, state, and regional health groups and agencies.

_____ 9. COMPLETES OPERATIONAL REQUIREMENTS
by
scheduling and assigning employees; following up on work results.

_____ 10. MAINTAINS MEDICAL STAFF
by
recruiting, selecting, orienting, and training employees.

_____ 11. MAINTAINS MEDICAL STAFF JOB RESULTS
by
coaching, counseling, and disciplining employees; planning, monitoring, and appraising job results.

_____ 12. MAINTAINS PROFESSIONAL AND TECHNICAL KNOWLEDGE
by
attending medical workshops; reviewing professional publications; establishing personal networks; participating in medical and health societies.

_____ 13. ACHIEVES FINANCIAL OBJECTIVES
by
preparing the annual medical budget; scheduling expenditures; analyzing variances; initiating corrective actions.

_____ 14. CONTRIBUTES TO TEAM EFFORT
by
accomplishing related results as needed.

JOB TITLE: Medical Records Technician

JOB PURPOSE: **MAINTAINS RECORD OF PATIENT CARE**

by

compiling, reviewing, and filing documentation of patient's condition, treatment, and health outcome.

ESSENTIAL JOB RESULTS:

% of Time

____ 1. MAINTAINS MEDICAL RECORDS OPERATIONS
by
following policies and procedures; reporting needed changes.

____ 2. INITIATES MEDICAL RECORD
by
searching master patient index; identifying existing patient records or need to assign a new number; interacting with registration areas and physicians' offices for information verification; processing or creating the record folder.

____ 3. ENSURES MEDICAL RECORD AVAILABILITY
by
routing records to admissions and emergency departments, physicians, and other authorized hospital staff; maintaining chart location systems.

____ 4. COMPLETES MEDICAL RECORD
by
reviewing information; notifying health care providers of record deficiencies; tracking outstanding records; notifying medical director of physicians in jeopardy of losing admitting privileges.

____ 5. RESOLVES MEDICAL RECORD DISCREPANCIES
by
collecting and analyzing information.

____ 6. MAINTAINS HISTORICAL REFERENCE
by
abstracting and coding clinical data, such as diseases, operations, procedures, and therapies, using standard classification systems; filing documents.

% of Time

____ 7. PREPARES STATISTICAL REPORTS
by
collecting and summarizing medical care and census information, such as types of diseases treated, surgery performed, and use of hospital beds.

____ 8. PROVIDES MEDICAL RECORD INFORMATION
by
answering questions and requests of patients, hospital staff, law firms, insurance companies, and government agencies.

____ 9. MAINTAINS PATIENT CONFIDENCE AND PROTECTS HOSPITAL OPERATIONS
by
keeping information confidential; following release-of-information protocols.

____ 10. MAINTAINS THE STABILITY AND REPUTATION OF THE HOSPITAL
by
complying with legal requirements.

____ 11. KEEPS EQUIPMENT OPERATIONAL
by
following manufacturer's instructions and established procedures.

____ 12. CONSERVES RESOURCES
by
using equipment and supplies as needed to accomplish job results.

____ 13. CONTRIBUTES TO TEAM EFFORT
by
accomplishing related results as needed.

JOB TITLE: Medical Technologist

JOB PURPOSE: **PROVIDES INFORMATION FOR DIAGNOSIS, TREATMENT, AND PREVENTION OF DISEASE**

by

conducting medical laboratory tests, procedures, experiments, and analyses.

ESSENTIAL JOB RESULTS:

% of Time

_____ 1. DETERMINES NORMAL AND ABNORMAL COMPONENTS OF BODY FLUIDS
by
conducting chemical analyses of blood, urine, spinal fluids, and gastric juices.

_____ 2. ANALYZES BLOOD CELLS
by
counting and identifying cells, using microscopic techniques and procedures.

_____ 3. PREPARES BLOOD, PLASMA, AND PLATELETS FOR TRANSFUSIONS
by
conducting blood group, type, and compatibility tests.

_____ 4. ENSURES OPERATION OF ANALYZERS, SPECTROPHOTOMETERS, COLORIMETERS, FLAME PHOTOMETERS, AND OTHER LABORATORY EQUIPMENT
by
calibrating; completing preventive maintenance requirements; following manufacturer's instructions; troubleshooting malfunctions; calling for repairs; maintaining equipment inventories; evaluating new equipment and techniques.

_____ 5. MAINTAINS LABORATORY SUPPLIES INVENTORY
by
checking stock to determine inventory level; anticipating needed supplies; placing and expediting orders for supplies; verifying receipt of supplies.

_____ 6. CONSERVES LABORATORY RESOURCES
by
using equipment and supplies as needed to accomplish job results.

% of Time

_____ 7. PROVIDES MEDICAL TECHNOLOGY INFORMATION
by
answering questions and requests.

_____ 8. PREPARES REPORTS OF TECHNOLOGICAL FINDINGS
by
collecting, analyzing, and summarizing information.

_____ 9. MAINTAINS PROFESSIONAL AND TECHNICAL KNOWLEDGE
by
attending educational workshops; reviewing professional publications; establishing personal networks; participating in professional societies.

_____ 10. MAINTAINS INTER- AND INTRADEPARTMENTAL WORK FLOW
by
fostering a spirit of cooperation.

_____ 11. MAINTAINS SAFE AND CLEAN WORKING ENVIRONMENT
by
complying with procedures, rules, and regulations.

_____ 12. PROTECTS PATIENTS AND EMPLOYEES
by
adhering to infection-control and hazardous waste policies and protocols; following identification procedures.

_____ 13. MAINTAINS PATIENT CONFIDENCE AND PROTECTS THE HOSPITAL
by
keeping information confidential.

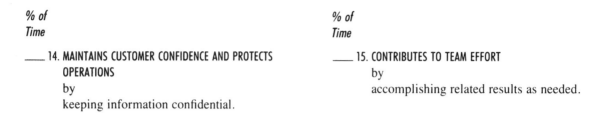

JOB TITLE: Medical Technologist

ESSENTIAL JOB RESULTS:

% of
Time

_____ 14. MAINTAINS CUSTOMER CONFIDENCE AND PROTECTS
OPERATIONS
by
keeping information confidential.

% of
Time

_____ 15. CONTRIBUTES TO TEAM EFFORT
by
accomplishing related results as needed.

JOB PURPOSE: PROVIDES A RECORD OF PATIENT CARE

by

transcribing and interpreting physicians' dictation into medical-legal documents.

ESSENTIAL JOB RESULTS:

% of Time

___ 1. PREPARES WORK TO BE ACCOMPLISHED

by

gathering and sorting transcription tapes and written instructions.

___ 2. DETERMINES FORMAT AND CONTENT

by

following written or dictated instructions.

___ 3. ESTABLISHES DOCUMENT FORMAT

by

entering commands for spacing, margins, type size, style and color, and other parameters.

___ 4. HELPS PHYSICIANS USE DICTATION EQUIPMENT

by

demonstrating dictation techniques and procedures.

___ 5. PREPARES DOCUMENTS

by

using transcription equipment; applying knowledge of medical terminology, anatomy, and physiology; employing listening skills to decipher various accents, dialects, and dictation styles; operating a word processor to input data.

___ 6. CORRECTS SPELLING AND MEDICAL TERMINOLOGY ERRORS

by

using dictionary and medical reference books.

% of Time

___ 7. EDITS DOCUMENTS

by

recognizing, interpreting, and evaluating repetitions, discrepancies, and inaccuracies in dictation; editing, revising, and clarifying without altering meaning and style.

___ 8. COMPLIES WITH MEDICAL-LEGAL POLICIES, PROCEDURES, AND PRIORITIES

by

perceiving medical documents as legal evidence, such as amendments of recordings; seeking clarification; recognizing and reporting problems, errors, and discrepancies to management.

___ 9. STORES COMPLETED DOCUMENTS

by

entering documents in data base.

___ 10. PRINTS DOCUMENTS

by

loading paper in printer; changing printing mechanisms; generating print commands.

___ 11. DISTRIBUTES DOCUMENTS

by

routing to physicians for editing and approvals.

___ 12. KEEPS EQUIPMENT OPERATIONAL

by

following manufacturer's instructions and established procedures.

```
┌──────────────────────────────────────────────────────────────┐
│ JOB TITLE: Medical Transcriptionist                          │
└──────────────────────────────────────────────────────────────┘
```

ESSENTIAL JOB RESULTS:

% of
Time

_____ 13. MAINTAINS SUPPLIES INVENTORY
      by
      checking stock to determine inventory level;
      anticipating needed supplies; placing and
      expediting orders for supplies; verifying
      receipt of supplies.

_____ 14. MAINTAINS PATIENT CONFIDENCE AND PROTECTS
      OPERATIONS
      by
      keeping information confidential.

% of
Time

_____ 15. CONTRIBUTES TO TEAM EFFORT
      by
      accomplishing related results as needed.

JOB TITLE: Methods and Procedures Analyst

JOB PURPOSE: **IMPROVES OPERATING EFFICIENCY**

by

developing and maintaining methods and procedures.

ESSENTIAL JOB RESULTS:

% of
Time

____ 1. IDENTIFIES OPERATIONAL OBJECTIVES
by
studying functions and requirements;
conferring with managers and employees.

____ 2. RECOMMENDS OPERATIONAL CONTROLS AND GUIDELINES
by
describing methods and writing procedures.

____ 3. OBTAINS APPROVAL OF OPERATIONAL CONTROLS AND GUIDELINES
by
submitting methods and procedures for approval.

____ 4. MAINTAINS REFERENCE OF METHODS AND PROCEDURES
by
filing documents, manuals, and instructions.

____ 5. RECOMMENDS CHANGES
by
identifying problems; developing improvements.

____ 6. COMMUNICATES CHANGES
by
distributing new and updated guidelines.

____ 7. SUPPORTS INFORMATION ANALYSIS PROJECTS
by
participating in development of project scope, analysis of operation function, and development of procedures.

% of
Time

____ 8. SUPPORTS TRAINING AND DEVELOPMENT PROGRAMS
by
reviewing training materials for conformance to established methods and procedures; recommending integration of approaches.

____ 9. RECOMMENDS EQUIPMENT
by
identifying operational objectives; studying requirements and proposed solutions.

____ 10. RECOMMENDS WORK STANDARDS
by
studying operational requirements and methods; applying standard measurements.

____ 11. CONTROLS PAPERWORK
by
designing, revising, consolidating, purchasing, or preparing forms.

____ 12. CONTRIBUTES TO TEAM EFFORT
by
accomplishing related results as needed.

JOB TITLE: Mixer

JOB PURPOSE: **PRODUCES PRODUCT**

by

mixing raw materials.

ESSENTIAL JOB RESULTS:

% of
Time

____ 1. CONTROLS RAW MATERIALS
by
ordering product requirements; receiving and
verifying order; recording raw materials
usage.

____ 2. PREPARES MIXER
by
setting equipment controls; weighing and
loading raw materials into the mixer.

____ 3. PRODUCES PRODUCT
by
mixing raw materials; monitoring and
adjusting the mixing process.

____ 4. PREPARES PRODUCT FOR NEXT PROCESS
by
unloading and storing the finished batch.

____ 5. MAINTAINS QUALITY STANDARDS
by
verifying weight and contents of raw
materials; conducting in-process batch
inspections; documenting all process events;
approving product for next step in
manufacturing process.

% of
Time

____ 6. PREPARES FOR NEXT BATCH
by
cleaning mixing equipment.

____ 7. MAINTAINS OPERATIONS
by
following policies and procedures; reporting
needed changes.

____ 8. MAINTAINS SAFE AND CLEAN WORKING ENVIRONMENT
by
complying with procedures, rules, and
regulations.

____ 9. CONTRIBUTES TO TEAM EFFORT
by
accomplishing related results as needed.

JOB PURPOSE: **PROMOTES AND RESTORES PATIENTS' HEALTH**

by

developing day-to-day management and long-term planning of the patient care area; directing and developing staff; collaborating with physicians and multidisciplinary professional staffs; providing physical and psychological support for patients, friends, and families.

ESSENTIAL JOB RESULTS:

% of Time

____ 1. IDENTIFIES PATIENT SERVICE REQUIREMENTS
by
establishing personal rapport with potential and actual patients and other persons in a position to understand service requirements.

____ 2. MAINTAINS NURSING GUIDELINES
by
writing and updating policies and procedures.

____ 3. MAINTAINS NURSING OPERATIONS
by
initiating, coordinating, and enforcing program, operational, and personnel policies and procedures.

____ 4. ASSURES QUALITY OF CARE
by
developing and interpreting hospital and nursing division's philosophies and standards of care; enforcing adherence to state board of nursing and State Nurse Practice Act requirements and to other governing agency regulations; measuring health outcomes against standards; making or recommending adjustments.

____ 5. MAINTAINS NURSING STAFF
by
recruiting, selecting, orienting, and training nurses and auxiliary staff.

____ 6. COMPLETES PATIENT CARE REQUIREMENTS
by
scheduling and assigning nursing and staff; following up on work results.

% of Time

____ 7. MAINTAINS NURSING STAFF JOB RESULTS
by
coaching, counseling, and disciplining employees; planning, monitoring, and appraising job results.

____ 8. MAINTAINS PROFESSIONAL AND TECHNICAL KNOWLEDGE
by
attending educational workshops; reviewing professional publications; establishing personal networks; participating in professional societies.

____ 9. ESTABLISHES A COMPASSIONATE ENVIRONMENT
by
providing emotional, psychological, and spiritual support to patients, friends, and families.

____ 10. PROMOTES PATIENT'S INDEPENDENCE
by
establishing patient care goals; teaching and counseling patient, friends, and family and reinforcing their understanding of disease, medications, and self-care skills.

____ 11. PROVIDES INFORMATION TO PATIENTS AND HEALTH CARE TEAM
by
answering questions and requests.

____ 12. RESOLVES PATIENT NEEDS
by
utilizing multidisciplinary team strategies.

JOB TITLE: Nurse Manager

ESSENTIAL JOB RESULTS:

*% of
Time*

_____ 13. MAINTAINS SAFE AND CLEAN WORKING ENVIRONMENT
by
designing and implementing procedures, rules, and regulations; calling for assistance from other health care professionals.

_____ 14. PROTECTS PATIENTS AND EMPLOYEES
by
developing and interpreting infection-control policies and protocols; enforcing medication administration, storage procedures, and controlled substance regulations.

_____ 15. MAINTAINS PATIENT CONFIDENCE AND PROTECTS OPERATIONS
by
monitoring confidential information processing.

_____ 16. MAINTAINS DOCUMENTATION OF PATIENT CARE SERVICES
by
auditing patient and department records.

_____ 17. ACHIEVES FINANCIAL OBJECTIVES
by
preparing an annual budget; scheduling expenditures; analyzing variances; initiating corrective actions.

_____ 18. ENSURES OPERATION OF MEDICAL AND ADMINISTRATIVE EQUIPMENT
by
verifying emergency equipment availability; completing preventive maintenance requirements; following manufacturer's instructions; troubleshooting malfunctions; calling for repairs; maintaining equipment inventories; evaluating new equipment and techniques.

*% of
Time*

_____ 19. MAINTAINS NURSING SUPPLIES INVENTORY
by
studying usage reports; identifying trends; anticipating needed supplies; approving requisitions and cost allocations.

_____ 20. CONSERVES NURSING RESOURCES
by
using equipment and supplies as needed to accomplish job results.

_____ 21. MAINTAINS PROFESSIONAL AND TECHNICAL KNOWLEDGE
by
attending educational workshops; reviewing professional publications; establishing personal networks; participating in professional societies.

_____ 22. MAINTAINS A COOPERATIVE RELATIONSHIP AMONG HEALTH CARE TEAMS
by
communicating information; responding to requests; building rapport; participating in team problem-solving methods.

_____ 23. CONTRIBUTES TO TEAM EFFORT
by
accomplishing related results as needed.

JOB PURPOSE: PROMOTES AND RESTORES PATIENTS' HEALTH

by

completing the nursing process; collaborating with physicians and multidisciplinary team members; providing physical and psychological support to patients, friends, and families; supervising assigned team members.

ESSENTIAL JOB RESULTS:

*% of
Time*

____ 1. IDENTIFIES PATIENT CARE REQUIREMENTS
by
establishing personal rapport with potential and actual patients and other persons in a position to understand care requirements.

____ 2. ESTABLISHES A COMPASSIONATE ENVIRONMENT
by
providing emotional, psychological, and spiritual support to patients, friends, and families.

____ 3. PROMOTES PATIENT'S INDEPENDENCE
by
establishing patient care goals; teaching patient, friends, and family to understand condition, medications, and self-care skills; answering questions.

____ 4. ASSURES QUALITY OF CARE
by
adhering to therapeutic standards; measuring health outcomes against patient care goals and standards; making or recommending necessary adjustments; following hospital and nursing division's philosophies and standards of care set by state board of nursing, State Nurse Practice Act, and other governing agency regulations.

____ 5. RESOLVES PATIENT PROBLEMS AND NEEDS
by
utilizing multidisciplinary team strategies.

*% of
Time*

____ 6. MAINTAINS SAFE AND CLEAN WORKING ENVIRONMENT
by
complying with procedures, rules, and regulations; calling for assistance from health care support personnel.

____ 7. PROTECTS PATIENTS AND EMPLOYEES
by
adhering to infection-control policies and protocols, medication administration and storage procedures, and controlled substance regulations.

____ 8. DOCUMENTS PATIENT CARE SERVICES
by
charting in patient and department records.

____ 9. MAINTAINS CONTINUITY AMONG NURSING TEAMS
by
documenting and communicating actions, irregularities, and continuing needs.

____ 10. MAINTAINS PATIENT CONFIDENCE AND PROTECTS OPERATIONS
by
keeping information confidential.

____ 11. ENSURES OPERATION OF EQUIPMENT
by
completing preventive maintenance requirements; following manufacturer's instructions; troubleshooting malfunctions; calling for repairs; maintaining equipment inventories; evaluating new equipment and techniques.

JOB TITLE: Nurse, Registered

ESSENTIAL JOB RESULTS:

% of Time

____ 12. MAINTAINS NURSING SUPPLIES INVENTORY
by
checking stock to determine inventory level;
anticipating needed supplies; placing and
expediting orders for supplies; verifying
receipt of supplies; using equipment and
supplies as needed to accomplish job results.

____ 13. MAINTAINS PROFESSIONAL AND TECHNICAL KNOWLEDGE
by
attending educational workshops; reviewing
professional publications; establishing
personal networks; participating in
professional societies.

% of Time

____ 14. MAINTAINS A COOPERATIVE RELATIONSHIP AMONG HEALTH CARE TEAMS
by
communicating information; responding to
requests; building rapport; participating in
team problem-solving methods.

____ 15. CONTRIBUTES TO TEAM EFFORT
by
accomplishing related results as needed.

JOB TITLE: Occupational Therapist

JOB PURPOSE: **FACILITATES DEVELOPMENT AND REHABILITATION OF PATIENTS WITH MENTAL, EMOTIONAL, AND PHYSICAL DISABILITIES**

by

planning and administering medically prescribed occupational therapy.

ESSENTIAL JOB RESULTS:

% of Time

_____ 1. MEETS THE PATIENT'S GOALS AND NEEDS AND PROVIDES QUALITY CARE

by

assessing and interpreting evaluations and test results; determining occupational therapy treatment plans in consultation with physicians or by prescription.

_____ 2. HELPS PATIENT DEVELOP OR REGAIN PHYSICAL OR MENTAL FUNCTIONING OR ADJUST TO DISABILITIES

by

implementing programs involving manual arts and crafts, practice in functional, prevocational, vocational, and homemaking skills, activities of daily living, and sensorimotor, educational, recreational, and social activities; directing aides, technicians, and assistants.

_____ 3. PROMOTES MAXIMUM INDEPENDENCE

by

selecting and constructing therapies according to individual's physical capacity, intelligence level, and interest.

_____ 4. PREPARES PATIENT FOR RETURN TO EMPLOYMENT

by

consulting with employers; determining potential employee difficulties; retraining employees; helping employers understand necessary physical and job result accommodations.

_____ 5. EVALUATES RESULTS OF OCCUPATIONAL THERAPY

by

observing, noting, and evaluating patient's progress; recommending and implementing adjustments and modifications.

% of Time

_____ 6. COMPLETES DISCHARGE PLANNING

by

consulting with physicians, nurses, social workers, and other health care workers; contributing to patient care conferences.

_____ 7. ASSURES CONTINUATION OF THERAPEUTIC PLAN FOLLOWING DISCHARGE

by

designing and instructing patients, families, and caregivers in home exercise programs; recommending and/or providing assistive equipment; recommending outpatient or home health follow-up programs.

_____ 8. DOCUMENTS PATIENT CARE SERVICES

by

charting in patient and department records.

_____ 9. MAINTAINS PATIENT CONFIDENCE AND PROTECTS HOSPITAL OPERATIONS

by

keeping information confidential.

_____ 10. MAINTAINS SAFE AND CLEAN WORKING ENVIRONMENT

by

complying with procedures, rules, and regulations.

_____ 11. PROTECTS PATIENTS AND EMPLOYEES

by

adhering to infection-control policies and protocols.

JOB TITLE: **Occupational Therapist**

ESSENTIAL JOB RESULTS:

% of
Time

____ 12. ENSURES OPERATION OF EQUIPMENT
by
completing preventive maintenance
requirements; following manufacturer's
instructions; troubleshooting malfunctions;
calling for repairs.

____ 13. MAINTAINS PROFESSIONAL AND TECHNICAL KNOWLEDGE
by
attending educational workshops; reviewing
professional publications; establishing
personal networks; participating in
professional societies.

____ 14. DEVELOPS OCCUPATIONAL THERAPY STAFF
by
providing information; developing and
conducting in-service training programs.

% of
Time

____ 15. COMPLIES WITH FEDERAL, STATE, AND LOCAL LEGAL AND
CERTIFICATION REQUIREMENTS
by
studying existing and new legislation;
anticipating future legislation; enforcing
adherence to requirements; advising
management on needed actions.

____ 16. CONTRIBUTES TO TEAM EFFORT
by
accomplishing related results as needed.

JOB TITLE: Office Manager

JOB PURPOSE: SUPPORTS COMPANY OPERATIONS

by

maintaining office systems; supervising staff.

ESSENTIAL JOB RESULTS:

% of
Time

_____ 1. MAINTAINS OFFICE SERVICES

by

organizing office operations and procedures; preparing payroll; controlling correspondence; designing filing systems; reviewing and approving supply requisitions; assigning and monitoring clerical functions.

_____ 2. PROVIDES HISTORICAL REFERENCE

by

defining procedures for retention, protection, retrieval, transfer, and disposal of records.

_____ 3. MAINTAINS OFFICE EFFICIENCY

by

planning and implementing office systems, layouts, and equipment procurement.

_____ 4. DESIGNS AND IMPLEMENTS OFFICE POLICIES

by

establishing standards and procedures; measuring results against standards; making necessary adjustments.

_____ 5. COMPLETES OPERATIONAL REQUIREMENTS

by

scheduling and assigning employees; following up on work results.

_____ 6. KEEPS MANAGEMENT INFORMED

by

reviewing and analyzing special reports; summarizing information; identifying trends.

% of
Time

_____ 7. MAINTAINS OFFICE STAFF

by

recruiting, selecting, orienting, and training employees.

_____ 8. MAINTAINS OFFICE STAFF JOB RESULTS

by

coaching, counseling, and disciplining employees; planning, monitoring, and appraising job results.

_____ 9. MAINTAINS PROFESSIONAL AND TECHNICAL KNOWLEDGE

by

attending educational workshops; reviewing professional publications; establishing personal networks; participating in professional societies.

_____ 10. ACHIEVES FINANCIAL OBJECTIVES

by

preparing an annual budget; scheduling expenditures; analyzing variances; initiating corrective actions.

_____ 11. CONTRIBUTES TO TEAM EFFORT

by

accomplishing related results as needed.

JOB TITLE: Operations Manager

JOB PURPOSE: **MAINTAINS BANK OPERATIONS**

by

training, scheduling, and monitoring staff; enforcing standards and procedures.

ESSENTIAL JOB RESULTS:

% of Time

_____ 1. COMPLETES OPERATIONAL REQUIREMENTS
by
scheduling and assigning employees; following up on work results.

_____ 2. MAINTAINS OPERATIONS
by
initiating, coordinating, and enforcing standards and procedures.

_____ 3. ENSURES COMPLIANCE WITH INTERNAL CONTROLS
by
auditing and verifying records, reports, and practices.

_____ 4. MEETS CASH REQUIREMENTS
by
adjusting supply of money on hand.

_____ 5. COMPLIES WITH FEDERAL, STATE, AND LOCAL LEGAL REQUIREMENTS
by
studying existing and new legislation; anticipating future legislation; enforcing adherence to requirements; advising management on needed actions.

_____ 6. PREPARES AUDIT REPORTS
by
collecting, analyzing, and summarizing information and trends.

% of Time

_____ 7. MAINTAINS HISTORICAL RECORDS
by
filing documents.

_____ 8. MAINTAINS OPERATIONS STAFF
by
recruiting, selecting, orienting, and training employees.

_____ 9. MAINTAINS OPERATIONS STAFF JOB RESULTS
by
coaching, counseling, and disciplining employees; planning, monitoring, and appraising job results.

_____ 10. MAINTAINS PROFESSIONAL AND TECHNICAL KNOWLEDGE
by
attending educational workshops; reviewing professional publications; establishing personal networks; participating in professional societies.

_____ 11. ACHIEVES FINANCIAL OBJECTIVES
by
preparing the operations budget; scheduling expenditures; analyzing variances; initiating corrective actions.

_____ 12. CONTRIBUTES TO TEAM EFFORT
by
accomplishing related results as needed.

JOB PURPOSE: DELIVERS MERCHANDISE TO CUSTOMERS

by

filling orders.

ESSENTIAL JOB RESULTS:

% of
Time

____ 1. PREPARES WORK TO BE ACCOMPLISHED
by
gathering and sorting documents.

____ 2. RECEIVES ORDERS
by
reading mail and facsimiles; answering the
telephone.

____ 3. COMPLETES ORDERS
by
editing for price and nomenclature;
calculating unit prices and shipping costs;
verifying product availability.

____ 4. KEEPS CUSTOMERS INFORMED
by
confirming and clarifying orders; noting
shipping or back-order delays.

____ 5. ENSURES DELIVERY
by
routing orders to departments for filling;
initiating purchase orders; tracking delayed
orders.

% of
Time

____ 6. PROVIDES INFORMATION
by
answering questions.

____ 7. MAINTAINS HISTORICAL RECORDS
by
filing orders and related documents.

____ 8. MAINTAINS OPERATIONS
by
following policies and procedures; reporting
needed changes.

____ 9. PREPARES REPORTS
by
collecting, analyzing, and summarizing
information.

____ 10. MAINTAINS WORK FLOW
by
sorting and delivering information.

____ 11. CONTRIBUTES TO TEAM EFFORT
by
accomplishing related results as needed.

JOB TITLE: Organization Development Consultant

JOB PURPOSE: **IMPROVES ORGANIZATIONAL RESULTS**

by

assessing performance; diagnosing problems; recommending courses of action.

ESSENTIAL JOB RESULTS:

% of Time

_____ 1. ASSESSES EFFECTIVENESS OF ORGANIZATION STRUCTURE
by
studying clarity of mission, strategy, objectives, priorities, division of work, accountabilities, and communication systems.

_____ 2. ASSESSES UTILIZATION OF HUMAN RESOURCES
by
studying staffing resources, job result outcomes, succession plans, and career development.

_____ 3. DIAGNOSES ORGANIZATION PROBLEMS
by
examining performance records; surveying and interviewing managers and employees regarding efficiency, effectiveness, morale, climate, and profitability.

_____ 4. RESOLVES ORGANIZATION PROBLEMS
by
presenting and evaluating options; guiding decisions; recommending courses of action.

% of Time

_____ 5. IMPROVES ORGANIZATION RESULTS
by
identifying potential projects; introducing new practices; presenting action plans; defining and recommending policies and procedures; designing and conducting team building and management training.

_____ 6. MAINTAINS PROFESSIONAL AND TECHNICAL KNOWLEDGE
by
attending educational workshops; reviewing professional publications; establishing personal networks; participating in professional societies.

_____ 7. CONTRIBUTES TO TEAM EFFORT
by
accomplishing related results as needed.

JOB TITLE: Packaging Engineer

JOB PURPOSE: **PROTECTS PRODUCT AND CONSUMER**

by

designing and developing packaging containers.

ESSENTIAL JOB RESULTS:

% of Time

____ 1. DESIGNS AND DEVELOPS PACKAGING CONTAINERS
by
studying engineering drawings, physical characteristics of product, handling and safety requirements, consumer preferences, and materials; applying knowledge of packaging methods.

____ 2. DETERMINES FEASIBILITY OF PACKAGING CONTAINERS
by
building models; testing methods and containers; determining equipment requirements and costs.

____ 3. CONFIRMS PACKAGING DESIGN
by
conferring and collaborating with purchasing, production, and marketing departments.

____ 4. MAINTAINS PROFESSIONAL AND TECHNICAL KNOWLEDGE
by
tracking packaging innovations; attending educational workshops; reviewing engineering and marketing publications; establishing personal networks; participating in professional societies.

% of Time

____ 5. COMPLIES WITH FEDERAL, STATE, AND LOCAL LEGAL REQUIREMENTS
by
studying existing and new packaging legislation; anticipating future legislation; enforcing adherence to requirements; advising management on needed actions.

____ 6. PREPARES REPORTS
by
collecting, analyzing, and summarizing information and trends.

____ 7. DOCUMENTS ACTIONS
by
completing engineering logs.

____ 8. CONTRIBUTES TO TEAM EFFORT
by
accomplishing related results as needed.

JOB TITLE: Parcel Post Clerk

JOB PURPOSE: **MAILS PACKAGES**

by

wrapping, inspecting, weighing, and affixing postage; following

company and postal regulations.

ESSENTIAL JOB RESULTS:

*% of
Time*

_____ 1. WRAPS OR INSPECTS PACKAGES
by
complying with company standards and
postal regulations.

_____ 2. AFFIXES POSTAGE
by
weighing packages; referring to parcel post
zone book for charges and insurance rates.

_____ 3. MAINTAINS PARCEL POST LOG
by
recording value, charges, and destination of
packages.

_____ 4. IDENTIFIES C.O.D. CHARGES
by
verifying cost of order, shipping, and other
charges; completing and affixing C.O.D. card
to package.

_____ 5. ADDRESSES PACKAGES
by
entering data; comparing addresses to
records.

_____ 6. PREPARES PARCELS FOR SHIPMENT
by
referencing destinations; sorting by parcel
post zones.

*% of
Time*

_____ 7. PROVIDES PARCEL POST INFORMATION
by
answering questions and requests.

_____ 8. MAINTAINS PARCEL POST SUPPLIES INVENTORY
by
checking stock to determine inventory level;
anticipating needed supplies; placing and
expediting orders for supplies; verifying
receipt of supplies.

_____ 9. MAINTAINS OPERATIONS
by
following policies and procedures; reporting
needed changes.

_____ 10. KEEPS EQUIPMENT OPERATIONAL
by
following manufacturer's instructions and
established procedures.

_____ 11. CONTRIBUTES TO TEAM EFFORT
by
accomplishing related results as needed.

JOB TITLE: Patient Care Unit Clerk

JOB PURPOSE: SUPPORTS PATIENT CARE DELIVERY

by

providing clerical services.

ESSENTIAL JOB RESULTS:

% of Time

____ 1. HELPS PATIENTS

by

responding to intercom requests; obtaining needed services from nurses, licensed practical nurses, physicians, aides, and other hospital personnel.

____ 2. WELCOMES VISITORS

by

greeting visitors, in person or on the telephone; answering inquiries; relaying calls to patients; giving directions; referring inquiries to nursing and physician staff.

____ 3. PROVIDES INFORMATION

by

answering questions and requests.

____ 4. ESTABLISHES PATIENT RECORD

by

preparing folder; assigning patient number; completing patient identification information.

____ 5. DOCUMENTS PATIENT CARE SERVICES

by

copying nursing and physician notes to patient and department records.

____ 6. ARRANGES DISCHARGES

by

notifying business office and patient transporter service.

____ 7. MAINTAINS UNIT OPERATIONS

by

following policies and procedures; reporting needed changes.

____ 8. MAINTAINS PATIENT CONFIDENCE AND PROTECTS HOSPITAL OPERATIONS

by

keeping information confidential.

% of Time

____ 9. MAINTAINS UNIT SUPPLIES INVENTORY

by

checking stock to determine inventory level; anticipating needed supplies; placing and expediting orders for supplies; verifying receipt of supplies.

____ 10. KEEPS UNIT EQUIPMENT OPERATIONAL

by

following manufacturer's instructions and established procedures; calling for repairs.

____ 11. CONSERVES UNIT RESOURCES

by

using equipment and supplies as needed to accomplish job results.

____ 12. SECURES PATIENT INFORMATION

by

completing data base backups.

____ 13. MAINTAINS SAFE AND CLEAN WORKING ENVIRONMENT

by

complying with procedures, rules, and regulations; adhering to infection-control policies and protocols.

____ 14. MAINTAINS CONTINUITY AMONG WORK TEAMS

by

documenting and communicating actions, irregularities, and continuing needs.

____ 15. CONTRIBUTES TO TEAM EFFORT

by

accomplishing related results as needed.

JOB TITLE: Pattern Maker

JOB PURPOSE: **CONSTRUCTS MASTER PATTERN**

by

developing layout; forming materials.

ESSENTIAL JOB RESULTS:

*% of
Time*

_____ 1. DEVELOPS LAYOUT

by

planning sequence of operations; studying engineering data, sketches, and blueprints; applying knowledge of material-forming properties and practices.

_____ 2. FORMS FRAME

by

fabricating parts; locating and aligning skeleton and master contour templates with precision measuring instruments.

_____ 3. FORMS PATTERN

by

placing forming substance over frame; finishing shape to peripheral dimensions.

_____ 4. VERIFIES FINISHED DIMENSIONS

by

measuring pattern.

_____ 5. ESTABLISHES REFERENCES

by

scribing points and lines.

_____ 6. RESOLVES FORMING PROBLEMS

by

altering process to meet specifications; notifying supervisor to obtain additional resources.

*% of
Time*

_____ 7. ENSURES OPERATION OF EQUIPMENT

by

completing preventive maintenance requirements; following manufacturer's instructions; troubleshooting malfunctions; and calling for repairs.

_____ 8. MAINTAINS SUPPLIES INVENTORY

by

checking supplies to determine amount available; anticipating needed supplies; placing and expediting orders for supplies; verifying receipt of supplies.

_____ 9. MAINTAINS CONTINUITY AMONG WORK TEAMS

by

documenting and communicating actions, irregularities, and continuing needs.

_____ 10. DOCUMENTS ACTIONS

by

completing logs; recording changes on engineering drawings.

_____ 11. CONTRIBUTES TO TEAM EFFORT

by

accomplishing related results as needed.

JOB TITLE: Payroll Clerk

JOB PURPOSE: **PAYS EMPLOYEES**

by

calculating pay and deductions; issuing checks.

ESSENTIAL JOB RESULTS:

% of
Time

_____ 1. MAINTAINS PAYROLL INFORMATION
by
collecting, calculating, and entering data.

_____ 2. UPDATES PAYROLL RECORDS
by
entering changes in exemptions, insurance coverage, savings deductions, and job title and department/division transfers.

_____ 3. PREPARES REPORTS
by
compiling summaries of earnings, taxes, deductions, leave, disability, and nontaxable wages.

_____ 4. DETERMINES PAYROLL LIABILITIES
by
calculating employee federal and state income and social security taxes and employer's social security, unemployment, and workers compensation payments.

% of
Time

_____ 5. RESOLVES PAYROLL DISCREPANCIES
by
collecting and analyzing information.

_____ 6. PROVIDES PAYROLL INFORMATION
by
answering questions and requests.

_____ 7. MAINTAINS PAYROLL OPERATIONS
by
following policies and procedures; reporting needed changes.

_____ 8. MAINTAINS EMPLOYEE CONFIDENCE AND PROTECTS PAYROLL OPERATIONS
by
keeping information confidential.

_____ 9. CONTRIBUTES TO TEAM EFFORT
by
accomplishing related results as needed.

JOB TITLE: Payroll Manager

JOB PURPOSE: **PAYS EMPLOYEES AND COMPILES PAYROLL INFORMATION**

by

managing payroll preparation; completing reports; maintaining records.

ESSENTIAL JOB RESULTS:

% of Time

____ 1. MAINTAINS PAYROLL INFORMATION
by
designing systems; directing the collection, calculation, and entering of data.

____ 2. UPDATES PAYROLL RECORDS
by
reviewing and approving changes in exemptions, insurance coverage, savings deductions, and job titles, and department/ division transfers.

____ 3. PAYS EMPLOYEES
by
directing the production and issuance of paychecks or electronic transfers to bank accounts.

____ 4. PREPARES REPORTS
by
compiling summaries of earnings, taxes, deductions, leave, disability, and nontaxable wages.

____ 5. DETERMINES PAYROLL LIABILITIES
by
approving the calculation of employee federal and state income and social security taxes, and employer's social security, unemployment, and workers compensation payments.

____ 6. BALANCES THE PAYROLL ACCOUNTS
by
resolving payroll discrepancies.

____ 7. PROVIDES PAYROLL INFORMATION
by
answering questions and requests.

% of Time

____ 8. MAINTAINS PAYROLL GUIDELINES
by
writing and updating policies and procedures.

____ 9. COMPLIES WITH FEDERAL, STATE, AND LOCAL LEGAL REQUIREMENTS
by
studying existing and new legislation; enforcing adherence to requirements; advising management on needed actions.

____ 10. MAINTAINS EMPLOYEE CONFIDENCE AND PROTECTS PAYROLL OPERATIONS
by
keeping information confidential.

____ 11. MAINTAINS PROFESSIONAL AND TECHNICAL KNOWLEDGE
by
attending educational workshops; reviewing professional publications; establishing personal networks; participating in professional societies.

____ 12. COMPLETES OPERATIONAL REQUIREMENTS
by
scheduling and assigning employees; following up on work results.

____ 13. MAINTAINS PAYROLL STAFF
by
recruiting, selecting, orienting, and training employees.

____ 14. MAINTAINS PAYROLL STAFF JOB RESULTS
by
counseling and disciplining employees; planning, monitoring, and appraising job results.

JOB TITLE: Payroll Manager

ESSENTIAL JOB RESULTS:

% of
Time

_____ 15. MAINTAINS PROFESSIONAL AND TECHNICAL KNOWLEDGE
  by
  attending educational workshops; reviewing
  professional publications; establishing
  personal networks; participating in
  professional societies.

% of
Time

_____ 16. CONTRIBUTES TO TEAM EFFORT
  by
  accomplishing related results as needed.

JOB TITLE: Pharmacist

JOB PURPOSE:
SERVES PATIENTS

by

preparing medications; giving pharmacological information to multidisciplinary health care team; monitoring patient drug therapies.

ESSENTIAL JOB RESULTS:

% of Time

_____ 1. PREPARES MEDICATIONS

by

reviewing and interpreting physician orders; detecting therapeutic incompatibilities.

_____ 2. DISPENSES MEDICATIONS

by

compounding, packaging, and labeling pharmaceuticals.

_____ 3. CONTROLS MEDICATIONS

by

monitoring drug therapies; advising interventions.

_____ 4. COMPLETES PHARMACY OPERATIONAL REQUIREMENTS

by

organizing and directing technicians' work flow; verifying their preparation and labeling of pharmaceuticals; verifying order entries, charges, and inspections.

_____ 5. PROVIDES PHARMACOLOGICAL INFORMATION

by

answering questions and requests of health care professionals; counseling patients on drug therapies.

_____ 6. DEVELOPS HOSPITAL STAFF'S PHARMACOLOGICAL KNOWLEDGE

by

participating in clinical programs; training pharmacy staff, students, interns, externs, residents, and health care professionals.

% of Time

_____ 7. COMPLIES WITH STATE AND FEDERAL DRUG LAWS AS REGULATED BY THE STATE BOARD OF PHARMACY, THE DRUG ENFORCEMENT ADMINISTRATION, AND THE FOOD AND DRUG ADMINISTRATION

by

monitoring nursing unit inspections; maintaining records for controlled substances; removing outdated and damaged drugs from the pharmacy inventory; supervising the work results of support personnel; maintaining current registration; studying existing and new legislation; anticipating legislation; advising management on needed actions.

_____ 8. PROTECTS PATIENTS AND TECHNICIANS

by

adhering to infection-control protocols.

_____ 9. MAINTAINS SAFE AND CLEAN WORKING ENVIRONMENT

by

complying with procedures, rules, and regulations.

_____ 10. MAINTAINS PHARMACOLOGICAL KNOWLEDGE

by

attending educational workshops; reviewing professional publications; establishing personal networks; participating in professional societies.

_____ 11. CONTRIBUTES TO TEAM EFFORT

by

accomplishing related results as needed.

JOB TITLE: Pharmacy Technician

JOB PURPOSE: **SUPPORTS PHARMACOLOGICAL SERVICES**
by
stocking, assembling, and distributing medications.

ESSENTIAL JOB RESULTS:

*% of
Time*

_____ 1. HELPS HEALTH CARE PROVIDERS AND PATIENTS
by
greeting them in person and by phone;
answering questions and requests; referring
inquiries to the pharmacist.

_____ 2. MAINTAINS PHARMACY INVENTORY
by
checking pharmaceutical stock to determine
inventory level; anticipating needed
medications and supplies; placing and
expediting orders; verifying receipt;
removing outdated drugs.

_____ 3. MAINTAINS A SAFE AND CLEAN PHARMACY
by
complying with procedures, rules, and
regulations.

_____ 4. PROTECTS PATIENTS AND EMPLOYEES
by
adhering to infection-control policies and
protocols.

_____ 5. ORGANIZES MEDICATIONS FOR PHARMACIST TO DISPENSE
by
reading medication orders and prescriptions;
preparing labels; calculating quantities;
assembling intravenous solutions and other
pharmaceutical therapies.

*% of
Time*

_____ 6. MAINTAINS RECORDS
by
recording and filing physicians' orders and
prescriptions.

_____ 7. GENERATES REVENUES
by
calculating, recording, and issuing charges.

_____ 8. ENSURES MEDICATION AVAILABILITY
by
delivering medications to patients and
departments.

_____ 9. PREPARES REPORTS
by
collecting and summarizing information.

_____ 10. CONTRIBUTES TO TEAM EFFORT
by
accomplishing related results as needed.

JOB TITLE: Physical Therapist

JOB PURPOSE:

RESTORES PATIENT'S FUNCTION, ALLEVIATES PAIN, AND PREVENTS DISABILITIES

by

planning and administering medically prescribed physical therapy.

ESSENTIAL JOB RESULTS:

% of Time

____ 1. MEETS THE PATIENT'S GOALS AND NEEDS AND PROVIDES QUALITY CARE

by

assessing and interpreting evaluations and test results; determining physical therapy treatment plans in consultation with physicians or by prescription.

____ 2. HELPS PATIENT ACCOMPLISH TREATMENT PLAN AND ACCEPT THERAPEUTIC DEVICES

by

administering manual exercises; instructing, encouraging, and assisting patients in performing physical activities, such as nonmanual exercises, ambulatory functional activities, and daily-living activities and in using assistive and supportive devices, such as crutches, canes, and prostheses.

____ 3. ADMINISTERS PHYSICAL THERAPY TREATMENTS

by

giving massages; initiating traction; applying physical agents; utilizing hydrotherapy tanks and whirlpool baths, moist packs, ultraviolet and infrared lamps, and ultrasound machines; directing treatments given by aides, technicians, and assistants.

____ 4. EVALUATES EFFECTS OF PHYSICAL THERAPY TREATMENTS AND FIT OF PROSTHETIC AND ORTHOTIC DEVICES

by

observing, noting, and evaluating patient's progress; recommending adjustments and modifications.

% of Time

____ 5. COMPLETES DISCHARGE PLANNING

by

consulting with physicians, nurses, social workers, and other health care workers; contributing to patient care conferences.

____ 6. ASSURES CONTINUATION OF THERAPEUTIC PLAN FOLLOWING DISCHARGE

by

designing home exercise programs; instructing patients, families, and caregivers in home exercise programs; recommending and/or providing assistive equipment; recommending outpatient or home health follow-up programs.

____ 7. DOCUMENTS PATIENT CARE SERVICES

by

charting in patient and department records.

____ 8. MAINTAINS PATIENT CONFIDENCE AND PROTECTS HOSPITAL OPERATIONS

by

keeping information confidential.

____ 9. MAINTAINS SAFE AND CLEAN WORKING ENVIRONMENT

by

complying with procedures, rules, and regulations.

____ 10. PROTECTS PATIENTS AND EMPLOYEES

by

adhering to infection-control policies and protocols.

JOB TITLE: Physical Therapist

ESSENTIAL JOB RESULTS:

*% of
Time*

____ 11. ENSURES OPERATION OF EQUIPMENT
    by
    completing preventive maintenance
    requirements; following manufacturer's
    instructions; troubleshooting malfunctions;
    calling for repairs.

____ 12. MAINTAINS PROFESSIONAL AND TECHNICAL KNOWLEDGE
    by
    attending educational workshops; reviewing
    professional publications; establishing
    personal networks; participating in
    professional societies.

____ 13. DEVELOPS PHYSICAL THERAPY STAFF
    by
    providing information; developing and
    conducting in-service training programs.

*% of
Time*

____ 14. COMPLIES WITH FEDERAL, STATE, AND LOCAL LEGAL AND
    PROFESSIONAL REQUIREMENTS
    by
    studying existing and new legislation;
    anticipating future legislation; enforcing
    adherence to requirements; advising
    management on needed actions.

____ 15. CONTRIBUTES TO TEAM EFFORT
    by
    accomplishing related results as needed.

JOB PURPOSE: **PROMOTES AND MAINTAINS HEALTH**

by

providing medical services under the supervision of a physician.

ESSENTIAL JOB RESULTS:

*% of
Time*

____ 1. CONTRIBUTES TO PHYSICIAN'S EFFECTIVENESS
by
identifying short-term and long-range patient care issues that must be addressed; providing information and commentary pertinent to deliberations; recommending options and courses of action; implementing physician directives.

____ 2. ASSESSES PATIENT HEALTH
by
interviewing patients; performing physical examinations; obtaining, updating, and studying medical histories.

____ 3. DETERMINES ABNORMAL CONDITIONS
by
administering or ordering diagnostic tests, such as x-rays, electrocardiograms, and laboratory studies; interpreting test results.

____ 4. DOCUMENTS PATIENT CARE SERVICES
by
charting in patient and department records.

____ 5. PERFORMS THERAPEUTIC PROCEDURES
by
administering injections and immunizations; suturing; managing wounds and infections.

____ 6. INSTRUCTS AND COUNSELS PATIENTS
by
describing therapeutic regimens; giving normal growth and development information; discussing family planning; providing counseling on emotional problems of daily living; promoting wellness and health maintenance.

____ 7. PROVIDES CONTINUITY OF CARE
by
developing and implementing patient management plans.

*% of
Time*

____ 8. MAINTAINS SAFE AND CLEAN WORKING ENVIRONMENT
by
complying with procedures, rules, and regulations.

____ 9. PROTECTS PATIENTS AND EMPLOYEES
by
adhering to infection-control policies and protocols.

____ 10. COMPLIES WITH FEDERAL, STATE, AND LOCAL LEGAL AND PROFESSIONAL REQUIREMENTS
by
studying existing and new legislation; anticipating future legislation; enforcing adherence to requirements; advising management on needed actions.

____ 11. MAINTAINS PROFESSIONAL AND TECHNICAL KNOWLEDGE
by
attending educational workshops; reviewing professional publications; establishing personal networks; participating in professional societies.

____ 12. DEVELOPS HEALTH CARE TEAM STAFF
by
providing information, educational opportunities, and experiential growth opportunities.

____ 13. CONTRIBUTES TO TEAM EFFORT
by
accomplishing related results as needed.

JOB PURPOSE:

MAINTAINS THE FLOW OF WATER, AIR AND OTHER GASES, AND DRAINAGE

by

assembling, installing, and repairing pipes, fittings, and plumbing fixtures.

ESSENTIAL JOB RESULTS:

% of Time

___ 1. PRODUCES PLUMBING SYSTEMS
by
establishing standards and procedures; measuring results against standards; making necessary adjustments.

___ 2. DETERMINES SEQUENCE OF INSTALLATIONS
by studying building plans and working drawings.

___ 3. IDENTIFIES OBSTRUCTIONS TO BE AVOIDED
by
inspecting structure.

___ 4. LOCATES POSITION OF PIPE AND PIPE CONNECTIONS AND PASSAGE HOLES
by
marking structure, using ruler, level, and plumb bob.

___ 5. ACCOMMODATES PIPES AND PIPE FITTINGS
by
cutting openings in floors and walls, using hand tools and power tools.

___ 6. CUTS, THREADS, AND BENDS PIPE
by
using cutters, cutting torch, threading machine, and bending machine.

___ 7. INSTALLS PLUMBING SYSTEMS
by
assembling, positioning, and sealing valves, pipe fittings, and pipes.

% of Time

___ 8. TESTS PLUMBING SYSTEMS
by
filling system with water or gas; identifying leaks.

___ 9. REPAIRS AND MAINTAINS PLUMBING SYSTEMS
by
replacing washers; mending burst pipes; opening clogged drains.

___ 10. COMPLIES WITH FEDERAL, STATE, AND LOCAL BUILDING AND PLUMBING CODES
by
enforcing adherence to requirements.

___ 11. KEEPS PLUMBING EQUIPMENT AND TOOLS OPERATIONAL
by
following manufacturer's instructions and established procedures.

___ 12. MAINTAINS PLUMBING SUPPLIES INVENTORY
by
checking stock to determine inventory level; anticipating needed supplies; placing and expediting orders for supplies; verifying receipt of supplies.

___ 13. CONSERVES PLUMBING RESOURCES
by
using equipment and supplies as needed to accomplish job results.

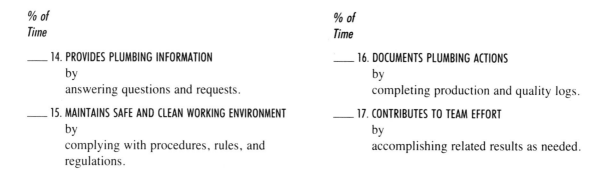

JOB TITLE: Plumber

ESSENTIAL JOB RESULTS:

% of
Time

____ 14. PROVIDES PLUMBING INFORMATION
   by
   answering questions and requests.

____ 15. MAINTAINS SAFE AND CLEAN WORKING ENVIRONMENT
   by
   complying with procedures, rules, and
   regulations.

% of
Time

____ 16. DOCUMENTS PLUMBING ACTIONS
   by
   completing production and quality logs.

____ 17. CONTRIBUTES TO TEAM EFFORT
   by
   accomplishing related results as needed.

JOB TITLE: Police Officer

JOB PURPOSE: **PROTECTS CITIZENS**

by

preventing crime; enforcing laws; apprehending suspects; monitoring traffic.

ESSENTIAL JOB RESULTS:

% of
Time

____ 1. PREVENTS CRIME

by

explaining and enforcing applicable federal, state, and local laws and ordinances; teaching preventive, protective, and defensive tactics; mediating disputes; patrolling assigned area; responding to notices of disturbances; conducting searches; observing suspicious activities; detaining suspects.

____ 2. APPREHENDS SUSPECTS

by

responding to complaints and calls for help; observing violations; making arrests.

____ 3. CONDUCTS CRIMINAL INVESTIGATIONS

by

gathering evidence; interviewing victims and witnesses; interrogating suspects.

____ 4. DOCUMENTS OBSERVATIONS AND ACTIONS

by

radioing information; completing reports.

____ 5. REPORTS OBSERVATIONS AND ACTIONS

by

testifying in court.

____ 6. FULFILLS COURT ORDERS

by

serving warrants and commitments.

____ 7. MAINTAINS SAFE TRAFFIC CONDITIONS

by

monitoring and directing traffic; enforcing laws and ordinances; investigating accidents; providing escort; reporting unsafe streets and facilities.

% of
Time

____ 8. MINIMIZES PERSONAL INJURY

by

rescuing and reviving victims; radioing for medical assistance.

____ 9. MAINTAINS OPERATIONS

by

following department policies and procedures; recommending changes.

____ 10. ENSURES OPERATION OF EQUIPMENT

by

practicing use; completing preventive maintenance requirements; following manufacturer's instructions; troubleshooting malfunctions; notifying supervisor of needed repairs; evaluating new equipment and techniques.

____ 11. MAINTAINS PROFESSIONAL AND TECHNICAL KNOWLEDGE

by

studying applicable federal, state, and local laws and ordinances; attending educational workshops; reviewing professional publications; practicing skills; participating in professional societies.

____ 12. CONTRIBUTES TO TEAM EFFORT

by

accomplishing related results as needed.

JOB TITLE: Printer

JOB PURPOSE: **PRODUCES PRINTED MATERIALS**

by

operating printing and binding equipment.

ESSENTIAL JOB RESULTS:

% of
Time

____ 1. PREPARES WORK TO BE ACCOMPLISHED
by
reviewing work order; assembling materials.

____ 2. PREPARES PRESS FOR USE
by
loading stock and adjusting for size; setting
feedboard, side guides, register board, and
delivery mechanism; setting impression
cylinder; mounting plates; loading ink;
setting ink fountain.

____ 3. ESTABLISHES QUALITY
by
pulling proof copy; adjusting settings.

____ 4. MAINTAINS PRODUCTION AND QUALITY
by
monitoring output; adjusting settings.

____ 5. PREPARES FOR NEXT WORK ORDER
by
returning supplies to stock; cleaning
equipment.

____ 6. ENSURES OPERATION OF EQUIPMENT
by
completing preventive maintenance
requirements; following manufacturer's
instructions; troubleshooting malfunctions;
calling for repairs; maintaining equipment
inventories; evaluating new equipment and
techniques.

% of
Time

____ 7. MAINTAINS SUPPLIES INVENTORY
by
checking stock to determine inventory level;
anticipating needed supplies; placing and
expediting orders for supplies; verifying
receipt of supplies.

____ 8. COMPLETES BINDERY REQUIREMENTS
by
operating cutter, collator, bander, stapler,
drill, etc.

____ 9. CONTRIBUTES TO TEAM EFFORT
by
accomplishing related results as needed.

JOB TITLE: Product Manager

JOB PURPOSE: **DEVELOPS PRODUCTS**

by

identifying potential products; determining specifications, manufacturing timetables, pricing, and time-integrated plans for product introduction; developing marketing strategies.

ESSENTIAL JOB RESULTS:

% of
Time

____ 1. DETERMINES CUSTOMERS' NEEDS AND DESIRES AND PRODUCT PRICING
by
specifying the research needed to obtain market information.

____ 2. RECOMMENDS THE NATURE AND SCOPE OF PRESENT AND FUTURE PRODUCT LINES
by
appraising new product ideas and/or product or packaging changes.

____ 3. ASSESSES MARKET COMPETITION
by
comparing the company's product to competitors' products.

____ 4. PROVIDES SOURCE DATA FOR PRODUCT LINE COMMUNICATIONS
by
defining product marketing communication objectives.

____ 5. OBTAINS PRODUCT MARKET SHARE
by
working with sales director to develop product sales strategies.

____ 6. ASSESSES PRODUCT MARKET DATA
by
calling on customers with field salespeople and evaluating sales call results.

____ 7. PROVIDES INFORMATION FOR MANAGEMENT
by
preparing short-term and long-term product sales forecasts and special reports and analyses; answering questions and requests.

% of
Time

____ 8. FACILITATES INVENTORY TURNOVER AND PRODUCT AVAILABILITY
by
reviewing and adjusting inventory levels and production schedules.

____ 9. BRINGS NEW PRODUCTS TO MARKET
by
analyzing proposed product development programs; preparing return-on-investment analyses; establishing time schedules with engineering and manufacturing.

____ 10. INTRODUCES AND MARKETS NEW PRODUCTS
by
developing time-integrated plans with sales, advertising, and production.

____ 11. DETERMINES PRODUCT PRICING
by
utilizing market research data; reviewing production and sales costs; anticipating volume; costing special and customized orders.

____ 12. COMPLETES OPERATIONAL REQUIREMENTS
by
scheduling and assigning employees; following up on work results.

____ 13. MAINTAINS PRODUCT MANAGEMENT STAFF
by
recruiting, selecting, orienting, and training employees.

ESSENTIAL JOB RESULTS:

% of
Time

_____ 14. MAINTAINS PRODUCT MANAGEMENT STAFF JOB RESULTS
by
counseling and disciplining employees;
planning, monitoring, and appraising job
results.

_____ 15. MAINTAINS PROFESSIONAL AND TECHNICAL
KNOWLEDGE
by
attending educational workshops; reviewing
professional publications; establishing
personal networks; participating in
professional societies.

% of
Time

_____ 16. CONTRIBUTES TO TEAM EFFORT
by
accomplishing related results as needed.

JOB TITLE: Production Control Clerk

JOB PURPOSE: **PROVIDES MANUFACTURING DECISION-MAKING INFORMATION**

by

compiling and reporting production data.

ESSENTIAL JOB RESULTS:

% of Time

_____ 1. COMPILES PRODUCTION INFORMATION
by
collecting and sorting production records.

_____ 2. MAINTAINS PRODUCTION DATA BASE
by
entering data.

_____ 3. EXTENDS AND SUMMARIZES DATA
by
calculating items produced, materials used, scrap, waste, and defects produced, production rates, etc.

_____ 4. PREPARES PRODUCTION REPORTS
by
collecting, analyzing, and summarizing information and trends.

% of Time

_____ 5. MAINTAINS MATERIALS INVENTORY RECORDS
by
calculating material usage; entering data.

_____ 6. RESOLVES DISCREPANCIES
by
collecting and analyzing production information.

_____ 7. SECURES INFORMATION
by
completing data base backups.

_____ 8. CONTRIBUTES TO TEAM EFFORT
by
accomplishing related results as needed.

229

JOB TITLE: Production Equipment Technician

JOB PURPOSE: **MAINTAINS PRODUCTION**

by

redesigning, modifying, installing, and repairing components in production equipment.

ESSENTIAL JOB RESULTS:

% of Time

____ 1. KEEPS PRODUCTION EQUIPMENT READY FOR USE
by
completing preventive maintenance schedules.

____ 2. SETS UP PRODUCTION EQUIPMENT
by
completing equipment changeovers.

____ 3. RESTARTS PRODUCTION
by
troubleshooting equipment breakdowns; making repairs.

____ 4. ENHANCES EQUIPMENT PERFORMANCE
by
installing modifications; making adjustments; recommending improvements.

____ 5. PRODUCES SPARE PARTS, JIGS, AND FIXTURES
by
studying requirements or drawings; operating shop equipment.

____ 6. MAINTAINS SHOP EQUIPMENT
by
completing preventive maintenance requirements; requesting repairs.

% of Time

____ 7. MAINTAINS PARTS AND MATERIALS INVENTORY
by
checking stock to determine inventory level; anticipating needed parts and materials; requesting resupply and expediting orders; verifying receipt of parts and materials.

____ 8. MAINTAINS EQUIPMENT HISTORICAL REFERENCE
by
documenting actions.

____ 9. SHARES KNOWLEDGE OF EQUIPMENT
by
training and coaching fellow employees.

____ 10. MAINTAINS SAFE AND CLEAN WORKING ENVIRONMENT
by
complying with procedures, rules, and regulations.

____ 11. CONTRIBUTES TO TEAM EFFORT
by
accomplishing related results as needed.

JOB TITLE: Production Inventory Clerk

JOB PURPOSE: **MAINTAINS PRODUCTION**

by

verifying staged orders.

ESSENTIAL JOB RESULTS:

% of
Time

_____ 1. VERIFIES ORDERS
by
checking components and quantities against packaging order.

_____ 2. MAINTAINS STATUS OF STAGED ORDERS
by
logging orders and material movement; notifying production planning.

_____ 3. MAINTAINS PRODUCTION
by
identifying space for staged components; delivering components to work centers; requisitioning and verifying additional components.

_____ 4. MAINTAINS COMPONENT INVENTORY
by
verifying and completing credit returns and requisitions.

% of
Time

_____ 5. COMPLETES PRODUCTION RECORD
by
recording and delivering pallets of finished stock to the warehouse.

_____ 6. MAINTAINS FINISHED GOODS INVENTORY
by
entering production into data base.

_____ 7. MAINTAINS A SAFE WORKING ENVIRONMENT
by
following safety rules and regulations.

_____ 8. CONTRIBUTES TO TEAM EFFORT
by
accomplishing related results as needed.

JOB TITLE: Production Operator

JOB PURPOSE: **PRODUCES PRODUCT**

by

monitoring and adjusting production line operations.

ESSENTIAL JOB RESULTS:

% of Time

____ 1. PREPARES PRODUCTION EQUIPMENT FOR OPERATION
by
making equipment setup adjustments; assisting with equipment changeovers.

____ 2. DOCUMENTS PRODUCTION AND PRODUCTION PROCESS
by
completing production logs; calculating production statistics; noting the receipt, flow, and return of materials; noting bins, racks, deliveries, move tickets and log sheets.

____ 3. MAINTAINS QUALITY STANDARDS
by
conducting first-piece and line-clearance inspection; completing production control charts; analyzing recordings and statistics; making equipment adjustments.

____ 4. HELPS PREPARE OTHERS FOR PRODUCTION JOB RESPONSIBILITIES
by
demonstrating operational procedures.

% of Time

____ 5. MAINTAINS PRODUCTION LINE OPERATION
by
solving production process problems; making equipment adjustments; reporting production and quality data; reporting decisions made; referring questions to the supervisor.

____ 6. MAINTAINS PRODUCTION OPERATIONS
by
following policies and procedures (equipment, raw and in-process materials, and finished goods); reporting needed changes.

____ 7. MAINTAINS SAFE AND CLEAN WORKING ENVIRONMENT
by
complying with procedures, rules, and regulations.

____ 8. CONTRIBUTES TO TEAM EFFORT
by
accomplishing related results as needed.

JOB TITLE: Production Scheduler

JOB PURPOSE: **EXPEDITES PRODUCTION**

by

organizing and monitoring schedules.

ESSENTIAL JOB RESULTS:

% of
Time

_____ 1. DETERMINES PRODUCTION PRIORITIES
by
studying master production schedule and
customer requirements.

_____ 2. ORGANIZES PRODUCTION SCHEDULE
by
studying work order specifications, current
schedule, and availability of equipment,
materials, and employees.

_____ 3. PUBLISHES PRODUCTION SCHEDULE
by
identifying products, equipment, sequence,
completion dates, etc.

_____ 4. MONITORS PRODUCTION
by
collecting production logs; comparing
progress to schedule.

_____ 5. RESOLVES SCHEDULING PROBLEMS
by
collecting and analyzing information;
coordinating solutions.

% of
Time

_____ 6. PREPARES REPORTS
by
compiling and summarizing production and
downtime data.

_____ 7. MAINTAINS PRODUCTION DATA BASE
by
entering data.

_____ 8. SECURES INFORMATION
by
completing data base backups.

_____ 9. CONTRIBUTES TO TEAM EFFORT
by
accomplishing related results as needed.

JOB TITLE: Project Director

JOB PURPOSE: COMPLETES ENGINEERING PROJECTS
by
developing and evaluating project plans and progress.

ESSENTIAL JOB RESULTS:

*% of
Time*

____ 1. ESTABLISHES PROJECT OBJECTIVES
by
analyzing project proposal; collaborating
with management.

____ 2. ESTABLISHES PROJECT PLAN
by
determining time frame, funding, and
staffing; approving project schedule.

____ 3. ORGANIZES PROJECT STAFF
by
recruiting, selecting, orienting, and training
staff members; assigning responsibilities;
approving contractors.

____ 4. ESTABLISHES AND ACHIEVES FINANCIAL OBJECTIVES
by
preparing a project budget; scheduling and
approving expenditures; analyzing variances;
initiating corrective actions.

____ 5. APPROVES PROJECT SPECIFICATIONS
by
analyzing product design, customer
requirements, and performance standards;
authorizing technical studies.

____ 6. CONFIRMS PRODUCT PERFORMANCE
by
establishing standards; testing requirements.

____ 7. CONTROLS PROJECT PLAN
by
approving design, specifications, and plan
and schedule changes.

____ 8. PREPARES PROJECT STATUS REPORTS
by
collecting, analyzing, and summarizing
information and trends.

*% of
Time*

____ 9. MAINTAINS PROJECT STAFF JOB RESULTS
by
coaching, counseling, and disciplining
employees; planning, monitoring, and
appraising job results.

____ 10. MAINTAINS PROFESSIONAL AND TECHNICAL KNOWLEDGE
by
attending educational workshops; reviewing
professional publications; establishing
personal networks; participating in
professional societies.

____ 11. MAINTAINS SAFE AND CLEAN WORKING ENVIRONMENT
by
establishing and enforcing procedures, rules,
and regulations.

____ 12. MAINTAINS PROJECT DATA BASE
by
developing information requirements;
designing an information system.

____ 13. MAINTAINS PRODUCT AND COMPANY REPUTATION
by
complying with federal and state regulations;
coordinating with government regulatory
agencies.

____ 14. CONTRIBUTES TO TEAM EFFORT
by
accomplishing related results as needed.

JOB TITLE: Project Engineer

JOB PURPOSE: **COMPLETES ENGINEERING PROJECTS**

by

organizing and controlling project elements.

ESSENTIAL JOB RESULTS:

% of
Time

____ 1. DEVELOPS PROJECT OBJECTIVES

by

reviewing project proposals and plans; conferring with management.

____ 2. DETERMINES PROJECT RESPONSIBILITIES

by

identifying project phases and elements; assigning personnel to phases and elements; reviewing bids from contractors.

____ 3. DETERMINES PROJECT SPECIFICATIONS

by

studying product design, customer requirements, and performance standards; completing technical studies; preparing cost estimates.

____ 4. CONFIRMS PRODUCT PERFORMANCE

by

designing and conducting tests.

____ 5. DETERMINES PROJECT SCHEDULE

by

studying project plan and specifications; calculating time requirements; sequencing project elements.

____ 6. MAINTAINS PROJECT SCHEDULE

by

monitoring project progress; coordinating activities; resolving problems.

____ 7. CONTROLS PROJECT PLAN

by

reviewing design, specifications, and plan and schedule changes; recommending actions.

% of
Time

____ 8. CONTROLS PROJECT COSTS

by

approving expenditures; administering contractor contracts.

____ 9. PREPARES PROJECT STATUS REPORTS

by

collecting, analyzing, and summarizing information and trends; recommending actions.

____ 10. MAINTAINS SAFE AND CLEAN WORKING ENVIRONMENT

by

enforcing procedures, rules, and regulations.

____ 11. MAINTAINS PROJECT DATA BASE

by

writing computer programs; entering and backing up data.

____ 12. MAINTAINS PRODUCT AND COMPANY REPUTATION

by

complying with federal and state regulations.

____ 13. CONTRIBUTES TO TEAM EFFORT

by

accomplishing related results as needed.

JOB TITLE: Public Health Educator

JOB PURPOSE: **EDUCATES PUBLIC ON HEALTH ISSUES**

by

preparing informational materials; designing and conducting training sessions.

ESSENTIAL JOB RESULTS:

% of Time

____ 1. IDENTIFIES PUBLIC HEALTH INFORMATION NEEDS
by
establishing personal rapport with potential and actual trainees and other persons in a position to understand health information requirements.

____ 2. DETERMINES AVAILABILITY OF HEALTH SERVICES
by
maintaining relationships with public, civic, professional, and voluntary agencies.

____ 3. DESIGNS TRAINING PROGRAMS
by
conducting and analyzing community surveys; collaborating with health specialists, civic organizations, and educational systems.

____ 4. PRESENTS TRAINING PROGRAMS
by
identifying learning objectives; selecting instructional methodologies.

____ 5. PROVIDES HEALTH INFORMATION
by
preparing and distributing educational and informational materials; conducting educational programs; answering questions and requests.

% of Time

____ 6. EVALUATES TRAINING EFFECTIVENESS
by
assessing application of learning; recommending future training programs.

____ 7. MAINTAINS PROFESSIONAL AND TECHNICAL KNOWLEDGE
by
attending educational workshops; reviewing professional publications; establishing personal networks; participating in professional societies.

____ 8. CONTRIBUTES TO AGENCY EFFECTIVENESS
by
identifying short-term and long-range issues that must be addressed; providing information and commentary pertinent to deliberations; recommending options and courses of action; implementing directives.

____ 9. CONTRIBUTES TO TEAM EFFORT
by
accomplishing related results as needed.

JOB TITLE: Public Relations and Communications Manager

JOB PURPOSE: **MAINTAINS PUBLIC AND EMPLOYEE AWARENESS OF ORGANIZATION ISSUES**

by

planning and directing external and internal information programs.

ESSENTIAL JOB RESULTS:

% of Time

_____ 1. SUPPORTS ORGANIZATION GOALS AND OBJECTIVES
by
developing external and internal information programs.

_____ 2. IDENTIFIES EXTERNAL AND INTERNAL INFORMATION NEEDS
by
researching trends; conducting and purchasing surveys and analyzing responses; studying information requests.

_____ 3. PLANS EXTERNAL AND INTERNAL INFORMATION PROGRAMS
by
identifying audiences and information needs; determining specific media approaches.

_____ 4. INFORMS PUBLIC AND EMPLOYEES
by
developing and disseminating information, including fact sheets, news releases, newsletters, photographs, films, recordings, personal appearances, etc.; purchasing advertising space and time.

_____ 5. RESPONDS TO MEDIA INQUIRIES
by
recommending information strategies to management; planning responses; providing information; arranging interviews and tours; editing copy; coaching responders.

_____ 6. MAINTAINS RAPPORT WITH MEDIA REPRESENTATIVES
by
arranging continuing contacts; resolving concerns.

% of Time

_____ 7. PROVIDES OPINION, OFFERS SUPPORT, AND GATHERS INFORMATION
by
representing the organization at public, social, and business events.

_____ 8. ACCOMPLISHES SPECIFIC INFORMATION OBJECTIVES
by
designing and conducting special projects; establishing relationships with lobbyists, consultants, and others.

_____ 9. MAINTAINS HISTORICAL REFERENCE
by
establishing and maintaining a filing and retrieval system.

_____ 10. ACHIEVES FINANCIAL OBJECTIVES
by
preparing an annual budget; scheduling expenditures; analyzing variances; initiating corrective actions.

_____ 11. COMPLETES PUBLIC RELATIONS AND COMMUNICATIONS OPERATIONAL REQUIREMENTS
by
scheduling and assigning employees; following up on work results.

_____ 12. MAINTAINS PUBLIC RELATIONS AND COMMUNICATIONS STAFF
by
recruiting, selecting, orienting, and training employees.

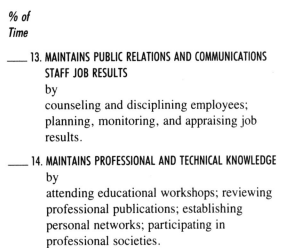

JOB TITLE: **Public Relations and Communications Manager**

ESSENTIAL JOB RESULTS:

% of Time

_____ 13. MAINTAINS PUBLIC RELATIONS AND COMMUNICATIONS STAFF JOB RESULTS

by

counseling and disciplining employees; planning, monitoring, and appraising job results.

_____ 14. MAINTAINS PROFESSIONAL AND TECHNICAL KNOWLEDGE

by

attending educational workshops; reviewing professional publications; establishing personal networks; participating in professional societies.

% of Time

_____ 15. CONTRIBUTES TO TEAM EFFORT

by

accomplishing related results as needed.

JOB TITLE: Purchasing Director

JOB PURPOSE: **OBTAINS SUPPLIES, SERVICES, AND EQUIPMENT**
by
directing procurement, contractual services, disbursement, and warehousing programs; supervising staff.

ESSENTIAL JOB RESULTS:

% of Time

____ 1. DEVELOPS SOURCES FOR THE PROCUREMENT OF SUPPLIES, SERVICES, AND EQUIPMENT
by
attending demonstrations; contacting vendors; attending educational workshops; reviewing professional publications; establishing personal networks; participating in professional societies.

____ 2. PROCURES SUPPLIES, SERVICES, AND EQUIPMENT
by
establishing minimum and maximum inventory levels and reorder quantities; reviewing supply requisitions for authorization and/or unusual usage; conferring with vendors; selecting products and equipment by testing, observing, or examining items and estimating values of market price; determining method of procurement, i.e., direct purchase, lease, or bid.

____ 3. PROVIDES INFORMATION REGARDING SUPPLY, SERVICE, AND EQUIPMENT SELECTION
by
responding to requests; leading conferences involving suppliers, engineers, purchasers, inspectors, and other company personnel; facilitating material inspection, substitution, standardization, and vendor/company partnering.

____ 4. MAINTAINS PROCUREMENT AND RECEIVING OPERATIONS
by
developing policies and procedures; designing forms and systems; ensuring verification of incoming shipments, costs, delivery, product quality or performance, and inventories.

% of Time

____ 5. MAINTAINS QUALITY OF SUPPLIES, SERVICES, AND EQUIPMENT
by
defining quality standards; discussing defective or unacceptable goods, services, or equipment with users, vendors, and others; determining source of trouble; resolving disputes.

____ 6. KEEPS EQUIPMENT OPERATIONAL
by
soliciting, procuring, and monitoring service agreements.

____ 7. MAINTAINS OPERATIONS
by
operating supply and equipment warehouse and distribution systems.

____ 8. MAINTAINS DEPRECIATION SCHEDULES
by
initiating procedures to track and monitor capital equipment purchases/transfers/ disposals.

____ 9. PREPARES PROCUREMENT AND USAGE REPORTS
by
collecting and analyzing cost, quality, user, vendor, and other information.

____ 10. COMPLETES OPERATIONAL REQUIREMENTS
by
scheduling and assigning employees; following up on work results.

JOB TITLE: **JOB TITLE: Purchasing Director**

ESSENTIAL JOB RESULTS:

% of
Time

_____ 11. MAINTAINS PURCHASING STAFF
　　　by
　　　recruiting, selecting, orienting, and training
　　　employees.

_____ 12. MAINTAINS PURCHASING STAFF JOB RESULTS
　　　by
　　　counseling and disciplining employees;
　　　planning, monitoring, and appraising job
　　　results.

% of
Time

_____ 13. CONTRIBUTES TO TEAM EFFORT
　　　by
　　　accomplishing related results as needed.

JOB TITLE: Purchasing Specialist

JOB PURPOSE: **MAINTAINS INVENTORY**

by

preparing purchase orders and bid requests; adding received goods to inventory; maintaining information systems and historical references.

ESSENTIAL JOB RESULTS:

% of Time

____ 1. MAINTAINS MASTER FILE OF STOCK ITEMS
by
assigning numbers to new stock items; updating specification files; recording reorder point information.

____ 2. PROVIDES INFORMATION
by
opening and distributing mail; answering questions and requests; making copies; updating and generating reports.

____ 3. COMPLETES PURCHASE REQUESTS
by
verifying inventory and specifications of purchase requests; preparing stock and equipment requisitions; inputting purchase orders and bid and service requests; expediting deliveries.

____ 4. MAINTAINS SERVICE CONTRACTS FOR OFFICE EQUIPMENT
by
accepting requests; contacting vendors; recording contract billing.

% of Time

____ 5. VERIFIES WAREHOUSE INVENTORY
by
inputting and adding supplies received to current inventory levels.

____ 6. MAINTAINS HISTORICAL REFERENCE OF SUPPLIES, EQUIPMENT, AND SERVICES
by
keeping records of items and services purchased, prices, delivery and shipping costs, and product or service acceptability.

____ 7. RECOMMENDS BILLS FOR PAYMENT
by
verifying bills from suppliers against bids and purchase orders.

____ 8. CONTRIBUTES TO TEAM EFFORT
by
accomplishing related results as needed.

JOB TITLE: Quality Assurance Director

JOB PURPOSE: **ASSURES QUALITY PRODUCTS AND PROCESSES**
by
establishing and enforcing quality standards; testing materials and
product.

ESSENTIAL JOB RESULTS:

*% of
Time*

____ 1. ESTABLISHES QUALITY AND RELIABILITY STANDARDS
by
studying product and consumer requirements
with other members of management and with
production operators, technicians, and
engineers.

____ 2. ESTABLISHES RAW MATERIAL STANDARDS
by
studying manufacturing and engineering
requirements; conferring and negotiating
with suppliers; devising testing methods and
procedures.

____ 3. ESTABLISHES IN-PROCESS PRODUCT INSPECTION
STANDARDS
by
studying manufacturing methods; devising
testing methods and procedures.

____ 4. ESTABLISHES STANDARDS FOR THE DISPOSITION OF
FINISHED PRODUCT
by
devising evaluation tests, methods, and
procedures.

____ 5. ESTABLISHES REWORK STANDARDS
by
devising inspection and physical testing
methods and procedures.

____ 6. ESTABLISHES PRODUCT QUALITY DOCUMENTATION
SYSTEM
by
writing and updating quality assurance
procedures.

*% of
Time*

____ 7. MAINTAINS PRODUCT QUALITY
by
enforcing quality assurance policies and
procedures and government requirements;
collaborating with other members of
management to develop new product and
engineering designs and manufacturing and
training methods.

____ 8. PREPARES PRODUCT AND PROCESS QUALITY REPORTS
by
collecting, analyzing, and summarizing
information and trends.

____ 9. COMPLETES QUALITY ASSURANCE OPERATIONAL
REQUIREMENTS
by
scheduling and assigning employees;
following up on work results.

____ 10. MAINTAINS QUALITY ASSURANCE STAFF
by
recruiting, selecting, orienting, and training
employees.

____ 11. MAINTAINS QUALITY ASSURANCE STAFF JOB RESULTS
by
coaching, counseling, and disciplining
employees; planning, monitoring, and
appraising job results.

____ 12. MAINTAINS PROFESSIONAL AND TECHNICAL KNOWLEDGE
by
attending educational workshops; reviewing
professional publications; establishing
personal networks; participating in
professional societies.

JOB TITLE: Quality Assurance Director

ESSENTIAL JOB RESULTS:

% of
Time

_____ 13. ACHIEVES FINANCIAL OBJECTIVES
   by
   preparing the quality assurance budget;
   scheduling expenditures; analyzing variances;
   initiating corrective actions.

% of
Time

_____ 14. CONTRIBUTES TO TEAM EFFORT
   by
   accomplishing related results as needed.

243

JOB TITLE: Quality Assurance Technician

JOB PURPOSE: **ASSURES QUALITY PRODUCT**

by

conducting in-process inspections; evaluating finished product.

ESSENTIAL JOB RESULTS:

% of Time

____ 1. DETERMINES QUALITY AND RELIABILITY STANDARDS
by
studying drawings and formulas; verifying specifications with engineering staff.

____ 2. IDENTIFIES RAW MATERIAL CONDITION
by
collecting materials samples; conducting inspections and physical tests of materials.

____ 3. IDENTIFIES IN-PROCESS PRODUCT CONDITION
by
collecting samples during production process; conducting in-process inspections and physical tests.

____ 4. DETERMINES DISPOSITION OF FINISHED PRODUCT
by
collecting, classifying, analyzing, and interpreting production and quality data; judging product acceptability in comparison to specifications.

____ 5. DETERMINES ACCEPTABILITY OF REWORK
by
conducting inspections and physical tests of reworked product.

% of Time

____ 6. DOCUMENTS FINISHED PRODUCT STATUS
by
recording and summarizing raw materials, in-process, and finished-product inspection and physical test data; updating quality assurance data base.

____ 7. MAINTAINS PRODUCT QUALITY DOCUMENTATION SYSTEM
by
writing or rewriting quality assurance procedures.

____ 8. MAINTAINS QUALITY ASSURANCE OPERATIONS
by
following quality assurance policies and procedures; reporting needed changes.

____ 9. CONTRIBUTES TO TEAM EFFORT
by
accomplishing related results as needed.

JOB TITLE: Radiologic Technologist

JOB PURPOSE: **PROVIDES INFORMATION TO DIAGNOSE PATIENT ILLNESSES**

by

operating radiologic equipment to produce radiographs.

ESSENTIAL JOB RESULTS:

% of Time

____ 1. IDENTIFIES PATIENT SERVICE REQUIREMENTS
by
establishing personal rapport with potential and actual patients and other persons in a position to understand service requirements.

____ 2. ENSURES OPERATION OF RADIOLOGY EQUIPMENT
by
completing preventive maintenance requirements; following manufacturer's instructions; troubleshooting malfunctions; calling for repairs; maintaining equipment inventories; evaluating new equipment and techniques.

____ 3. MAINTAINS RADIOLOGY SUPPLIES INVENTORY
by
checking stock to determine inventory level; anticipating needed supplies; placing and expediting orders for supplies; verifying receipt of supplies.

____ 4. COMPLIES WITH FEDERAL, STATE, AND LOCAL LEGAL AND PROFESSIONAL REQUIREMENTS
by
studying existing and new legislation; anticipating future legislation; enforcing adherence to requirements; advising management on needed actions.

____ 5. MAINTAINS PROFESSIONAL AND TECHNICAL KNOWLEDGE
by
attending educational workshops; reviewing professional publications; establishing personal networks; participating in professional societies.

____ 6. MAINTAINS SAFE AND CLEAN WORKING ENVIRONMENT
by
complying with procedures, rules, and regulations.

% of Time

____ 7. GAINS PATIENT COOPERATION
by
reducing anxieties; providing explanations of treatment; answering questions.

____ 8. PREPARES PATIENT FOR RADIOLOGICAL PROCEDURE
by
positioning patient; adjusting immobilization devices; moving equipment into specified position; adjusting equipment controls to set exposure factors.

____ 9. MINIMIZES RADIATION TO PATIENT AND STAFF
by
practicing radiation protection techniques, using beam restrictive devices, patient shielding, and knowledge of exposure factors.

____ 10. PROTECTS PATIENTS AND EMPLOYEES
by
adhering to infection-control policies and protocols; following drug protocols in case of reactions to drugs, such as contrast media, administering first aid, and using the emergency cart.

____ 11. MAINTAINS PRODUCTION AND QUALITY OF RADIOGRAPHS
by
following established standards and procedures; developing radiographs; observing radiographic results; making necessary adjustments.

____ 12. DOCUMENTS PATIENT CARE SERVICES
by
charting in patient and department records.

____ 13. CONTRIBUTES TO TEAM EFFORT
by
accomplishing related results as needed.

JOB TITLE: Receptionist

JOB PURPOSE: **SERVES VISITORS**

by

greeting, welcoming, and directing them; notifying company personnel of visitors' arrival; maintaining security and telecommunications system.

ESSENTIAL JOB RESULTS:

% of
Time

____ 1. WELCOMES VISITORS
by
greeting them, in person or on the telephone; answering or referring inquiries.

____ 2. DIRECTS VISITORS
by
maintaining employee and department directories; giving instructions.

____ 3. MAINTAINS SECURITY
by
following procedures; monitoring logbook; issuing visitor badges.

____ 4. MAINTAINS TELECOMMUNICATION SYSTEM
by
following manufacturer's instructions for house phone and console operation.

% of
Time

____ 5. MAINTAINS SAFE AND CLEAN RECEPTION AREA
by
complying with procedures, rules, and regulations.

____ 6. MAINTAINS CONTINUITY AMONG WORK TEAMS
by
documenting and communicating actions, irregularities, and continuing needs.

____ 7. CONTRIBUTES TO TEAM EFFORT
by
accomplishing related results as needed.

JOB TITLE: Receptionist, Medical Office

JOB PURPOSE:
SERVES PATIENTS

by

greeting and helping them; scheduling appointments; maintaining records and accounts.

ESSENTIAL JOB RESULTS:

% of Time

____ 1. WELCOMES PATIENTS AND VISITORS

by

greeting patients and visitors, in person or on the telephone; answering or referring inquiries.

____ 2. OPTIMIZES PATIENTS' SATISFACTION, PROVIDER TIME, AND TREATMENT ROOM UTILIZATION

by

scheduling appointments in person or by telephone.

____ 3. KEEPS PATIENT APPOINTMENTS ON SCHEDULE

by

notifying provider of patient's arrival; reviewing service delivery compared to schedule; reminding provider of service delays.

____ 4. COMFORTS PATIENTS

by

anticipating patients' anxieties; answering patients' questions; maintaining the reception area.

____ 5. ENSURES AVAILABILITY OF TREATMENT INFORMATION

by

filing and retrieving patient records.

____ 6. MAINTAINS PATIENT ACCOUNTS

by

obtaining, recording, and updating personal and financial information.

% of Time

____ 7. OBTAINS REVENUE

by

recording and updating financial information; recording and collecting patient charges; controlling credit extended to patients; filing, collecting, and expediting third-party claims.

____ 8. MAINTAINS BUSINESS OFFICE INVENTORY AND EQUIPMENT

by

checking stock to determine inventory level; anticipating needed supplies; placing and expediting orders for supplies; verifying receipt of supplies; scheduling equipment service and repairs.

____ 9. HELPS PATIENTS IN DISTRESS

by

responding to emergencies.

____ 10. PROTECTS PATIENTS' RIGHTS

by

maintaining confidentiality of personal and financial information.

____ 11. MAINTAINS OPERATIONS

by

following policies and procedures; reporting needed changes.

____ 12. CONTRIBUTES TO TEAM EFFORT

by

accomplishing related results as needed.

JOB TITLE: Records Clerk

JOB PURPOSE: **CONTRIBUTES TO STATISTICAL STUDIES**

by

compiling data; computing statistics; preparing reports.

ESSENTIAL JOB RESULTS:

*% of
Time*

____ 1. COMPILES STATISTICS
by
reviewing, verifying, and utilizing source
materials.

____ 2. ASSEMBLES AND CLASSIFIES STATISTICS
by
following prescribed procedures.

____ 3. COMPUTES STATISTICAL DATA
by
utilizing statistical software and prescribed
formulas.

____ 4. RESOLVES STATISTICAL DISCREPANCIES
by
collecting and analyzing information.

*% of
Time*

____ 5. PROVIDES STATISTICAL INFORMATION
by
answering questions and requests; preparing
reports.

____ 6. MAINTAINS HISTORICAL RECORDS
by
filing documents.

____ 7. CONTRIBUTES TO TEAM EFFORT
by
accomplishing related results as needed.

JOB TITLE: Records Management Analyst

JOB PURPOSE: **CONTROLS THE USE, PROTECTION, AND DISPOSITION OF BUSINESS RECORDS AND INFORMATION**

by

examining and evaluating the records management system.

ESSENTIAL JOB RESULTS:

% of Time

____ 1. MAINTAINS RECORDS MANAGEMENT SYSTEM

by

examining and evaluating existing and new methods for using, protecting, and disposing of records.

____ 2. ASCERTAINS STORAGE MEDIA

by

studying records and reports.

____ 3. DETERMINES BUILDING LAYOUT

by

plotting locations of equipment; reviewing physical storage needs; identifying records for off-site storage.

____ 4. DETECTS RECORDS MANAGEMENT PROBLEMS AND SYSTEM IMPROVEMENTS

by

conferring with clerical and supervisory personnel.

____ 5. ESTABLISHES RECORD RETENTION SCHEDULES

by

scheduling transfer of action records to inactive or archival storage; reducing paper records to micrographic form; destroying obsolete records.

____ 6. RECOMMENDS PURCHASE OF STORAGE, RETRIEVAL, OR DISPOSAL EQUIPMENT

by

studying and evaluating equipment capability and cost.

____ 7. COMPLETES OPERATIONAL REQUIREMENTS

by

scheduling and assigning employees; following up on work results.

% of Time

____ 8. MAINTAINS RECORDS MANAGEMENT STAFF

by

recruiting, selecting, orienting, and training employees.

____ 9. MAINTAINS RECORDS MANAGEMENT STAFF JOB RESULTS

by

coaching, counseling, and disciplining employees; planning, monitoring, and appraising job results.

____ 10. MAINTAINS PROFESSIONAL AND TECHNICAL KNOWLEDGE

by

attending educational workshops; reviewing professional publications; establishing personal networks; participating in professional societies.

____ 11. ACHIEVES FINANCIAL OBJECTIVES

by

preparing an annual budget; scheduling expenditures; analyzing variances; initiating corrective actions.

____ 12. PROTECTS RECORDS MANAGEMENT OPERATIONS

by

enforcing procedures; keeping information confidential.

____ 13. MAINTAINS INTER- AND INTRADEPARTMENTAL WORK FLOW

by

fostering a spirit of cooperation.

____ 14. CONTRIBUTES TO TEAM EFFORT

by

accomplishing related results as needed.

JOB TITLE: Recreation Supervisor

JOB PURPOSE: **PROVIDES RECREATION FOR CITIZENS**

by

planning, organizing, promoting, and evaluating recreational programs and facilities.

ESSENTIAL JOB RESULTS:

*% of
Time*

_____ 1. IDENTIFIES COMMUNITY NEEDS AND INTERESTS
by
surveying individual citizens and civic groups; developing and evaluating options; determining costs; recommending programs and facilities.

_____ 2. COMPLETES OPERATIONAL REQUIREMENTS
by
scheduling and assigning employees; following up on work results; scheduling the use of facilities.

_____ 3. MAINTAINS RECREATION AND PARK STAFF
by
recruiting, selecting, orienting, and training employees.

_____ 4. MAINTAINS RECREATION AND PARK STAFF JOB RESULTS
by
coaching, counseling, and disciplining employees; planning, monitoring, and appraising job results.

_____ 5. ACHIEVES FINANCIAL OBJECTIVES
by
preparing an annual budget; scheduling expenditures; analyzing variances; initiating corrective actions.

_____ 6. ENSURES OPERATION OF EQUIPMENT AND FACILITIES
by
directing preventive maintenance program; enforcing manufacturer's instructions; arranging for repairs and restoration; maintaining equipment inventories; evaluating adequacy to meet future use; testing new equipment and techniques.

*% of
Time*

_____ 7. PROMOTES USE OF PROGRAMS AND FACILITIES
by
advertising availability and schedules; notifying special interests groups; coordinating and cooperating with federal, state, and local units of government.

_____ 8. MAINTAINS SAFE AND CLEAN FACILITIES AND EQUIPMENT
by
developing and enforcing procedures, rules, and regulations; providing training programs and instructions for users.

_____ 9. SUPPORTS THE PARKS AND RECREATION COMMISSION
by
advising on the management of recreational programs and facilities; developing and evaluating options, recommending courses of action; keeping members informed; remaining accessible; answering questions; providing information.

_____ 10. PREPARES REPORTS
by
collecting, analyzing, and summarizing information and trends.

_____ 11. MAINTAINS PROFESSIONAL AND TECHNICAL KNOWLEDGE
by
attending educational workshops; reviewing professional publications; establishing personal networks; participating in professional societies.

_____ 12. CONTRIBUTES TO TEAM EFFORT
by
accomplishing related results as needed.

JOB TITLE: Recreation Therapist

JOB PURPOSE: **FACILITATES REHABILITATION AND DEVELOPMENT OF PATIENTS WITH ILLNESSES AND PHYSICAL DISABILITIES**

by

planning and administering medically prescribed recreational therapy.

ESSENTIAL JOB RESULTS:

% of Time

____ 1. MEETS PATIENT'S GOALS AND NEEDS AND PROVIDES QUALITY CARE

by

assessing and interpreting evaluations and test results; determining recreational therapy treatment plans in consultation with physicians or by prescription.

____ 2. HELPS PATIENT DEVELOP INTERPERSONAL RELATIONSHIPS AND CONFIDENCE FOR GROUP ACTIVITIES

by

implementing programs involving sports, dramatics, games, and arts and crafts.

____ 3. ADMINISTERS RECREATIONAL THERAPY

by

teaching relaxation techniques; instructing patients in calisthenics, stretching and limbering exercises, and individual and group sports; organizing and conducting special outings, such as ball games, sightseeing, and picnics; directing treatments given by aides, technicians, and assistants.

____ 4. PROMOTES MAXIMUM INDEPENDENCE

by

selecting and constructing therapies according to patient's physical capacity, intelligence level, and interest.

____ 5. EVALUATES RESULTS OF RECREATIONAL THERAPY

by

observing, noting, and evaluating patient's progress; recommending and implementing adjustments and modifications.

% of Time

____ 6. COMPLETES DISCHARGE PLANNING

by

consulting with physicians, nurses, social workers, and other health care workers; contributing to patient care conferences.

____ 7. ASSURES CONTINUATION OF THERAPEUTIC PLAN FOLLOWING DISCHARGE

by

designing home exercise programs; instructing patients, families, and caregivers in home exercise programs; recommending and/or providing assistive equipment; recommending outpatient or home health follow-up programs.

____ 8. DOCUMENTS PATIENT CARE SERVICES

by

charting in patient and department records.

____ 9. MAINTAINS PATIENT CONFIDENCE AND PROTECTS HOSPITAL OPERATIONS

by

keeping information confidential.

____ 10. MAINTAINS SAFE AND CLEAN WORKING ENVIRONMENT

by

complying with procedures, rules, and regulations.

____ 11. PROTECTS PATIENTS AND EMPLOYEES

by

adhering to infection-control policies and protocols.

JOB TITLE: Recreation Therapist

ESSENTIAL JOB RESULTS:

% of
Time

____ 12. ENSURES OPERATION OF EQUIPMENT
by
completing preventive maintenance
requirements; following manufacturer's
instructions; troubleshooting malfunctions;
calling for repairs.

____ 13. MAINTAINS PROFESSIONAL AND TECHNICAL KNOWLEDGE
by
attending educational workshops; reviewing
professional publications; establishing
personal networks; participating in
professional societies.

____ 14. DEVELOPS RECREATION THERAPY STAFF
by
providing information; developing and
conducting in-service training programs.

% of
Time

____ 15. COMPLIES WITH FEDERAL, STATE, AND LOCAL LEGAL AND
PROFESSIONAL REQUIREMENTS
by
studying existing and new legislation;
anticipating future legislation; enforcing
adherence to requirements; advising
management on needed actions.

____ 16. CONTRIBUTES TO TEAM EFFORT
by
accomplishing related results as needed.

JOB TITLE: Refinery Operator

JOB PURPOSE: **PRODUCES PRODUCT**

by

monitoring and adjusting process.

ESSENTIAL JOB RESULTS:

*% of
Time*

_____ 1. SETS PROCESSING VARIABLES
by
reading processing schedule; studying test results of samples and laboratory recommendations; adjusting controls.

_____ 2. MONITORS PROCESSING
by
observing control panels and warning signals; completing operating logs.

_____ 3. REGULATES PROCESSING UNITS
by
reviewing operating logs; adjusting controls.

_____ 4. DIRECTS FLOW OF PRODUCT
by
regulating values, pumps, compressors, and auxiliary equipment.

_____ 5. MAINTAINS PROCESSING SYSTEM
by
reporting malfunctioning units; obtaining and testing product samples; conducting inspections; scheduling maintenance.

_____ 6. MAINTAINS SAFE PROCESSING ENVIRONMENT
by
complying with procedures, rules, and regulations; patrolling unit.

*% of
Time*

_____ 7. ENSURES OPERATION OF PROCESSING SYSTEM
by
completing preventive maintenance requirements; following manufacturer's instructions; troubleshooting malfunctions; calling for repairs.

_____ 8. PREPARES SYSTEM FOR NEW PRODUCT
by
circulating cleaning chemicals.

_____ 9. MAINTAINS CONTINUITY AMONG WORK TEAMS
by
documenting and communicating actions, irregularities, and continuing needs.

_____ 10. PREPARES PROCESSING REPORTS
by
collecting, analyzing, and summarizing information and trends.

_____ 11. CONTRIBUTES TO TEAM EFFORT
by
accomplishing related results as needed.

JOB TITLE: Reservation Clerk

JOB PURPOSE: **COMPLETES TRAVEL ARRANGEMENTS**
by
planning itineraries; obtaining tickets.

ESSENTIAL JOB RESULTS:

% of
Time

____ 1. PROVIDES TRAVEL OPTIONS
by
assembling literature, commentaries, and
schedules; answering inquiries; reviewing
preferences; offering suggestions.

____ 2. DEVELOPS ITINERARY
by
planning and identifying route, carriers,
lodging, and dining; verifying space.

____ 3. OBTAINS TICKETS
by
entering requirements; confirming rates.

____ 4. COMPLETES FOREIGN TRAVEL REQUIREMENTS
by
obtaining visa, permit, and medical
information; completing forms; providing
information regarding currency.

____ 5. PREPARES TRAVEL PACKET
by
assembling itinerary, maps, tickets,
confirmations, visas and related documents,
baggage tags, emergency resources,
insurance options, etc.

% of
Time

____ 6. APPROVES INVOICES
by
verifying charges.

____ 7. MAINTAINS INFORMATION RESOURCES
by
obtaining, filing, and updating directories,
brochures, pamphlets, guides, timetables,
etc.

____ 8. OBTAINS REFUNDS AND ADJUSTMENTS
by
completing claim forms.

____ 9. PREPARES REPORTS
by
collecting information.

____ 10. CONTRIBUTES TO TEAM EFFORT
by
accomplishing related results as needed.

JOB PURPOSE: **RESTORES PATIENT'S PULMONARY FUNCTION;
ALLEVIATES PAIN; SUPPORTS LIFE**

by

planning and administering medically prescribed respiratory therapy.

ESSENTIAL JOB RESULTS:

*% of
Time*

___ 1. MEETS PATIENT'S GOALS AND NEEDS AND PROVIDES QUALITY CARE

by

conducting pulmonary function tests; assessing and interpreting evaluations and test results; determining respiratory therapy treatment plans in consultation with physicians and by prescription.

___ 2. HELPS PATIENT ACCOMPLISH TREATMENT PLAN AND SUPPORTS LIFE

by

administering inhalants; operating mechanical ventilators, therapeutic gas administration apparatus, environmental control systems, and aerosol generators.

___ 3. ADMINISTERS RESPIRATORY THERAPY TREATMENTS

by

performing bronchopulmonary drainage; assisting with breathing exercises; monitoring physiological responses to therapy, such as vital signs, arterial blood gases, and blood chemistry changes; directing treatments given by aides, technicians and assistants.

___ 4. EVALUATES EFFECTS OF RESPIRATORY THERAPY TREATMENT PLAN

by

observing, noting, and evaluating patient's progress; recommending adjustments and modifications.

___ 5. COMPLETES DISCHARGE PLANNING

by

consulting with physicians, nurses, social workers, and other health care workers; contributing to patient care conferences.

*% of
Time*

___ 6. ASSURES CONTINUATION OF THERAPEUTIC PLAN FOLLOWING DISCHARGE

by

designing home exercise programs; instructing patients, families, and caregivers in home exercise programs; recommending and/or providing assistive equipment; recommending outpatient or home health follow-up programs.

___ 7. DOCUMENTS PATIENT CARE SERVICES

by

charting in patient and department records.

___ 8. MAINTAINS PATIENT CONFIDENCE AND PROTECTS HOSPITAL OPERATIONS

by

keeping information confidential.

___ 9. MAINTAINS SAFE AND CLEAN WORKING ENVIRONMENT

by

complying with procedures, rules, and regulations.

___ 10. PROTECTS PATIENTS AND EMPLOYEES

by

adhering to infection-control policies and protocols.

___ 11. ENSURES OPERATION OF EQUIPMENT

by

completing preventive maintenance requirements; following manufacturer's instructions; troubleshooting malfunctions; calling for repairs.

ESSENTIAL JOB RESULTS:

% of
Time

___ 12. MAINTAINS PROFESSIONAL AND TECHNICAL KNOWLEDGE
by
attending educational workshops; reviewing professional publications; establishing personal networks; participating in professional societies.

___ 13. DEVELOPS RESPIRATORY THERAPY STAFF
by
providing information; developing and conducting in-service training programs.

___ 14. COMPLIES WITH FEDERAL, STATE, AND LOCAL LEGAL AND CERTIFICATION REQUIREMENTS
by
studying existing and new legislation; anticipating future legislation; enforcing adherence to requirements; advising management on needed actions.

% of
Time

___ 15. CONTRIBUTES TO TEAM EFFORT
by
accomplishing related results as needed.

JOB PURPOSE:

SERVES CUSTOMERS

by

providing merchandise; supervising staff.

ESSENTIAL JOB RESULTS:

*% of
Time*

____ 1. COMPLETES STORE OPERATIONAL REQUIREMENTS
by
scheduling and assigning employees;
following up on work results.

____ 2. MAINTAINS STORE STAFF
by
recruiting, selecting, orienting, and training
employees.

____ 3. MAINTAINS STORE STAFF JOB RESULTS
by
coaching, counseling, and disciplining
employees; planning, monitoring, and
appraising job results.

____ 4. ACHIEVES FINANCIAL OBJECTIVES
by
preparing an annual budget; scheduling
expenditures; analyzing variances; initiating
corrective actions.

____ 5. IDENTIFIES CURRENT AND FUTURE CUSTOMER
REQUIREMENTS
by
establishing rapport with potential and actual
customers and other persons in a position to
understand service requirements.

____ 6. ENSURES AVAILABILITY OF MERCHANDISE AND SERVICES
by
approving contracts; maintaining inventories.

____ 7. FORMULATES PRICING POLICIES
by
reviewing merchandising activities;
determining additional needed sales
promotion; authorizing clearance sales;
studying trends.

*% of
Time*

____ 8. MARKETS MERCHANDISE
by
studying advertising, sales promotion, and
display plans; analyzing operating and
financial statements for profitability ratios.

____ 9. SECURES MERCHANDISE
by
implementing security systems and measures.

____ 10. PROTECTS EMPLOYEES AND CUSTOMERS
by
providing a safe and clean store environment.

____ 11. MAINTAINS THE STABILITY AND REPUTATION OF THE
STORE
by
complying with legal requirements.

____ 12. DETERMINES MARKETING STRATEGY CHANGES
by
reviewing operating and financial statements
and departmental sales records.

____ 13. MAINTAINS PROFESSIONAL AND TECHNICAL KNOWLEDGE
by
attending educational workshops; reviewing
professional publications; establishing
personal networks; participating in
professional societies.

____ 14. MAINTAINS OPERATIONS
by
initiating, coordinating, and enforcing
program, operational, and personnel policies
and procedures.

____ 15. CONTRIBUTES TO TEAM EFFORT
by
accomplishing related results as needed.

JOB TITLE: Returned-Goods Clerk

JOB PURPOSE: **PROCESSES RETURNED GOODS**

by

receiving; inspecting; making dispositions.

ESSENTIAL JOB RESULTS:

% of
Time

____ 1. RECEIVES RETURNED GOODS
by
unpacking goods; verifying bills of lading.

____ 2. VERIFIES CUSTOMER'S REASONS FOR RETURN
by
studying accompanying correspondence;
inspecting goods.

____ 3. DETERMINES DISPOSITION OF RETURNS
by
assessing damage and defects.

____ 4. DISPOSES OF GOODS
by
routing to inventory, salvage, or repair.

____ 5. DOCUMENTS RETURNED-GOODS INFORMATION
by
entering return data into order-tracking
system.

% of
Time

____ 6. MAINTAINS SAFE AND CLEAN WORKING ENVIRONMENT
by
complying with procedures, rules, and
regulations.

____ 7. PROVIDES RETURNED-GOODS INFORMATION
by
answering questions and requests.

____ 8. CONTRIBUTES TO TEAM EFFORT
by
accomplishing related results as needed.

JOB TITLE: Returned-Items Clerk

JOB PURPOSE: **MAINTAINS CUSTOMER ACCOUNT STATUS**

by

receiving and recording returned checks.

ESSENTIAL JOB RESULTS:

% of Time

_____ 1. VERIFIES INCOMING CASH LETTERS
by
reconciling documents.

_____ 2. PREPARES WORK TO BE ACCOMPLISHED
by
gathering and sorting checks and documents.

_____ 3. MAINTAINS HISTORICAL RECORDS
by
logging, filming, and filing checks and documents.

_____ 4. MAINTAINS ACCOUNT STATUS
by
placing audio and written holds; notifying correspondent banks and branches of large-dollar returns.

_____ 5. MAINTAINS GENERAL LEDGER
by
forwarding credits.

% of Time

_____ 6. ANSWERS INQUIRIES AND RESOLVES DISCREPANCIES
by
collecting, researching, analyzing, copying, and mailing data and documents.

_____ 7. NOTIFIES CUSTOMERS OF RETURNED ITEMS
by
mail or telephone.

_____ 8. MAINTAINS CUSTOMER CONFIDENCE AND PROTECTS BANK OPERATIONS
by
keeping information confidential.

_____ 9. MAINTAINS OPERATIONS
by
following policies and procedures; reporting needed changes.

_____ 10. CONTRIBUTES TO TEAM EFFORT
by
accomplishing related results as needed.

JOB TITLE: Right-of-Way Engineer

JOB PURPOSE: **PROTECTS PROPERTY RIGHT-OF-WAY OWNERSHIP**
by
investigating usage, ownership, installations, and complaints.

ESSENTIAL JOB RESULTS:

*% of
Time*

_____ 1. INVESTIGATES REQUESTS FOR RIGHT-OF-WAY USAGE
by
studying engineering and maintenance impact.

_____ 2. VERIFIES CLEARANCES
by
studying proposed installations.

_____ 3. DETERMINES RIGHT-OF-WAY OWNERSHIP
by
studying deeds and easements.

_____ 4. RESPONDS TO RIGHT-OF-WAY COMPLAINTS
by
forwarding information to appropriate department.

_____ 5. MAINTAINS RIGHT-OF-WAY DATA BASE
by
entering and backing up data.

_____ 6. APPROVES INSTALLATIONS IN RIGHT-OF-WAY.
by
conducting inspections; comparing work to codes and specifications.

*% of
Time*

_____ 7. MAINTAINS SERVICE AND COMPANY REPUTATION
by
complying with federal and state regulations.

_____ 8. PROVIDES INFORMATION
by
answering questions and requests.

_____ 9. PREPARES REPORTS
by
collecting, analyzing, and summarizing information and trends.

_____ 10. REPRESENTS THE ORGANIZATION
by
collecting data; presenting information at hearings.

_____ 11. CONTRIBUTES TO TEAM EFFORT
by
accomplishing related results as needed.

JOB PURPOSE: **CONTROLS RISKS AND LOSSES**

by

planning, directing, and coordinating risk and insurance programs.

ESSENTIAL JOB RESULTS:

% of Time

____ 1. DETERMINES FINANCIAL IMPACT OF RISK ON COMPANY

by

analyzing and classifying risks as to frequency and potential severity.

____ 2. MINIMIZES LOSSES

by

reducing chance of loss; reducing frequency and severity of loss; utilizing self-insurance and planned noninsurance; increasing predictability of loss; placing property, activity, or risk with other establishments or insurers.

____ 3. PLACES INSURANCE

by

directing insurance negotiations; selecting insurance brokers and carriers.

____ 4. CONTROLS PROGRAMS

by

studying existing and new fidelity, surety, liability, property, group life, medical, pension plans, and workers compensation insurance regulations and trends; anticipating changes.

____ 5. COMPLIES WITH FEDERAL, STATE, AND LOCAL LEGAL REQUIREMENTS

by

studying existing and new legislation; anticipating future legislation; enforcing adherence to requirements; advising management on needed actions.

____ 6. ALLOCATES PROGRAM COSTS

by

preparing operational and risk reports for analyses.

% of Time

____ 7. DIRECTS LOSS PREVENTION AND SAFETY PROGRAMS

by

selecting and directing safety activities, engineering, and loss prevention experts.

____ 8. COMPLETES RISK MANAGEMENT OPERATIONAL REQUIREMENTS

by

scheduling and assigning employees; following up on work results.

____ 9. MAINTAINS RISK MANAGEMENT STAFF

by

recruiting, selecting, orienting, and training employees.

____ 10. MAINTAINS RISK MANAGEMENT STAFF JOB RESULTS

by

coaching, counseling, and disciplining employees; planning, monitoring, and appraising job results.

____ 11. MAINTAINS PROFESSIONAL AND TECHNICAL KNOWLEDGE

by

attending educational workshops; reviewing professional publications; establishing personal networks; participating in professional societies.

____ 12. ACHIEVES RISK MANAGEMENT FINANCIAL OBJECTIVES

by

preparing an annual budget; scheduling expenditures; analyzing variances; initiating corrective actions.

____ 13. CONTRIBUTES TO TEAM EFFORT

by

accomplishing related results as needed.

JOB TITLE: Safe Deposit Box Custodian

JOB PURPOSE: SECURES CUSTOMERS' VALUABLES

by

controlling vault access; helping customers.

ESSENTIAL JOB RESULTS:

% of Time

___ 1. SECURES SAFE DEPOSIT AREA
by
identifying customers; unlocking and locking drawer; setting vault alarm times.

___ 2. RENTS BOXES
by
preparing forms and contracts; issuing boxes; charging, collecting, and recording fees; completing forms; resetting locks; issuing keys.

___ 3. SERVES CUSTOMERS
by
answering questions and requests; completing information change forms; contacting vendors to open boxes for customers who have lost keys; assisting probate attorneys and state revenue officers with audits of deceased renters' box contents; consoling customers.

___ 4. MAINTAINS RECORDS
by
retaining signature cards, rental agreements, payment receipts, and access logs.

% of Time

___ 5. COMPLIES WITH FEDERAL, STATE, AND LOCAL BANKING REGULATIONS
by
following guidelines and procedures.

___ 6. MAINTAINS CUSTOMER CONFIDENCE AND PROTECTS OPERATIONS
by
keeping information confidential.

___ 7. MAINTAINS SAFE AND CLEAN WORKING ENVIRONMENT
by
complying with procedures, rules, and regulations.

___ 8. CONTRIBUTES TO TEAM EFFORT
by
accomplishing related results as needed.

```
┌─────────────────────────────────────────────────────────────┐
│ JOB TITLE: Safety Director                                    │
└─────────────────────────────────────────────────────────────┘
```

JOB PURPOSE: MAINTAINS SAFE AND HEALTHFUL ENVIRONMENT

by

identifying and anticipating concerns and hazards; developing and enforcing systems, policies, and procedures.

ESSENTIAL JOB RESULTS:

% of Time

_____ 1. IDENTIFIES AND ANTICIPATES SAFETY AND HEALTH CONCERNS AND HAZARDS

by

surveying environmental, operational, and occupational conditions; rendering opinions on new equipment and procedures; investigating violations; recommending preventive programs.

_____ 2. GUIDES AND PROMOTES SAFE WORK PERFORMANCE

by

developing safety systems, policies, and procedures; developing safety campaigns, communications, and recognitions; training managers and employees.

_____ 3. COMPLIES WITH FEDERAL, STATE, AND LOCAL SAFETY REGULATIONS

by

studying existing and new legislation; anticipating future legislation; interpreting standards; enforcing adherence to regulations; advising management on needed actions.

_____ 4. ENFORCES SAFETY POLICIES

by

conducting inspections; reporting statistics; counseling managers and employees.

_____ 5. PROMOTES A SAFE ENVIRONMENT

by

coordinating and cooperating with local, state, and regional safety groups and agencies.

_____ 6. REPRESENTS THE ORGANIZATION

by

collecting data; presenting information at hearings; coordinating with claims adjusters.

% of Time

_____ 7. MAINTAINS SAFETY INFORMATION DATA BASE

by

developing information requirements; designing an information system.

_____ 8. COMPLETES OPERATIONAL REQUIREMENTS

by

scheduling and assigning employees; following up on work results.

_____ 9. MAINTAINS SAFETY STAFF

by

recruiting, selecting, orienting, and training employees.

_____ 10. MAINTAINS SAFETY STAFF JOB RESULTS

by

coaching, counseling, and disciplining employees; planning, monitoring, and appraising job results.

_____ 11. MAINTAINS PROFESSIONAL AND TECHNICAL KNOWLEDGE

by

attending educational workshops; reviewing professional publications; establishing personal networks; participating in professional societies.

_____ 12. ACHIEVES FINANCIAL OBJECTIVES

by

preparing an annual budget; scheduling expenditures; analyzing variances; initiating corrective actions.

_____ 13. CONTRIBUTES TO TEAM EFFORT

by

accomplishing related results as needed.

JOB TITLE: Safety Engineer

JOB PURPOSE: **MAINTAINS SAFE AND HEALTHFUL ENVIRONMENT**
by
conducting studies and investigations; devising safe procedures and
equipment.

ESSENTIAL JOB RESULTS:

% of Time

____ 1. IDENTIFIES POTENTIAL FIRE AND SAFETY HAZARDS
by
inspecting current and proposed facilities,
machinery, equipment, tools, and personnel
practices.

____ 2. IDENTIFIES ACTUAL FIRE AND SAFETY HAZARDS AND
UNSAFE PRACTICES
by
investigating accidents and near-accidents.

____ 3. GUIDES AND PROMOTES SAFE WORK PERFORMANCE
by
enforcing safety policies; implementing
safety campaigns; training managers and
employees in safe practices and first aid.

____ 4. ELIMINATES OR MINIMIZES HAZARDOUS SITUATIONS
by
developing and recommending safety policies
and procedures; designing, building, and
installing safety devices on machinery;
designing personal safety clothing and
equipment.

____ 5. COMPLIES WITH FEDERAL, STATE, AND LOCAL SAFETY
REGULATIONS
by
interpreting standards; enforcing adherence to
regulations; advising management on needed
actions.

% of Time

____ 6. PROMOTES A SAFE WORK ENVIRONMENT
by
coordinating and cooperating with local,
state, and regional safety groups and
agencies.

____ 7. PREPARES SAFETY REPORTS
by
collecting, analyzing, and summarizing
information and trends.

____ 8. REPRESENTS THE ORGANIZATION
by
coordinating investigations with claims
adjusters.

____ 9. MAINTAINS SAFETY INFORMATION DATA BASE
by
writing computer programs; entering and
backing up data.

____ 10. CONTRIBUTES TO TEAM EFFORT
by
accomplishing related results as needed.

JOB TITLE: Sales Clerk

JOB PURPOSE: **SERVES CUSTOMERS**

by

displaying, promoting, and tagging merchandise; receiving and processing payments.

ESSENTIAL JOB RESULTS:

% of
Time

____ 1. DISPLAYS MERCHANDISE
   by
   stocking shelves, counters, racks, and tables.

____ 2. PROMOTES SALES
   by
   setting up advertising displays.

____ 3. PRICES MERCHANDISE
   by
   stamping, marking, and tagging.

____ 4. HELPS CUSTOMERS
   by
   providing information; answering questions;
   obtaining merchandise requested by
   customers; receiving merchandise selected by
   customers.

% of
Time

____ 5. ISSUES BILLS AND RECEIPTS
   by
   listing and totaling purchases.

____ 6. OBTAINS PAYMENTS
   by
   processing cash, checks, sales discounts, and
   credit cards.

____ 7. PREPARES MERCHANDISE FOR DELIVERY
   by
   removing tags, wrapping, and bagging.

____ 8. CONTRIBUTES TO TEAM EFFORT
   by
   accomplishing related results as needed.

JOB TITLE: Sales Engineer

JOB PURPOSE: **SERVES CUSTOMERS**

by

identifying their needs; engineering adaptations of products, equipment, and services.

ESSENTIAL JOB RESULTS:

% of
Time

____ 1. IDENTIFIES CURRENT AND FUTURE CUSTOMER SERVICE REQUIREMENTS
by
establishing personal rapport with potential and actual customers and other persons in a position to understand service requirements.

____ 2. PROVIDES PRODUCT, SERVICE, OR EQUIPMENT TECHNICAL AND ENGINEERING INFORMATION
by
answering questions and requests.

____ 3. ESTABLISHES NEW ACCOUNTS AND SERVICES ACCOUNTS
by
identifying potential customers; planning and organizing sales call schedule.

____ 4. PREPARES COST ESTIMATES
by
studying blueprints, plans, and related customer documents; consulting with engineers, architects, and other professional and technical personnel.

____ 5. DETERMINES IMPROVEMENTS
by
analyzing cost-benefit ratios of equipment, supplies, or service applications in customer environment; engineering or proposing changes in equipment, processes, or use of materials or services.

____ 6. GAINS CUSTOMER ACCEPTANCE
by
explaining or demonstrating cost reductions and operations improvements.

____ 7. SUBMITS ORDERS
by
conferring with technical support staff; costing engineering changes.

% of
Time

____ 8. DEVELOPS CUSTOMER'S STAFF
by
providing technical information and training.

____ 9. COMPLIES WITH FEDERAL, STATE, AND LOCAL LEGAL REQUIREMENTS
by
studying existing and new legislation; anticipating future legislation; advising customer on product, service, or equipment adherence to requirements; advising customer on needed actions.

____ 10. PREPARES SALES ENGINEERING REPORTS
by
collecting, analyzing, and summarizing sales information and engineering and application trends.

____ 11. MAINTAINS PROFESSIONAL AND TECHNICAL KNOWLEDGE
by
attending educational workshops; reviewing professional publications; establishing personal networks; participating in professional societies.

____ 12. CONTRIBUTES TO SALES ENGINEERING EFFECTIVENESS
by
identifying short-term and long-range issues that must be addressed; providing information and commentary pertinent to deliberations; recommending options and courses of action; implementing directives.

____ 13. CONTRIBUTES TO TEAM EFFORT
by
accomplishing related results as needed.

JOB TITLE: Sales Manager

JOB PURPOSE: **SELLS PRODUCTS**

by

implementing national sales plans; supervising regional sales managers.

ESSENTIAL JOB RESULTS:

*% of
Time*

____ 1. DETERMINES ANNUAL UNIT AND GROSS-PROFIT PLANS
by
implementing marketing strategies; analyzing trends and results.

____ 2. ESTABLISHES SALES OBJECTIVES
by
forecasting and developing annual sales quotas for regions and territories; projecting expected sales volume and profit for existing and new products.

____ 3. IMPLEMENTS NATIONAL SALES PROGRAMS
by
developing field sales action plans.

____ 4. MAINTAINS SALES VOLUME, PRODUCT MIX, AND SELLING PRICE
by
keeping current with supply and demand, changing trends, economic indicators, and competitors.

____ 5. ESTABLISHES AND ADJUSTS SELLING PRICES
by
monitoring costs, competition, and supply and demand.

*% of
Time*

____ 6. COMPLETES NATIONAL SALES OPERATIONAL REQUIREMENTS
by
scheduling and assigning employees; following up on work results.

____ 7. MAINTAINS NATIONAL SALES STAFF
by
recruiting, selecting, orienting, and training employees.

____ 8. MAINTAINS NATIONAL SALES STAFF JOB RESULTS
by
counseling and disciplining employees; planning, monitoring, and appraising job results.

____ 9. MAINTAINS PROFESSIONAL AND TECHNICAL KNOWLEDGE
by
attending educational workshops; reviewing professional publications; establishing personal networks; participating in professional societies.

____ 10. CONTRIBUTES TO TEAM EFFORT
by
accomplishing related results as needed.

JOB TITLE: **Sales Promotion Manager**

JOB PURPOSE: **PRODUCES WRITTEN AND VISUAL PROMOTIONAL MATERIALS**

by

defining and controlling internal and external production schedules.

ESSENTIAL JOB RESULTS:

% of Time

____ 1. COMPLETES PRELIMINARY RESEARCH
by
studying files; reviewing marketing research.

____ 2. CREATES PROMOTIONAL MATERIALS
by
designing and composing letters, brochures, and video scripts.

____ 3. SERVES MARKET SEGMENTS AND SPECIFIC PRODUCT NEEDS
by
responding to field requests for market- or product-specific materials.

____ 4. COMPLETES OPERATIONAL REQUIREMENTS
by
coordinating internal and external graphic arts, printing, and video vendors with field and home office personnel.

____ 5. SCHEDULES AND MONITORS PRODUCTION OF MAILINGS, PROMOTIONS, VIDEOS, AND OTHER PROJECTS
by
determining production time requirements; maintaining flowcharts; tracking projects to completion.

____ 6. COMPLETES SALES PROMOTION OPERATIONAL REQUIREMENTS
by
scheduling and assigning employees; following up on work results.

% of Time

____ 7. MAINTAINS SALES PROMOTION STAFF
by
recruiting, selecting, orienting, and training employees.

____ 8. MAINTAINS SALES PROMOTION STAFF JOB RESULTS
by
counseling and disciplining employees; planning, monitoring, and appraising job results.

____ 9. MAINTAINS PROFESSIONAL AND TECHNICAL KNOWLEDGE
by
attending educational workshops; reviewing professional publications; establishing personal networks; participating in professional societies.

____ 10. MAINTAINS EXTERNAL VENDOR RELATIONS
by
providing direction, guidance, and information; resolving concerns.

____ 11. ACHIEVES FINANCIAL OBJECTIVES
by
preparing an annual budget; scheduling expenditures; analyzing variances; initiating corrective actions.

____ 12. CONTRIBUTES TO TEAM EFFORT
by
accomplishing related results as needed.

JOB TITLE: Sales Representative

JOB PURPOSE: SERVES CUSTOMERS

by

selling products; meeting customer needs.

ESSENTIAL JOB RESULTS:

% of Time

____ 1. SERVICES EXISTING ACCOUNTS, OBTAINS ORDERS, AND ESTABLISHES NEW ACCOUNTS
by
planning and organizing daily work schedule to call on existing or potential sales outlets and other trade factors.

____ 2. ADJUSTS CONTENT OF SALES PRESENTATIONS
by
studying the type of sales outlet or trade factor.

____ 3. FOCUSES SALES EFFORTS
by
studying existing and potential volume of dealers.

____ 4. SUBMITS ORDERS
by
referring to price lists and product literature.

____ 5. KEEPS MANAGEMENT INFORMED
by
submitting activity and results reports, such as daily call reports, weekly work plans, and monthly and annual territory analyses.

____ 6. MONITORS COMPETITION
by
gathering current marketplace information on pricing, products, new products, delivery schedules, merchandising techniques, etc.

____ 7. RECOMMENDS CHANGES IN PRODUCTS, SERVICE, AND POLICY
by
evaluating results and competitive developments.

% of Time

____ 8. RESOLVES CUSTOMER COMPLAINTS
by
investigating problems; developing solutions; preparing reports; making recommendations to management.

____ 9. PREPARES SALES OUTLET PERSONNEL, CONTRACTORS, AND OTHER TRADE FACTORS WITH PRODUCT KNOWLEDGE AND SELLING SKILLS
by
conducting and/or participating in sales promotion and educational meetings.

____ 10. MAINTAINS PROFESSIONAL AND TECHNICAL KNOWLEDGE
by
attending educational workshops; reviewing professional publications; establishing personal networks; participating in professional societies.

____ 11. PROVIDES HISTORICAL RECORDS
by
maintaining records on area and customer sales.

____ 12. CONTRIBUTES TO TEAM EFFORT
by
accomplishing related results as needed.

JOB TITLE: Salesperson, Apparel

JOB PURPOSE: **SERVES CUSTOMERS**

by

helping them select appearance-enhancing apparel.

ESSENTIAL JOB RESULTS:

% of
Time

____ 1. WELCOMES CUSTOMERS
by
greeting them; learning their shopping
purpose.

____ 2. DIRECTS CUSTOMERS
by
escorting them to racks and counters;
suggesting items.

____ 3. ADVISES CUSTOMERS
by
providing information on current fashions.

____ 4. HELPS CUSTOMERS
by
accessorizing fashions.

____ 5. GIVES FABRIC ADVICE
by
answering questions regarding washability,
durability, and colorfastness.

____ 6. ANALYZES STYLE CHOICES
by
assessing shape and size of customer.

____ 7. SUGGESTS COLORS, TONES, AND COLOR COMBINATIONS
by
assessing customer's skin, hair, and eye
colors.

% of
Time

____ 8. HELPS CUSTOMER MAKE SELECTIONS
by
building customer confidence; offering
suggestions and opinions.

____ 9. CUSTOMIZES GARMENT FIT
by
demonstrating effect of alterations; calling on
alteration department for implementation.

____ 10. PROCESSES PAYMENTS
by
totaling purchases; processing checks, cash,
and store or other credit cards.

____ 11. DOCUMENTS SALE
by
creating or adding to customer profile
records.

____ 12. KEEPS CLIENTELE INFORMED
by
notifying them of preferred customer sales
and future merchandise of potential interest.

____ 13. CONTRIBUTES TO TEAM EFFORT
by
accomplishing related results as needed.

JOB TITLE: Secretary

JOB PURPOSE: **ENHANCES (DEPARTMENT) EFFECTIVENESS**

by

providing information-management support.

ESSENTIAL JOB RESULTS:

*% of
Time*

____ 1. PRODUCES INFORMATION
by
transcribing, formatting, inputting, editing,
retrieving, copying, and transmitting text,
data, and graphics.

____ 2. ORGANIZES WORK
by
reading and routing correspondence;
collecting information; initiating
telecommunications.

____ 3. MAINTAINS DEPARTMENT'S SCHEDULE
by
maintaining calendars for department
personnel; arranging meetings, conferences,
teleconferences, and travel.

____ 4. COMPLETES REQUESTS
by
greeting customers, in person or on the
telephone; answering or referring inquiries.

____ 5. MAINTAINS CUSTOMER CONFIDENCE AND PROTECTS
OPERATIONS
by
keeping information confidential.

____ 6. PREPARES REPORTS
by
collecting information.

*% of
Time*

____ 7. MAINTAINS OFFICE SUPPLIES INVENTORY
by
checking stock to determine inventory level;
anticipating needed supplies; placing and
expediting orders for supplies; verifying
receipt of supplies.

____ 8. KEEPS EQUIPMENT OPERATIONAL
by
following manufacturer's instructions and
established procedures.

____ 9. SECURES INFORMATION
by
completing data base backups.

____ 10. PROVIDES HISTORICAL REFERENCE
by
utilizing filing and retrieval systems.

____ 11. MAINTAINS TECHNICAL KNOWLEDGE
by
attending educational workshops; reading
secretarial publications.

____ 12. CONTRIBUTES TO TEAM EFFORT
by
accomplishing related results as needed.

JOB TITLE: Secretary, Executive

JOB PURPOSE: **ENHANCES EXECUTIVE'S EFFECTIVENESS**

by

providing information-management support; representing the executive to others.

ESSENTIAL JOB RESULTS:

% of Time

____ 1. PRODUCES INFORMATION
by
transcribing, formatting, inputting, editing, retrieving, copying, and transmitting text, data, and graphics.

____ 2. CONSERVES EXECUTIVE'S TIME
by
reading, researching, and routing correspondence; drafting letters and documents; collecting and analyzing information; initiating telecommunications.

____ 3. MAINTAINS EXECUTIVE'S APPOINTMENT SCHEDULE
by
planning and scheduling meetings, conferences, teleconferences, and travel.

____ 4. REPRESENTS THE EXECUTIVE
by
attending meetings in the executive's absence; speaking for the executive.

____ 5. WELCOMES GUESTS AND CUSTOMERS
by
greeting them, in person or on the telephone; answering or directing inquiries.

____ 6. MAINTAINS CUSTOMER CONFIDENCE AND PROTECTS OPERATIONS
by
keeping information confidential.

____ 7. COMPLETES PROJECTS
by
assigning work to clerical staff; following up on results.

____ 8. PREPARES REPORTS
by
collecting and analyzing information.

% of Time

____ 9. SECURES INFORMATION
by
completing data base backups.

____ 10. PROVIDES HISTORICAL REFERENCE
by
developing and utilizing filing and retrieval systems; recording meeting discussions.

____ 11. MAINTAINS OFFICE SUPPLIES INVENTORY
by
checking stock to determine inventory level; anticipating needed supplies; evaluating new office products; placing and expediting orders for supplies; verifying receipt of supplies.

____ 12. ENSURES OPERATION OF EQUIPMENT
by
completing preventive maintenance requirements; following manufacturer's instructions; troubleshooting malfunctions; calling for repairs; maintaining equipment inventories; evaluating new equipment and techniques.

____ 13. MAINTAINS PROFESSIONAL AND TECHNICAL KNOWLEDGE
by
attending educational workshops; reviewing professional publications; establishing personal networks; participating in professional societies.

____ 14. CONTRIBUTES TO TEAM EFFORT
by
accomplishing related results as needed.

JOB TITLE: Securities Broker

JOB PURPOSE: MEETS CLIENT'S INVESTMENT NEEDS

by

managing investment portfolios.

ESSENTIAL JOB RESULTS:

% of
Time

____ 1. IDENTIFIES CURRENT AND FUTURE CLIENT SERVICE REQUIREMENTS
by
establishing personal rapport with potential and actual clients and other persons in a position to understand service requirements.

____ 2. MARKETS FINANCIAL SERVICES
by
soliciting prospective and current clients; ascertaining their needs; explaining products and services; making sales presentations to groups.

____ 3. MANAGES INVESTMENT PORTFOLIOS
by
analyzing investment opportunities; purchasing and selling securities.

____ 4. COMPLIES WITH SECURITIES AND EXCHANGE COMMISSION REGULATIONS AND STATE AND LOCAL REQUIREMENTS AND PRACTICES
by
studying existing and new legislation; anticipating future legislation; adhering to requirements; advising clients on needed actions.

____ 5. MAINTAINS CLIENT CONFIDENCE AND PROTECTS OPERATIONS
by
keeping investment information confidential.

____ 6. DETERMINES TIMING OF TRANSACTIONS
by
analyzing market conditions and trends.

% of
Time

____ 7. EXECUTES TRANSACTIONS
by
studying market quotations; assessing competitiveness.

____ 8. DOCUMENTS TRANSACTIONS
by
completing buy and sell orders.

____ 9. RESOLVES DISCREPANCIES
by
collecting and analyzing order and transaction information.

____ 10. KEEPS CLIENTS INFORMED
by
communicating market fluctuations; reporting securities transactions affecting accounts; recommending future investment strategies.

____ 11. MAINTAINS OPERATIONS
by
following policies and procedures; reporting needed changes.

____ 12. MAINTAINS PROFESSIONAL AND TECHNICAL KNOWLEDGE
by
attending educational workshops; reviewing professional publications; establishing personal networks; participating in professional societies.

____ 13. CONTRIBUTES TO TEAM EFFORT
by
accomplishing related results as needed.

JOB TITLE: Security Director

JOB PURPOSE: **MAINTAINS A SAFE AND SECURE ENVIRONMENT FOR CUSTOMERS AND EMPLOYEES**

by

establishing and enforcing security policies and procedures; supervising the security guard force.

ESSENTIAL JOB RESULTS:

% of Time

____ 1. DETERMINES AND COMMUNICATES SECURITY POLICIES AND PROCEDURES

by

studying organization operations and executive schedules; establishing internal controls; conducting inspections; preparing and updating a security manual; conducting training sessions.

____ 2. COMPLIES WITH FEDERAL, STATE, AND LOCAL LEGAL REGULATIONS

by

studying existing and new requirements; anticipating future requirements; enforcing adherence to requirements; coordinating and cooperating with government agencies and representatives; advising management on needed actions.

____ 3. SECURES FACILITIES, EQUIPMENT, ASSETS, AND PERSONNEL

by

laying out observation and warning systems; reviewing activities logs; completing personnel security clearances.

____ 4. COMPLETES INVESTIGATIONS

by

gathering evidence; conducting interviews; collecting documents; coordinating with law enforcement personnel; presenting evidence at hearings and trials.

% of Time

____ 5. RESOLVES EMERGENCY SITUATIONS

by

directing actions on location; coordinating with management, public relations, government, and first-aid personnel.

____ 6. MAINTAINS CUSTOMER CONFIDENCE AND PROTECTS OPERATIONS

by

keeping information confidential.

____ 7. COMPLETES SECURITY OPERATIONS REQUIREMENTS

by

scheduling and assigning employees; following up on work results.

____ 8. MAINTAINS SECURITY STAFF

by

recruiting, selecting, orienting, and training employees.

____ 9. MAINTAINS SECURITY STAFF JOB RESULTS

by

coaching, counseling, and disciplining employees; planning, monitoring, and appraising job results.

____ 10. MAINTAINS PROFESSIONAL AND TECHNICAL KNOWLEDGE

by

attending educational workshops; reviewing professional publications; establishing personal networks; participating in professional societies.

ESSENTIAL JOB RESULTS:

% of
Time

____ 11. ACHIEVES FINANCIAL OBJECTIVES
     by
     preparing the security budget; scheduling
     expenditures; analyzing variances; initiating
     corrective actions.

____ 12. PREPARES SECURITY REPORTS
     by
     collecting, analyzing, and summarizing
     information and trends.

% of
Time

____ 13. CONTRIBUTES TO TEAM EFFORT
     by
     accomplishing related results as needed.

JOB TITLE: Security Guard

JOB PURPOSE: **MAINTAINS SAFE AND SECURE ENVIRONMENT FOR CUSTOMERS AND EMPLOYEES**

by

patrolling and monitoring premises and personnel.

ESSENTIAL JOB RESULTS:

*% of
Time*

_____ 1. SECURES PREMISES AND PERSONNEL

by

patrolling property; monitoring surveillance equipment; inspecting buildings, equipment, and access points; permitting entry.

_____ 2. OBTAINS HELP

by

sounding alarms.

_____ 3. PREVENTS LOSSES AND DAMAGE

by

reporting irregularities; informing violators of policy and procedures; restraining trespassers.

_____ 4. CONTROLS TRAFFIC

by

directing drivers.

_____ 5. COMPLETES REPORTS

by

recording observations, information, occurrences, and surveillance activities; interviewing witnesses; obtaining signatures.

*% of
Time*

_____ 6. MAINTAINS ENVIRONMENT

by

monitoring and setting building and equipment controls.

_____ 7. MAINTAINS ORGANIZATION'S STABILITY AND REPUTATION

by

complying with legal requirements.

_____ 8. ENSURES OPERATION OF EQUIPMENT

by

completing preventive maintenance requirements; following manufacturer's instructions; troubleshooting malfunctions; calling for repairs; evaluating new equipment and techniques.

_____ 9. CONTRIBUTES TO TEAM EFFORT

by

accomplishing related results as needed.

JOB TITLE: Security Supervisor

JOB PURPOSE: **MAINTAINS SAFE AND SECURE ENVIRONMENT FOR CUSTOMERS AND EMPLOYEES**

by

scheduling and completing security assignments.

ESSENTIAL JOB RESULTS:

% of Time

____ 1. COMPLETES SECURITY OPERATIONS REQUIREMENTS

by

designing routes; monitoring timetables; scheduling and assigning security guards to posts and routes; inspecting work results.

____ 2. MAINTAINS SECURITY STAFF

by

recruiting, selecting, orienting, and training security guards.

____ 3. MAINTAINS SECURITY STAFF JOB RESULTS

by

coaching, counseling, and disciplining security guards; planning, monitoring, and appraising job results.

____ 4. MAINTAINS PROFESSIONAL AND TECHNICAL KNOWLEDGE

by

attending educational workshops; reviewing professional publications; establishing personal networks; participating in professional societies.

____ 5. SECURES FACILITIES, OPERATIONS, AND PERSONNEL

by

surveying and testing alarms; maintaining surveillance; conducting inspections; reporting irregularities; issuing security badges; responding to emergencies.

____ 6. MAINTAINS SECURITY FLEET

by

compiling and analyzing vehicle logs; identifying maintenance and repair requirements; scheduling service appointments; recommending purchases of new vehicles.

% of Time

____ 7. MAINTAINS OPERATIONS

by

interpreting and enforcing policies and procedures; reporting needed changes.

____ 8. MAINTAINS RAPPORT WITH LOCAL LAW ENFORCEMENT, CIVIL DEFENSE, AND FIRST-AID AGENCIES

by

establishing personal contact; cooperating to resolve situations.

____ 9. MAINTAINS CUSTOMER CONFIDENCE AND PROTECTS OPERATIONS

by

keeping information confidential.

____ 10. PREPARES SECURITY REPORTS

by

collecting, analyzing, and summarizing information and trends.

____ 11. MAINTAINS SUPPLIES INVENTORY

by

checking stock to determine inventory level; anticipating needed supplies; placing and expediting orders for supplies; verifying receipt of supplies.

____ 12. CONTRIBUTES TO TEAM EFFORT

by

accomplishing related results as needed.

JOB PURPOSE: **JOINS, REINFORCES, OR DECORATES MATERIALS**

by

operating a sewing machine.

ESSENTIAL JOB RESULTS:

% of
Time

_____ 1. PREPARES WORK TO BE ACCOMPLISHED
by
gathering and sorting materials.

_____ 2. PREPARES MACHINE
by
changing needles and thread; securing
attachments.

_____ 3. APPROVES MATERIALS
by
inspecting materials for flaws.

_____ 4. SEWS MATERIALS TOGETHER
by
guiding material under machine needle.

_____ 5. ADJUSTS MACHINE PERFORMANCE ON MATERIAL
by
observing machine operation; detecting
malfunctions; adjusting settings.

_____ 6. MAINTAINS QUALITY
by
inspecting finished product.

_____ 7. ENSURES OPERATION OF EQUIPMENT
by
completing preventive maintenance
requirements; following manufacturer's
instructions; troubleshooting malfunctions;
calling for repairs.

% of
Time

_____ 8. MAINTAINS MATERIALS AND SUPPLIES INVENTORY
by
checking materials and supplies to determine
inventory level; anticipating needed materials
and supplies; placing and expediting orders
for materials and supplies; verifying receipt
of materials and supplies.

_____ 9. RESOLVES ASSEMBLY PROBLEMS
by
altering dimensions to meet specifications;
notifying supervisor to obtain additional
resources.

_____ 10. DOCUMENTS ACTIONS
by
completing production and quality logs.

_____ 11. CONTRIBUTES TO TEAM EFFORT
by
accomplishing related results as needed.

JOB TITLE: Shipping/Receiving Technician

JOB PURPOSE: ACCEPTS SHIPMENTS AND SHIPS PRODUCT

by

unloading, loading, and verifying shipments.

ESSENTIAL JOB RESULTS:

*% of
Time*

____ 1. RECEIVES ITEMS

by

unloading vehicles; accepting deliveries; unpacking containers.

____ 2. VERIFIES ITEMS RECEIVED

by

inspecting condition of items; comparing count/measure of items to purchase order and packing list; noting discrepancies.

____ 3. DOCUMENTS ITEMS RECEIVED

by

recording identifying information.

____ 4. TRANSFERS ORDERS RECEIVED

by

routing or delivering items to requesting department.

____ 5. REPLACES DAMAGED ITEMS AND SHORTAGES OR OBTAINS CREDIT

by

informing shipper and transporter of damage or shortage; returning damaged items; requesting new items or credit for shortages.

____ 6. RECEIVES CREDIT-RETURN MATERIALS FROM PRODUCTION

by

verifying identifying information and quantity of materials; placing materials in inventory.

*% of
Time*

____ 7. PREPARES SHIPMENTS

by

assembling, packing, protecting, and labeling containers.

____ 8. DETERMINES METHOD OF SHIPMENT

by

examining items to be shipped, destination, route, rate, and time of shipment.

____ 9. SHIPS ITEMS

by

verifying identifying information and quantity and condition of items; loading and protecting items.

____ 10. DOCUMENTS ITEMS SHIPPED

by

recording identifying information of items and transport information.

____ 11. MAINTAINS SHIPPING AND RECEIVING MATERIALS

by

checking stock to determine inventory level; anticipating needed materials; placing and expediting orders for materials; verifying receipt of materials.

____ 12. CONTRIBUTES TO TEAM EFFORT

by

accomplishing related results as needed.

279

```
┌─────────────────────────────────────────────────────────────────────┐
│                                                                       │
│   JOB TITLE: Social Worker                                            │
│                                                                       │
└─────────────────────────────────────────────────────────────────────┘
```

JOB PURPOSE: **HELP CLIENTS**

by

assessing their situation; setting goals; obtaining required services.

ESSENTIAL JOB RESULTS:

% of
Time

_____ 1. DETERMINES NATURE OF CLIENT'S SITUATION

by

interviewing client; assessing medical, psychological, emotional, and social information; making on-site visits.

_____ 2. ESTABLISHES COURSE OF ACTION

by

exploring options; setting goals with client.

_____ 3. OBTAINS ASSISTANCE FOR CLIENT

by

referring him/her to community resources; arranging for appointments; establishing rapport with other agencies.

_____ 4. FOSTERS CLIENT'S ACTION OR ADJUSTMENT

by

interpreting attitudes and patterns of behavior; explaining and pointing out new options.

_____ 5. MAINTAINS RECORD OF CASE

by

documenting client's situation and client's own actions.

% of
Time

_____ 6. MONITORS PLANNED ACTIONS

by

periodic follow-up.

_____ 7. MAINTAINS OPERATIONS

by

following policies and procedures; participating in quality reviews; reporting needed changes.

_____ 8. COMPLIES WITH FEDERAL, STATE, AND LOCAL LEGAL REQUIREMENTS

by

studying existing and new legislation; enforcing adherence to requirements; advising management on needed actions.

_____ 9. MAINTAINS CLIENT CONFIDENCE AND PROTECTS OPERATIONS

by

keeping information confidential.

_____ 10. CONTRIBUTES TO TEAM EFFORT

by

accomplishing related results as needed.

JOB PURPOSE: RESTORES OR DEVELOPS PATIENT'S ABILITY TO COMMUNICATE

by

planning and administering medically prescribed speech therapy.

ESSENTIAL JOB RESULTS:

% of Time

____ 1. MEETS PATIENT'S GOALS AND NEEDS AND PROVIDES QUALITY CARE

by

assessing patient's condition; interpreting evaluations and test results; identifying speech, language, voice, and swallowing disorders; determining speech therapy treatment plans in consultation with physicians or by prescription.

____ 2. HELPS PATIENTS ACCOMPLISH TREATMENT PLAN

by

training with audiovisual equipment, sound-activated computer systems, and electronic voice machines; providing counseling and guidance; providing development therapy; interpreting specialized hearing and speech tests; instructing individuals in monitoring their own speech; teaching manual sign language; providing ways to practice skills; directing aides, technicians, and assistants.

____ 3. EVALUATES EFFECTS OF SPEECH THERAPY

by

observing patient's progress; recommending adjustments and modifications.

____ 4. COMPLETES DISCHARGE PLANNING

by

consulting with physicians, nurses, social workers, and other health care workers; contributing to patient care conferences.

% of Time

____ 5. ASSURES CONTINUATION OF THERAPEUTIC PLAN FOLLOWING DISCHARGE

by

designing home exercise programs; instructing patients, families, and caregivers in home exercise programs; recommending and/or providing assistive equipment; recommending outpatient or home health follow-up programs.

____ 6. DOCUMENTS PATIENT CARE SERVICES

by

completing charting in patient and department records.

____ 7. MAINTAINS PATIENT CONFIDENCE AND PROTECTS HOSPITAL OPERATIONS

by

keeping information confidential.

____ 8. MAINTAINS SAFE AND CLEAN WORKING ENVIRONMENT

by

complying with procedures, rules, and regulations.

____ 9. PROTECTS PATIENTS AND EMPLOYEES

by

adhering to infection-control policies and protocols.

JOB TITLE: Speech Therapist

ESSENTIAL JOB RESULTS:

% of
Time

_____ 10. ENSURES OPERATION OF EQUIPMENT
by
completing preventive maintenance
requirements; following manufacturer's
instructions; troubleshooting malfunctions;
calling for repairs.

_____ 11. MAINTAINS PROFESSIONAL AND TECHNICAL KNOWLEDGE
by
attending educational workshops; reviewing
professional publications; establishing
personal networks; participating in
professional societies.

_____ 12. DEVELOPS SPEECH THERAPY AND HOSPITAL STAFF
by
providing information; developing and
conducting in-service training programs.

% of
Time

_____ 13. COMPLIES WITH FEDERAL, STATE, AND LOCAL LEGAL AND
CERTIFICATION REQUIREMENTS
by
studying existing and new legislation;
anticipating future legislation; enforcing
adherence to requirements; advising
management on needed actions.

_____ 14. CONTRIBUTES TO TEAM EFFORT
by
accomplishing related results as needed.

JOB TITLE: Statistical Analyst

JOB PURPOSE: **PROVIDES INFORMATION FOR SCIENTIFIC RESEARCH AND STATISTICAL ANALYSIS**

by

planning data collection; analyzing and interpreting data; applying statistical methodologies.

ESSENTIAL JOB RESULTS:

% of Time

____ 1. PLANS METHODS TO COLLECT INFORMATION
by
developing survey questionnaire techniques based on survey design.

____ 2. CONDUCTS SURVEYS
by
applying sampling techniques and counting responses.

____ 3. EVALUATES RELIABILITY OF SOURCE INFORMATION
by
weighting raw data; organizing results for analysis.

____ 4. PRESENTS DATA
by
computer readouts, graphs, charts, tables, written reports, or other methods.

____ 5. PREPARES CONCLUSIONS AND FORECASTS
by
analyzing and interpreting data summaries; identifying differences in relationships among sources of information; determining limitations on reliability and usability.

% of Time

____ 6. MAINTAINS HISTORICAL DATA RECORDS
by
organizing and filing statistical reports; developing formats for time-line analyses.

____ 7. MAINTAINS PROFESSIONAL AND TECHNICAL KNOWLEDGE
by
attending educational workshops; reviewing professional publications; establishing personal networks; participating in professional societies.

____ 8. CONTRIBUTES TO TEAM EFFORT
by
accomplishing related results as needed.

JOB TITLE: Stock Clerk

JOB PURPOSE: **FILLS INVENTORY REQUESTS**

by

receiving and dispensing supplies.

ESSENTIAL JOB RESULTS:

*% of
Time*

____ 1. RECEIVES MERCHANDISE
by
unloading vehicles; checking merchandise for
damage; verifying freight bill.

____ 2. FILLS ORDERS
by
identifying items requested; pulling items
from stock; packing and labeling items;
noting back orders; verifying completeness.

____ 3. PREPARES ORDERS FOR CARRIER SERVICE
by
packing and labeling merchandise; delivering
to carrier or arranging pickup; maintaining
carrier records.

____ 4. CONTROLS INVENTORY
by
conducting physical counts and reconciling
with inventory system; notifying purchasing
department when reorder points are reached;
retrieving unused or excess supplies and
equipment and reentering them to inventory.

____ 5. PROVIDES INFORMATION
by
answering questions; inputting and
generating data; completing forms.

*% of
Time*

____ 6. SUPPORTS OTHER DEPARTMENTS
by
establishing routine deliveries of standard
orders; determining other predictable supply
needs.

____ 7. MAINTAINS WAREHOUSE VEHICLES AND EQUIPMENT
by
cleaning; following manufacturer's standards
of use; performing and scheduling preventive
maintenance; reporting damage or
mechanical problems to supervisor.

____ 8. MAINTAINS SAFE AND CLEAN WORKING ENVIRONMENT
by
complying with procedures, rules, and
regulations.

____ 9. CONTRIBUTES TO TEAM EFFORT
by
accomplishing related results as needed.

JOB TITLE: Student Loan Officer

JOB PURPOSE: PROMOTES STUDENT LOANS

by

developing information programs; soliciting business.

ESSENTIAL JOB RESULTS:

*% of
Time*

_____ 1. IDENTIFIES MARKET PROSPECTS

by

obtaining students' names from schools, counselors, financial aid officers, mailing lists, and other sources.

_____ 2. DEVELOPS MARKETING PLAN

by

reviewing objectives, strategies, and media with marketing department.

_____ 3. DEVELOPS ADVERTISING PROGRAM

by

defining objectives; evaluating and selecting media; preparing media message.

_____ 4. DEVELOPS EXPLANATORY LITERATURE

by

stating program objectives, benefits, methods of application, requirements, and contract.

_____ 5. PROMOTES STUDENT LOAN PROGRAM

by

initiating direct-mail campaigns; conducting discussions; presenting programs; informing and training bank personnel who are in contact with customers.

_____ 6. EXPLAINS THE PROGRAM

by

answering questions and requests.

_____ 7. PREPARES ACTIVITY REPORTS

by

collecting, analyzing, and summarizing information and trends.

*% of
Time*

_____ 8. MAINTAINS KNOWLEDGE OF INDUSTRY DEVELOPMENT

by

attending educational workshops; reviewing professional publications; establishing personal networks; participating in professional societies.

_____ 9. COMPLIES WITH FEDERAL, STATE, AND LOCAL LEGAL REQUIREMENTS

by

studying existing and new legislation; anticipating future legislation; enforcing adherence to requirements; advising management on needed actions.

_____ 10. SUPPORTS COLLECTION OF DEFAULTS

by

providing account information.

_____ 11. SECURES INFORMATION

by

completing data base backups.

_____ 12. MAINTAINS CUSTOMER CONFIDENCE AND PROTECTS BANK OPERATIONS

by

keeping information confidential.

_____ 13. CONTRIBUTES TO TEAM EFFORT

by

accomplishing related results as needed.

┌───┐
│ **JOB TITLE:** Systems Analyst   │
└───┘

JOB PURPOSE: SOLVES CLIENTS' INFORMATION REQUIREMENTS
by
developing and maintaining software applications; helping clients use computer resources.

ESSENTIAL JOB RESULTS:

% of
Time

____ 1. IDENTIFIES CLIENT INFORMATION REQUIREMENTS
by
conferring with clients; analyzing operations; evaluating input and output requirements and formats.

____ 2. DESIGNS COMPUTER PROGRAM
by
describing and analyzing information requirements in a work flow chart and diagram; studying system capabilities; writing specifications for programmers.

____ 3. IMPROVES CURRENT SYSTEMS
by
studying practices, procedures, and problems; designing modifications.

____ 4. PROVIDES REFERENCE FOR CLIENTS
by
writing and maintaining user documentation; maintaining a help desk.

____ 5. PREPARES CLIENTS TO USE SYSTEM
by
conducting training sessions.

____ 6. MAINTAINS SYSTEM GUIDELINES
by
writing and updating policies and procedures.

% of
Time

____ 7. MAINTAINS PROFESSIONAL AND TECHNICAL KNOWLEDGE
by
attending educational workshops; reviewing professional publications; establishing personal networks; participating in professional societies.

____ 8. MAINTAINS CLIENT CONFIDENCE AND PROTECTS OPERATIONS
by
keeping information confidential.

____ 9. PREPARES TECHNICAL REPORTS
by
collecting, analyzing, and summarizing information and trends.

____ 10. COMPLETES PROJECTS
by
training and guiding specialists.

____ 11. CONTRIBUTES TO TEAM EFFORT
by
accomplishing related results as needed.

JOB TITLE: Systems Programmer

JOB PURPOSE: **PREPARES COMPUTER**

by

installing and modifying system software.

ESSENTIAL JOB RESULTS:

% of Time

____ 1. PREPARES SYSTEM SOFTWARE INSTALLATION
by
studying software capabilities and operations, including task scheduling, memory management, file system, and input and output requirements.

____ 2. INSTALLS SYSTEM SOFTWARE
by
loading software into computer.

____ 3. DETECTS WORK STOPPAGE OR ERRORS
by
conducting tests; monitoring output.

____ 4. CORRECTS WORK STOPPAGES OR ERRORS
by
entering code changes.

____ 5. OPTIMIZES SYSTEM EFFICIENCY
by
analyzing performance indicators; changing software.

____ 6. MAINTAINS HISTORICAL RECORDS
by
documenting system software changes and revisions.

____ 7. PREPARES REFERENCE FOR USERS
by
writing operating instructions.

% of Time

____ 8. MAINTAINS CLIENT CONFIDENCE AND PROTECTS OPERATIONS
by
keeping information confidential.

____ 9. CONTROLS ACCESS TO SYSTEM
by
monitoring program usage.

____ 10. ENSURES OPERATION OF EQUIPMENT
by
following manufacturer's instructions; troubleshooting malfunctions; calling for repairs; evaluating new equipment and techniques.

____ 11. MAINTAINS PROFESSIONAL AND TECHNICAL KNOWLEDGE
by
attending educational workshops; reviewing professional publications; establishing personal networks; participating in professional societies.

____ 12. CONTRIBUTES TO TEAM EFFORT
by
accomplishing related results as needed.

JOB TITLE: Tax Accountant

JOB PURPOSE: DETERMINES TAX LIABILITY

by

interpreting tax regulations; computing taxes; completing tax returns.

ESSENTIAL JOB RESULTS:

*% of
Time*

_____ 1. GUIDES MANAGEMENT'S TAX DECISIONS
by
examining and discussing tax consequences
of various financial options; recommending
optimal course of action.

_____ 2. DETERMINES IMPACT OF MANAGEMENT'S TAX DECISIONS
by
computing taxes.

_____ 3. RECOMMENDS STRATEGIES TO MINIMIZE TAX LIABILITY
by
studying tax regulations; searching out and
evaluating tax options.

_____ 4. PREPARES FEDERAL, STATE, AND LOCAL TAX RETURNS
by
collecting, analyzing, and formatting
financial information.

_____ 5. REMITS TAX PAYMENTS
by
requesting disbursements.

_____ 6. COMPLIES WITH FEDERAL, STATE, AND LOCAL TAX
REQUIREMENTS
by
studying existing regulations; enforcing
adherence to requirements; advising
management on needed actions; filing
required financial and related information.

_____ 7. MAINTAINS KNOWLEDGE OF TAX REQUIREMENTS
by
studying new tax regulations and directives;
obtaining tax opinions and interpretations;
attending tax seminars; studying proposed tax
legislation.

*% of
Time*

_____ 8. PREPARES SPECIAL TAX REPORTS
by
collecting and analyzing financial and related
information.

_____ 9. RECONCILES TAX DISCREPANCIES
by
collecting and analyzing financial
information.

_____ 10. REPRESENTS THE ORGANIZATION AT TAX HEARINGS
by
providing financial information; arguing the
organization's position.

_____ 11. SECURES TAX INFORMATION
by
completing data base backups.

_____ 12. MAINTAINS CUSTOMER CONFIDENCE AND PROTECTS
OPERATIONS
by
keeping tax information confidential.

_____ 13. CONTRIBUTES TO TEAM EFFORT
by
accomplishing related results as needed.

JOB PURPOSE: **DETERMINES TAX LIABILITY**

by

auditing financial records.

ESSENTIAL JOB RESULTS:

*% of
Time*

____ 1. VERIFIES REPORTED FINANCIAL STATUS
by
reviewing assets and liabilities.

____ 2. DETERMINES NATURE AND SCOPE OF INVESTIGATION
by
collecting and analyzing financial
information.

____ 3. DETERMINES TAX LIABILITY
by
evaluating and verifying evidence of taxpayer
financial status and transactions; interviewing
taxpayer and financial institutions;
conducting audits.

____ 4. NOTIFIES TAXPAYER OF TAX LIABILITY
by
preparing a report and explanation of the
investigation.

____ 5. NOTIFIES TAXPAYER OF APPEAL RIGHTS
by
explaining procedures.

____ 6. COMPLIES WITH FEDERAL, STATE, AND LOCAL LEGAL
REQUIREMENTS
by
studying existing and new legislation.

*% of
Time*

____ 7. MAINTAINS OPERATIONS
by
following policies and procedures; reporting
needed changes.

____ 8. MAINTAINS PROFESSIONAL AND TECHNICAL KNOWLEDGE
by
attending educational workshops; reviewing
professional publications; establishing
personal networks; participating in
professional societies.

____ 9. MAINTAINS TAXPAYER CONFIDENCE AND PROTECTS
OPERATIONS
by
keeping information confidential.

____ 10. CONTRIBUTES TO TEAM EFFORT
by
accomplishing related results as needed.

JOB TITLE: Technical Illustrator

JOB PURPOSE: **INTERPRETS TECHNOLOGY**

by

producing illustrations.

ESSENTIAL JOB RESULTS:

% of
Time

____ 1. PREPARES WORK TO BE ACCOMPLISHED
by
gathering information and materials.

____ 2. ILLUSTRATES CONCEPTS, ASSEMBLIES, AND COMPONENTS
by
designing and executing drawings, sketches,
prints, charts, and graphs.

____ 3. PREPARES PRESENTATIONS
by
designing and executing visual aids; taking
photographs.

____ 4. PREPARES PRINTED MATERIALS
by
designing and executing sketches and rough
and finished artwork.

____ 5. ENSURES OPERATION OF EQUIPMENT
by
completing preventive maintenance
requirements; following manufacturer's
instructions; troubleshooting malfunctions;
calling for repairs; maintaining equipment
inventories; evaluating new equipment.

% of
Time

____ 6. COMPLETES PROJECTS
by
coordinating with outside agencies, art
services, printers, etc.

____ 7. MAINTAINS TECHNICAL KNOWLEDGE
by
attending design workshops; reviewing
professional publications; participating in
professional societies.

____ 8. CONTRIBUTES TO TEAM EFFORT
by
accomplishing related results as needed.

JOB TITLE: Technical Support Specialist

JOB PURPOSE: MAXIMIZES COMPUTER SYSTEM CAPABILITIES
by

studying technical applications; making recommendations.

ESSENTIAL JOB RESULTS:

% of
Time

_____ 1. EVALUATES SYSTEM POTENTIAL
by
testing compatibility of new programs with existing programs.

_____ 2. EVALUATES EXPANSIONS OR ENHANCEMENTS
by
studying work load and capacity of computer system.

_____ 3. ACHIEVES COMPUTER SYSTEM OBJECTIVES
by
gathering pertinent data; identifying and evaluating options; recommending a course of action.

_____ 4. CONFIRMS PROGRAM OBJECTIVES AND SPECIFICATIONS
by
testing new programs; comparing programs with established standards; making modifications.

_____ 5. IMPROVES EXISTING PROGRAMS
by
reviewing objectives and specifications; evaluating proposed changes; recommending changes; making modifications.

_____ 6. EVALUATES VENDOR-SUPPLIED SOFTWARE
by
studying user objectives; testing software compatibility with existing hardware and programs.

_____ 7. PLACES SOFTWARE INTO PRODUCTION
by
loading software into computer; entering necessary commands.

% of
Time

_____ 8. PLACES HARDWARE INTO PRODUCTION
by
establishing connections; entering necessary commands.

_____ 9. MAXIMIZES USE OF HARDWARE AND SOFTWARE
by
training users; interpreting instructions; answering questions.

_____ 10. MAINTAINS SYSTEM CAPABILITY
by
testing computer components.

_____ 11. PREPARES REFERENCE FOR USERS
by
writing operating instructions.

_____ 12. MAINTAINS HISTORICAL RECORDS
by
documenting hardware and software changes and revisions.

_____ 13. MAINTAINS CLIENT CONFIDENCE AND PROTECTS OPERATIONS
by
keeping information confidential.

_____ 14. MAINTAINS PROFESSIONAL AND TECHNICAL KNOWLEDGE
by
attending educational workshops; reviewing professional publications; establishing personal networks; participating in professional societies.

_____ 15. CONTRIBUTES TO TEAM EFFORT
by
accomplishing related results as needed.

JOB TITLE: Technical Writer

JOB PURPOSE: **INTERPRETS TECHNOLOGY**

by

producing written descriptions and instructions.

ESSENTIAL JOB RESULTS:

% of
Time

_____ 1. PREPARES WORK TO BE ACCOMPLISHED
by
gathering information.

_____ 2. COMPREHENDS TECHNOLOGY
by
observing production and use; interviewing
engineers and designers; studying blueprints,
sketches, drawings, specifications, parts
lists, mock-ups, samples, etc.

_____ 3. PREPARES OUTLINE
by
organizing materials.

_____ 4. COMPLETES OUTLINE
by
composing language for nontechnical
consumers.

_____ 5. VERIFIES COMPREHENSION OF TECHNOLOGY AND
COMPOSITION
by
testing description and instructions.

% of
Time

_____ 6. OBTAINS APPROVAL OF INTERPRETATION
by
submitting draft for approval.

_____ 7. MAINTAINS RESOURCE OF TECHNICAL WRITING
by
filing publications.

_____ 8. COMPLETES PROJECTS
by
coordinating with agencies and typing and
printing services.

_____ 9. SUPPORTS DEVELOPMENT OF SPEECHES, ARTICLES AND
NEWS RELEASES
by
preparing technical descriptions.

_____ 10. CONTRIBUTES TO TEAM EFFORT
by
accomplishing related results as needed.

JOB PURPOSE: **HELPS PEOPLE COMMUNICATE**

by

referring telephone calls; maintaining telephone directories.

ESSENTIAL JOB RESULTS:

% of
Time

____ 1. HELPS CUSTOMERS, EMPLOYEES, VENDORS, AND OTHERS WHO HAVE BUSINESS WITH THE ORGANIZATION
by
referring telephone calls to requested individuals.

____ 2. MAINTAINS ORGANIZATION TELEPHONE DIRECTORY
by
updating files with additions, deletions, and changes.

____ 3. RESOLVES TELECOMMUNICATIONS PROBLEMS
by
recording complaints; calling repair services.

% of
Time

____ 4. APPLIES TELECOMMUNICATIONS EXPENDITURES TO COST CENTERS
by
separating charges on invoices.

____ 5. VERIFIES INVOICES FOR PAYMENT
by
verifying charges; reconciling charges.

____ 6. CONTRIBUTES TO TEAM EFFORT
by
accomplishing related results as needed.

JOB TITLE: Telemarketer

JOB PURPOSE: SOLICITS ORDERS FOR MERCHANDISE OR SERVICES

by

telephoning customers.

ESSENTIAL JOB RESULTS:

*% of
Time*

____ 1. IDENTIFIES PROSPECTS
  by
  reading telephone and zip code directories
  and other prepared listings.

____ 2. CALLS PROSPECTIVE CUSTOMERS
  by
  operating telephone equipment, automatic
  dialing systems, and other
  telecommunications technologies.

____ 3. INFLUENCES CUSTOMERS TO BUY SERVICES AND
  MERCHANDISE
  by
  following a prepared sales talk to give service
  and product information and price
  quotations.

____ 4. COMPLETES ORDERS
  by
  recording names, addresses, and purchases;
  referring orders for filling.

*% of
Time*

____ 5. KEEPS EQUIPMENT OPERATIONAL
  by
  following manufacturer's instructions and
  established procedures.

____ 6. SECURES INFORMATION
  by
  completing data base backups.

____ 7. MAINTAINS SAFE AND CLEAN WORKING ENVIRONMENT
  by
  complying with procedures, rules, and
  regulations.

____ 8. MAINTAINS OPERATIONS
  by
  following policies and procedures; reporting
  needed changes.

____ 9. CONTRIBUTES TO TEAM EFFORT
  by
  accomplishing related results as needed.

JOB TITLE: Teller

JOB PURPOSE:

SERVES CUSTOMERS

by

completing account transactions.

ESSENTIAL JOB RESULTS:

% of
Time

_____ 1. PROVIDES ACCOUNT SERVICES TO CUSTOMERS

by

receiving deposits and loan payments; cashing checks; issuing savings withdrawals; recording night and mail deposits; selling cashier's checks, traveler's checks, and Series E bonds; answering questions in person or on telephone; referring to other bank services.

_____ 2. RECORDS TRANSACTIONS

by

logging cashier's checks, traveler's checks, and other special services; preparing currency transaction reports.

_____ 3. CROSS-SELLS BANK PRODUCTS

by

answering inquiries; informing customers of new services and product promotions; ascertaining customers' needs; directing customers to a branch representative.

_____ 4. COMPLETES SPECIAL REQUESTS

by

closing accounts; taking orders for checks; opening and closing Christmas and vacation clubs; exchanging foreign currencies; providing special statements, copies, and referrals; completing safe-deposit box procedures.

% of
Time

_____ 5. RECONCILES CASH DRAWER

by

proving cash transactions; counting and packaging currency and coins; reconciling loan coupons and other transactions; turning in excess cash and mutilated currency to head teller; maintaining supply of cash and currency.

_____ 6. COMPLIES WITH BANK OPERATIONS AND SECURITY PROCEDURES

by

participating in all dual-control functions; maintaining customer traffic surveys; auditing other tellers' currency; assisting in certification of proof.

_____ 7. MAINTAINS CUSTOMER CONFIDENCE AND PROTECTS BANK OPERATIONS

by

keeping information confidential.

_____ 8. CONTRIBUTES TO TEAM EFFORT

by

accomplishing related results as needed.

JOB TITLE: Test Engineer

JOB PURPOSE:

EVALUATES PRODUCTS

by

designing and conducting performance, environmental, and operational tests.

ESSENTIAL JOB RESULTS:

% of Time

____ 1. DETERMINES TEST OBJECTIVES AND STANDARDS
by
studying product characteristics, customer requirements, and government regulations; conferring with management.

____ 2. MEETS TEST OBJECTIVES
by
determining testing methods, phases, and conditions; selecting or fabricating testing equipment and apparatus.

____ 3. IDENTIFIES PRODUCT CAPABILITY AND RELIABILITY
by
conducting performance, environmental, and operational tests.

____ 4. RESOLVES TESTING PROBLEMS
by
modifying testing methods during tests; conferring with management to revise test objectives and standards.

____ 5. COMPLETES TESTS
by
training and directing technicians.

____ 6. DOCUMENTS TEST OUTCOMES
by
devising observation and recording devices.

% of Time

____ 7. MAINTAINS TEST INFORMATION DATA BASE
by
developing information requirements; designing an information system; entering and securing data.

____ 8. REPORTS TEST OUTCOMES
by
collecting, analyzing, interpreting, summarizing, and displaying data; recommending product changes.

____ 9. MAINTAINS PROFESSIONAL AND TECHNICAL KNOWLEDGE
by
attending educational workshops; reviewing professional publications; establishing personal networks; participating in professional societies.

____ 10. MAINTAINS SAFE TEST ENVIRONMENT
by
enforcing and complying with procedures, rules, and regulations.

____ 11. CONTRIBUTES TO TEAM EFFORT
by
accomplishing related results as needed.

JOB TITLE: Test Technician

JOB PURPOSE: **EVALUATES PRODUCTS**

by

conducting performance, environmental, and operational tests.

ESSENTIAL JOB RESULTS:

% of
Time

____ 1. PREPARES TESTS

by
studying test objectives, standards, methods, conditions, and equipment.

____ 2. IDENTIFIES PRODUCT CAPABILITY AND RELIABILITY

by
conducting performance, environmental, and operational tests.

____ 3. RESOLVES TESTING PROBLEMS

by
altering testing methods during tests; notifying supervisor to obtain additional resources.

____ 4. DOCUMENTS TEST OUTCOMES

by
completing test logs.

____ 5. REPORTS TEST OUTCOMES

by
collecting data.

____ 6. MAINTAINS TECHNICAL KNOWLEDGE

by
attending educational workshops; reviewing professional publications.

% of
Time

____ 7. MAINTAINS SAFE TEST ENVIRONMENT

by
complying with procedures, rules, and regulations.

____ 8. MAINTAINS TEST INFORMATION DATA BASE

by
entering and backing up data.

____ 9. ENSURES OPERATION OF EQUIPMENT

by
completing preventive maintenance requirements; following manufacturer's instructions; troubleshooting malfunctions; calling for repairs; evaluating new equipment and techniques.

____ 10. MAINTAINS CONTINUITY AMONG WORK TEAMS

by
documenting and communicating actions, irregularities, and continuing needs.

____ 11. CONTRIBUTES TO TEAM EFFORT

by
accomplishing related results as needed.

JOB TITLE: Toolmaker

JOB PURPOSE: **FABRICATES AND REPAIRS TOOLS, JIGS, FIXTURES, GAUGES, OR HAND TOOLS**

by

studying requirements; machining materials.

ESSENTIAL JOB RESULTS:

% of Time

____ 1. DEVELOPS TOOLS, JIGS, FIXTURES, GAUGES, OR HAND TOOLS

by

studying blueprints, sketches, specifications, and descriptions; applying knowledge of materials, machining, and assembly methods and mathematics.

____ 2. PREPARES STOCK FOR MACHINING

by

measuring, marking, and scribing.

____ 3. MACHINES TOOLS, JIGS, FIXTURES, GAUGES, OR HAND TOOLS

by

setting up and operating lathe, mill, shaper, grinder, and related equipment.

____ 4. CONFIRMS TOOLS, JIGS, FIXTURES, GAUGES, OR HAND TOOLS

by

comparing measurements to specifications using micrometers, thickness gauges, gauge blocks, and other measurement tools.

____ 5. ASSEMBLES TOOLS, JIGS, FIXTURES, GAUGES, OR HAND TOOLS

by

shaping, smoothing, and fitting parts with grinders, files, stones, etc.

____ 6. STRENGTHENS TOOLS, JIGS, FIXTURES, GAUGES, OR HAND TOOLS

by

heat-treating materials.

% of Time

____ 7. RESOLVES FABRICATION AND ASSEMBLY PROBLEMS

by

altering process to meet specifications; notifying supervisor to obtain additional resources.

____ 8. ENSURES OPERATION OF EQUIPMENT

by

completing preventive maintenance requirements; following manufacturer's instructions; troubleshooting malfunctions; calling for repairs.

____ 9. MAINTAINS STOCK INVENTORY

by

checking stock to determine amount available; anticipating needed stock; placing and expediting orders for stock; verifying receipt of stock.

____ 10. MAINTAINS CONTINUITY AMONG WORK TEAMS

by

documenting and communicating actions, irregularities, and continuing needs.

____ 11. DOCUMENTS ACTIONS

by

completing logs; adjusting specifications.

____ 12. CONTRIBUTES TO TEAM EFFORT

by

accomplishing related results as needed.

Tractor/Trailer Truck Driver

JOB PURPOSE:

TRANSPORTS AND DELIVERS PRODUCT OR MATERIAL

by

operating a tractor/trailer truck.

ESSENTIAL JOB RESULTS:

% of
Time

_____ 1. DETERMINES CONDITION OF VEHICLE
by
inspecting vehicle before and after use;
logging inspection; reporting requirements.

_____ 2. ENSURES CORRECT LOADING OF VEHICLE
by
loading product or material; directing
material handlers.

_____ 3. DELIVERS PRODUCT OR MATERIAL TO DESTINATION
by
identifying destination; selecting route;
driving the vehicle.

_____ 4. ENSURES OPERATION OF EQUIPMENT
by
completing preventive maintenance
requirements; following manufacturer's
instructions; troubleshooting malfunctions;
calling for repairs; maintaining equipment
supplies; evaluating new equipment and
techniques.

% of
Time

_____ 5. MAINTAINS SAFE VEHICLE AND CONDITIONS AND
PROTECTS LOAD
by
complying with organization policies and
procedures and highway rules and
regulations.

_____ 6. CONSERVES RESOURCES
by
using equipment and supplies as needed to
accomplish job results.

_____ 7. MAINTAINS RECORDS
by
completing driver log; obtaining shipper and
receiver authorizations; filing documents.

_____ 8. CONTRIBUTES TO TEAM EFFORT
by
accomplishing related results as needed.

JOB PURPOSE: **TRANSPORTS RAW MATERIALS AND COMMODITIES**

by

determining modes of transportation and routing.

ESSENTIAL JOB RESULTS:

% of
Time

____ 1. DIRECTS TRANSPORTATION OF RAW MATERIALS AND COMMODITIES

by

developing methods and procedures for transportation of raw materials to processing and production areas and commodities from departments to customers and warehouses.

____ 2. DETERMINES ROUTING AND METHOD OF TRANSPORTATION

by

studying tariff manuals and motor freight and railroad guidebooks.

____ 3. CONTROLS SCHEDULING OF SHIPMENTS

by

notifying departments or customers of arrival dates.

____ 4. PROTECTS SHIPMENTS

by

investigating causes of damages or shortages in consignments or overcharges for freight or insurance.

____ 5. COMPLIES WITH FEDERAL, STATE, AND LOCAL LEGAL REQUIREMENTS

by

studying existing and new legislation; anticipating future legislation; enforcing adherence to requirements; advising management on needed actions.

____ 6. PROVIDES INFORMATION

by

answering questions and requests.

% of
Time

____ 7. PREPARES REPORTS

by

collecting, analyzing, and summarizing information and trends.

____ 8. COMPLETES OPERATIONAL REQUIREMENTS

by

scheduling and assigning employees; following up on work results.

____ 9. MAINTAINS INTER- AND INTRADEPARTMENTAL WORK FLOW

by

fostering a spirit of cooperation.

____ 10. MAINTAINS TRAFFIC DEPARTMENT STAFF

by

recruiting, selecting, orienting, and training employees.

____ 11. MAINTAINS TRAFFIC DEPARTMENT STAFF JOB RESULTS

by

coaching, counseling, and disciplining employees; planning, monitoring, and appraising job results.

____ 12. MAINTAINS PROFESSIONAL AND TECHNICAL KNOWLEDGE

by

attending educational workshops; reviewing professional publications; establishing personal networks; participating in professional societies.

____ 13. CONTRIBUTES TO TEAM EFFORT

by

accomplishing related results as needed.

JOB TITLE: Trainer

JOB PURPOSE: **PREPARES MANAGERS AND EMPLOYEES TO ACCOMPLISH JOB RESULTS**

by

presenting training and development programs.

ESSENTIAL JOB RESULTS:

% of Time

____ 1. SATISFIES TRAINING AND DEVELOPMENT NEEDS
by
researching, designing, or learning training programs.

____ 2. PRESENTS TRAINING AND DEVELOPMENT PROGRAMS
by
identifying learning objectives; selecting instructional methodologies.

____ 3. REINFORCES LEARNING
by
selecting and utilizing training media.

____ 4. EVALUATES TRAINING AND DEVELOPMENT EFFECTIVENESS
by
assessing application of learning to job performance; recommending future training and development programs.

____ 5. COUNSELS INDIVIDUAL MANAGERS AND EMPLOYEES
by
identifying learning requirements; designing an individual training or development program; coaching to improve performance.

% of Time

____ 6. PREPARES TRAINING AND RESOURCE MANUALS
by
identifying purpose; assembling and composing information.

____ 7. MAINTAINS KNOWLEDGE OF INSTRUCTIONAL TECHNOLOGIES
by
attending workshops; reviewing professional publications; establishing personal networks; participating in professional societies.

____ 8. CONTRIBUTES TO TEAM EFFORT
by
accomplishing related results as needed.

JOB TITLE: Training Manager

JOB PURPOSE: **PREPARES MANAGERS AND EMPLOYEES TO ACCOMPLISH JOB RESULTS**

by

identifying training needs; offering programs to meet the needs.

ESSENTIAL JOB RESULTS:

% of Time

_____ 1. IDENTIFIES TRAINING AND DEVELOPMENT NEEDS
by
analyzing organization results, job requirements, operational problems, plans and forecasts, and current training programs.

_____ 2. SATISFIES TRAINING AND DEVELOPMENT NEEDS
by
researching, designing, or purchasing training programs and media; introducing new trends in training and development.

_____ 3. PRESENTS TRAINING AND DEVELOPMENT PROGRAMS
by
identifying learning objectives; selecting instructional methodologies.

_____ 4. EVALUATES TRAINING AND DEVELOPMENT EFFECTIVENESS
by
assessing trainee performance; counseling managers and employees regarding future training and work restructuring.

_____ 5. SELECTS AND MAINTAINS TRAINING EQUIPMENT
by
evaluating equipment and service capabilities; arranging for repair or replacement.

_____ 6. DESIGNS AND MAINTAINS PHYSICAL FACILITIES
by
consulting with architects and designers; specifying requirements to support training activities.

% of Time

_____ 7. COMPLETES TRAINING REQUIREMENTS
by
scheduling and assigning trainees and instructors.

_____ 8. MAINTAINS TRAINING AND DEVELOPMENT STAFF
by
recruiting, selecting, orienting, and training instructors and support personnel.

_____ 9. MAINTAINS TRAINING AND DEVELOPMENT STAFF JOB RESULTS
by
coaching, counseling, and disciplining instructors and support personnel; planning, monitoring, and appraising job results.

_____ 10. MAINTAINS KNOWLEDGE OF INSTRUCTIONAL TECHNOLOGIES
by
attending workshops; reviewing professional publications; establishing personal networks; participating in professional societies.

_____ 11. ACHIEVES FINANCIAL OBJECTIVES
by
preparing the training and development budget; scheduling expenditures; approving educational requests; analyzing variances; initiating corrective actions.

_____ 12. CONTRIBUTES TO TEAM EFFORT
by
accomplishing related results as needed.

JOB PURPOSE: **GUIDES TRAVELERS**

by

identifying itineraries; booking reservations.

ESSENTIAL JOB RESULTS:

% of
Time

___ 1. CLARIFIES TRAVEL PREFERENCES

by
determining travel dates and destination, mode of transportation, and finances.

___ 2. DEVELOPS ITINERARY

by
assembling literature; offering personal experiences; commenting on local customs, points of interest, and special events; answering inquiries; offering suggestions.

___ 3. SCHEDULES ITINERARY

by
identifying, booking, and confirming route, carriers, lodging, and dining; verifying space and rates; issuing tickets.

___ 4. COMPLETES FOREIGN TRAVEL REQUIREMENTS

by
obtaining visa, permit, and medical regulations; completing forms; providing information to obtain currency.

___ 5. PREPARES TRAVEL PACKET

by
assembling itinerary, maps, tickets, confirmations, visas and related documents, baggage tags, emergency resources, insurance options, etc.

% of
Time

___ 6. COLLECTS PAYMENT

by
entering and verifying scheduled services and charges; computing total; obtaining credit card charge, check, or cash.

___ 7. MAINTAINS RESOURCE OF TRAVEL OPTIONS

by
traveling carriers and visiting destinations; assembling, filing, and updating directories, brochures, pamphlets, guides, timetables, etc.

___ 8. OBTAINS REFUNDS AND ADJUSTMENTS

by
completing claim forms.

___ 9. PROMOTES TRAVEL

by
selling tour packages and special events; speaking to community groups.

___ 10. CONTRIBUTES TO TEAM EFFORT

by
accomplishing related results as needed.

JOB TITLE: Trust Administrator

JOB PURPOSE: **SATISFIES CLIENT'S FIDUCIARY REQUIREMENTS**

by

establishing and administering trusts.

ESSENTIAL JOB RESULTS:

*% of
Time*

_____ 1. DEVELOPS NEW BUSINESS
by
meeting with existing and prospective
clients, attorneys, accountants, and other
financial professionals; explaining services.

_____ 2. ESTABLISHES TRUST ACCOUNT
by
clarifying objectives and procedures;
probating will; drafting legal documents;
locating, collecting, inventorying, and
valuing assets.

_____ 3. PRODUCES INCOME
by
setting income objectives; investing assets.

_____ 4. DISBURSES FUNDS
by
following the conditions of the trust;
notifying and examining the needs of the
beneficiary; determining cash requirements;
resolving claims; calculating, preparing, and
distributing settlements; paying debts and
taxes; recommending discretionary actions;
liquidating assets.

_____ 5. COMPLIES WITH FEDERAL, STATE, AND LOCAL LEGAL
REQUIREMENTS
by
filing tax returns; studying existing and new
legislation; anticipating future legislation;
enforcing adherence to requirements;
advising management on needed actions.

*% of
Time*

_____ 6. PREPARES ACTIVITY AND STATUS REPORTS
by
collecting, analyzing, and summarizing
information and trends.

_____ 7. MAINTAINS CLIENT CONFIDENCE AND PROTECTS BANK
OPERATIONS
by
keeping information confidential.

_____ 8. SECURES ACCOUNT INFORMATION
by
completing data base backups.

_____ 9. COMPLETES OPERATIONAL REQUIREMENTS
by
assigning projects to clerical staff; following
up on work results.

_____ 10. MAINTAINS PROFESSIONAL AND TECHNICAL KNOWLEDGE
AND INDUSTRY TRENDS
by
attending educational workshops; reviewing
professional publications; establishing
personal networks; participating in
professional societies.

_____ 11. CONTRIBUTES TO TEAM EFFORT
by
accomplishing related results as needed.

JOB TITLE: Underwriter

JOB PURPOSE: **MINIMIZES RISKS**

by

accepting and rejecting insurance applications; modifying insurance coverage.

ESSENTIAL JOB RESULTS:

% of Time

___ 1. COMPLETES INSURANCE APPLICATIONS
by
adhering to established underwriting standards.

___ 2. DETERMINES DEGREE OF RISK
by
examining application forms, inspection reports, actuarial reports, and medical reports.

___ 3. EVALUATES APPLICANT FACTORS
by
reviewing applicant financial standing, age, occupation, and accident experience and value and condition of property.

___ 4. EVALUATES POSSIBILITY OF LOSSES
by
determining amount of insurance in force on single risk or group of closely related risks; estimating possibility of losses from catastrophe or excessive insurance.

___ 5. DETERMINES DISTRIBUTION OF RISKS
by
using rate books, tables, code books, computer records, and other reference materials.

___ 6. GATHERS INFORMATION
by
communicating with field representatives, insurance brokers, medical personnel, and other insurance or inspection companies.

___ 7. PROVIDES INFORMATION
by
answering questions and requests; quoting rates; explaining company underwriting policies.

% of Time

___ 8. RESOLVES DISCREPANCIES
by
collecting and analyzing information.

___ 9. DETERMINES INSURANCE COVERAGE
by
declining excessive risks; authorizing reinsurance on high-risk policies; decreasing policy values; specifying applicable exclusions and endorsements.

___ 10. PREPARES REPORTS
by
collecting, analyzing, and summarizing information and trends.

___ 11. CONTRIBUTES TO ORGANIZATION EFFECTIVENESS
by
identifying short-term and long-range issues that must be addressed; providing information and commentary pertinent to deliberations; recommending options and courses of action; implementing directives

___ 12. MAINTAINS INTER- AND INTRADEPARTMENTAL WORK FLOW
by
fostering a spirit of cooperation.

___ 13. MAINTAINS PROFESSIONAL UNDERWRITING AND TECHNICAL KNOWLEDGE
by
attending educational workshops; reviewing professional publications; establishing personal networks; participating in professional societies.

___ 14. CONTRIBUTES TO TEAM EFFORT
by
accomplishing related results as needed.

JOB TITLE: Vending Machine Attendant

JOB PURPOSE: **SERVES CUSTOMERS**

by

maintaining vending machine supplies and equipment.

ESSENTIAL JOB RESULTS:

% of
Time

____ 1. TRANSPORTS FOOD TO CUSTOMERS
by
filling orders; stocking, loading, and driving a truck.

____ 2. MAINTAINS FOOD AND DRINK SUPPLIES IN VENDING MACHINES
by
determining inventory levels and freshness; replenishing according to supply levels.

____ 3. ENSURES OPERATION OF EQUIPMENT
by
adjusting temperature gauges; completing preventive maintenance requirements; calling for repairs.

____ 4. PROVIDES INFORMATION TO CUSTOMERS
by
answering questions and requests.

% of
Time

____ 5. MAINTAINS VENDING MACHINE DISPENSING AND CHANGE-MAKING OPERATIONS
by
following policies and procedures; reporting needed changes.

____ 6. MAINTAINS SAFE AND CLEAN WORKING ENVIRONMENT
by
complying with procedures, sanitation requirements, and other rules and regulations.

____ 7. GENERATES REVENUES
by
collecting coins from machines; preparing distribution reports and collection logs.

____ 8. CONTRIBUTES TO TEAM EFFORT
by
accomplishing related results as needed.

JOB TITLE: Videographer

JOB PURPOSE: PRODUCES VIDEOTAPE PROGRAMS

by

operating videotaping equipment; editing productions.

ESSENTIAL JOB RESULTS:

% of
Time

____ 1. ESTABLISHES PROGRAM DESIGN

by

studying program content; conferring with program managers to determine program outcomes.

____ 2. PREPARES SET

by

transporting equipment and supplies to location; positioning people, props, and equipment; adjusting lighting; placing microphones.

____ 3. PRODUCES PROGRAM

by

operating equipment; directing performers.

____ 4. OPERATES EQUIPMENT

by

following manufacturer's instructions.

____ 5. COMPLETES PRODUCTION

by

editing and packaging program.

____ 6. RECOMMENDS EQUIPMENT PURCHASES

by

studying equipment specifications; conducting tests.

% of
Time

____ 7. MAINTAINS TECHNICAL KNOWLEDGE

by

attending educational workshops; reviewing publications; establishing personal networks; participating in professional societies.

____ 8. ENSURES OPERATION OF EQUIPMENT

by

completing preventive maintenance requirements; troubleshooting malfunctions; calling for repairs.

____ 9. PROVIDES RESOURCE OF EQUIPMENT

by

issuing equipment; training users.

____ 10. MAINTAINS SUPPLIES INVENTORY

by

checking stock to determine inventory level; anticipating needed supplies; placing and expediting orders for supplies; verifying receipt of supplies.

____ 11. CONTRIBUTES TO TEAM EFFORT

by

accomplishing related results as needed.

JOB PURPOSE: SERVES PATRONS

by

providing information to help food and beverage selections; presenting
ordered choices; maintaining dining ambiance.

ESSENTIAL JOB RESULTS:

% of
Time

____ 1. PREPARES ROOM FOR DINING
by
clothing tables and setting decorations,
condiments, candles, napkins, service plates,
and utensils.

____ 2. PROTECTS ESTABLISHMENT AND PATRONS
by
adhering to sanitation, safety, and alcohol
beverage control policies.

____ 3. HELPS PATRONS SELECT FOOD AND BEVERAGES
by
presenting menu; offering cocktails and
aperitifs; suggesting courses; explaining the
chef's specialties; identifying appropriate
wines; answering food preparation questions.

____ 4. TRANSMITS ORDERS TO BAR AND KITCHEN
by
recording patrons' choices; identifying
patrons' special dietary needs and special
requests.

____ 5. KEEPS KITCHEN STAFF INFORMED
by
noting timing of meal progression.

____ 6. SERVES ORDERS
by
picking up and delivering patrons' choices
from bar and kitchen; delivering
accompaniments and condiments from
service bars.

% of
Time

____ 7. RESPONDS TO ADDITIONAL PATRON REQUIREMENTS
by
inquiring of needs; observing dining process.

____ 8. MAINTAINS TABLE SETTING
by
removing courses as completed; replenishing
utensils; refilling water glasses; being alert to
patron spills or other special needs.

____ 9. CONCLUDES DINING EXPERIENCE
by
acknowledging choice of restaurant; inviting
patrons to return.

____ 10. OBTAINS REVENUES
by
totaling charges; issuing bill; accepting
payment; delivering bill and payment to
hostperson; returning change or credit card
and signature slip to patrons.

____ 11. CONTRIBUTES TO TEAM EFFORT
by
accomplishing related results as needed.

JOB TITLE: Warehouse Manager

JOB PURPOSE: **PROVIDES MATERIALS, EQUIPMENT, AND SUPPLIES**
by
directing receiving, warehousing, and distribution services; supervising staff.

ESSENTIAL JOB RESULTS:

% of Time

____ 1. MAINTAINS RECEIVING, WAREHOUSING, AND DISTRIBUTION OPERATIONS
by
initiating, coordinating, and enforcing program, operational, and personnel policies and procedures.

____ 2. COMPLIES WITH FEDERAL, STATE, AND LOCAL WAREHOUSING, MATERIAL HANDLING, AND SHIPPING REQUIREMENTS
by
studying existing and new legislation; enforcing adherence to requirements; advising management on needed actions.

____ 3. SAFEGUARDS WAREHOUSE OPERATIONS AND CONTENTS
by
establishing and monitoring security procedures and protocols.

____ 4. CONTROLS INVENTORY LEVELS
by
conducting physical counts; reconciling with data storage system.

____ 5. MAINTAINS PHYSICAL CONDITION OF WAREHOUSE
by
planning and implementing new design layouts; inspecting equipment; issuing work orders for repair and requisitions for replacement.

____ 6. ACHIEVES FINANCIAL OBJECTIVES
by
preparing an annual budget; scheduling expenditures; analyzing variances; initiating corrective actions.

% of Time

____ 7. COMPLETES WAREHOUSE OPERATIONAL REQUIREMENTS
by
scheduling and assigning employees; following up on work results.

____ 8. MAINTAINS WAREHOUSE STAFF
by
recruiting, selecting, orienting, and training employees.

____ 9. MAINTAINS WAREHOUSE STAFF JOB RESULTS
by
coaching, counseling, and disciplining employees; planning, monitoring, and appraising job results.

____ 10. MAINTAINS PROFESSIONAL AND TECHNICAL KNOWLEDGE
by
attending educational workshops; reviewing professional publications; establishing personal networks; participating in professional societies.

____ 11. CONTRIBUTES TO TEAM EFFORT
by
accomplishing related results as needed.

JOB TITLE: Weight Reduction Specialist

JOB PURPOSE: **HELPS CLIENTS LOSE WEIGHT**

by

implementing and monitoring weight-loss programs.

ESSENTIAL JOB RESULTS:

% of Time

____ 1. ESTABLISHES CLIENT DATA BASE

by

weighing and measuring client; determining weight development history, eating habits, and medical restrictions.

____ 2. DEVELOPS AND IMPLEMENTS WEIGHT-LOSS PROGRAMS

by

blending client's goals and restrictions with established dietary programs and positive reinforcement procedures.

____ 3. EDUCATES CLIENTS

by

differentiating between nonnutritious, high-fat foods and nutritious foods with low fat content.

____ 4. PROVIDES INFORMATION

by

explaining programs and procedures for desired weight loss; answering questions.

____ 5. OVERSEES CLIENT'S PROGRESS

by

reviewing eating habits and weight-loss statistics.

% of Time

____ 6. ENCOURAGES CLIENTS

by

promoting goals; reinforcing positive results; offering comfort at setbacks.

____ 7. IDENTIFIES CLIENT SERVICE REQUIREMENTS

by

establishing personal contact and rapport with potential and actual clients and other persons in a position to understand service requirements.

____ 8. MAINTAINS PROFESSIONAL AND TECHNICAL KNOWLEDGE

by

attending educational workshops; reviewing professional publications; establishing personal networks; participating in professional societies.

____ 9. CONTRIBUTES TO TEAM EFFORT

by

accomplishing related results as needed.

```
┌─────────────────────────────────────────────────────────────┐
│  JOB TITLE: Wooden Frame Builder                             │
└─────────────────────────────────────────────────────────────┘
```

JOB PURPOSE: **FABRICATES WOODEN FRAMES**

by

assembling and adjusting parts.

ESSENTIAL JOB RESULTS:

*% of
Time*

____ 1. ARRANGES SEQUENCE OF OPERATIONS
by
studying work orders; gathering materials.

____ 2. PREPARES WORK
by
cutting parts.

____ 3. LAYS OUT FRAME
by
positioning sides, ends, braces, etc.

____ 4. ASSEMBLES FRAME
by
fastening parts.

____ 5. FINISHES FRAME
by
trimming and smoothing edges.

____ 6. COMPLETES ASSEMBLY
by
fastening materials to frame.

____ 7. MAINTAINS SPECIFICATIONS
by
inspecting and measuring parts and frame;
making alterations; notifying supervisor to
obtain additional resources.

*% of
Time*

____ 8. ENSURES OPERATION OF TOOLS
by
completing preventive maintenance
requirements; following manufacturer's
instructions; troubleshooting malfunctions;
calling for repairs.

____ 9. MAINTAINS STOCK INVENTORY
by
checking stock to determine amount
available; anticipating needed stock; placing
and expediting orders for stock; verifying
receipt of stock.

____ 10. MAINTAINS CONTINUITY AMONG WORK TEAMS
by
documenting and communicating actions,
irregularities, and continuing needs.

____ 11. DOCUMENTS ACTIONS
by
completing production and quality logs.

____ 12. CONTRIBUTES TO TEAM EFFORT
by
accomplishing related results as needed.

JOB TITLE: Word-Processing Operator

JOB PURPOSE: **PREPARES AND STORES DOCUMENTS**

by

operating word-processing equipment; using software.

ESSENTIAL JOB RESULTS:

*% of
Time*

____ 1. PREPARES WORK TO BE ACCOMPLISHED
by
gathering and sorting documents.

____ 2. DETERMINES FORMAT AND CONTENT
by
following oral or written instructions.

____ 3. ESTABLISHES SPACING, MARGINS, TYPE SIZE, STYLE AND
COLOR, AND OTHER PARAMETERS
by
entering commands.

____ 4. ENTERS AND MODIFIES TEXT
by
following rough draft, corrected copy,
recorded voice dictation, or previous version
displayed on screen.

____ 5. CORRECTS SPELLING ERRORS
by
using dictionary.

____ 6. EDITS DOCUMENT
by
proofreading for grammar, punctuation, and
format errors.

*% of
Time*

____ 7. STORES COMPLETED DOCUMENT
by
entering document in data base.

____ 8. PRINTS DOCUMENTS
by
loading paper in printer; changing printing
mechanisms; generating print commands.

____ 9. KEEPS EQUIPMENT OPERATIONAL
by
following manufacturer's operating and
maintenance instructions and established
procedures.

____ 10. CONTRIBUTES TO TEAM EFFORT
by
accomplishing related results as needed.